# The Impact of School Choice and Community

SUNY Series, Youth Social Services, Schooling, and Public Policy
Barry M. Franklin and José R. Rosario, editors

# The Impact of School Choice and Community

*In the Interest of Families and Schools*

Claire Smrekar

STATE UNIVERSITY OF NEW YORK PRESS

Published by
State University of New York Press, Albany

For information, address State University of New York Press,
State University Plaza, Albany, NY 12246

Production by Christine Lynch
Marketing by Nancy Farrell

**Library of Congress Cataloging-in-Publication Data**

Smrekar, Claire.
     The impact of school choice and community: in the interest of
families and schools / by Claire Smrekar.
          p.   cm. — (SUNY series, youth social services, schooling, and
public policy)
     Includes bibliographical references and index.
     ISBN 0–7914–2613–0 (acid-free paper). — ISBN 0–7914–2614–9 (pbk.
acid-free paper)
     1. Education—Parent participation—United States—Case studies.
2. School choice—United States—Case studies.  3. Community and
school—United States—Case studies.  4. Educational sociology—
United States—Case studies.  I. Title.  II. Series.
LC225.3.S64  1996
370.19'31'0973—dc20                                                            94-40526
                                                                                          CIP

10 9 8 7 6 5 4 3 2 1

# Contents

# 1

## *In Whose Interest?*

### INTRODUCTION

The promise of parent involvement is important for all families and critical to the aims of school improvement. As teachers and school administrators are squeezed by the dictates of bottom-up and top-down school reform plans, shifting expectations and reconstituted roles carve out new spaces for parents in their children's schooling (Murphy 1991). Changes in instruction, assessment, and governance highlighted in the decade-long march toward fundamental change in our nation's schools imply the need to consider parent involvement in the most expansive terms and broadest context.

The widespread appeal and perceived value of parent involvement is reflected in its prominent place across nearly every state and local policy proposal designed to improve the performance of schools. Repeated calls for "parent empowerment" identify home- and community-based involvement as a key weapon in the struggle to slow the downward slide in academic indicators. Goals 2000, the recently enacted legislative mandate for new and expanded federal action in public education, locates objectives for increased parent involvement side by side with strategies focused on curriculum content and student performance. Headlining the agendas of the nation's school systems and statehouses, the promise of parent involvement continues to capture the interest and attention of reform-minded school administrators, teachers, business leaders, and policy makers.

The problem with these policy endorsements and their unwavering faith in the power of parent involvement to improve schools is not that the strategy does not work. To be sure, there is accumulating evidence regarding the positive effects of both home- and school-based parent involvement programs for all parents, teachers, and students. Findings indicate that parent involvement enhances parents' attitudes about themselves, school, school personnel, and the role each plays in the development of the child (Becher 1986; Gordon 1979; Henderson 1981; Keesling & Melaragno 1983; Rich & Jones 1977). Teachers also benefit from parental involvement by gaining insights about their students and their home environment (Epstein 1983). This increased understanding promotes greater cooperation, commitment, and trust between the parents and teacher. Finally, substantial evidence suggests that students' achievement and cognitive development increases when effective parent involvement practices are in place (Stearns & Peterson 1973; Goodson & Hess 1975; Henderson 1987; Rich 1987; Comer 1980).

While these celebrated outcomes of parent involvement in schools explain the value attached to home-school partnership efforts, they ignore the failed promises of parent involvement. The rush to embrace parent involvement whole cloth without giving central consideration to the social context of family life has rapidly unraveled the authentic promise of parent involvement amidst persistent indications of negative and infrequent interactions between families and schools. Most disturbing may be the evidence which suggests that patterns of parent participation are related to differences in socioeconomic status: higher-income and more educated parents participate at higher rates than lower-class parents, both in terms of school-based activities and home-learning exercises (Baker & Stevenson 1986; Lareau 1989). These observations are routinely provided as evidence that low-income parents "just don't care about their kids" or "don't think education is important." Moreover, researchers (Baker & Stevenson 1986; Medrich et al. 1982; Stevenson & Baker 1987; Wilcox 1978) have identified educative enrichment activities (reading to children, taking children to the library, attending school events) which middle-class parents apparently engage in more frequently than lower-class parents. Despite these observations, the critical question of how and why social class affects patterns of parent action in schools is often overlooked—muted by more vocal voices promoting the value of parent involvement and strategies for increasing it.

## REALIZING THE PROMISE

This study and other research indicate that access to information concerning teacher reputations and specialized academic programs can pay profitable dividends to families by enhancing the educational opportunities of their children. Beyond the benefit of home-based activities (e.g., reading, math games) on children's learning, academic program, and promotion, there are strong indications of the connection between teachers' expectations for student performance and the actions and attitudes of parents. Decisions regarding retention/promotion and ability grouping may well hinge on teachers' perceptions of parental interest and commitment. Negotiating successfully the expectations and demands of teachers and administrators undergird the rhetoric and reward of parent involvement.

The promise of parent involvement may be fully realized if efforts are undertaken to examine the elements of family life which influence the ways in which parents interact with schools. This book offers a response to the policy failures associated with parent involvement in schools by amplifying the importance of parents' social networks in the discussion of family-school partnerships. The interaction between social structure and school organization provides compelling indications of the need to recast the problem of parent involvement as one of community building. We begin this effort by examining the influence of cultural capital on patterns of parent involvement.

## CULTURAL CAPITAL AND FAMILY-SCHOOL INTERACTIONS

This study applies Pierre Bourdieu's concept of cultural capital to understand varying levels of parent participation in schooling. Bourdieu argues that schools draw unevenly on the social and cultural resources of members of the society by invoking particular linguistic styles, authority patterns, and types of curricula (Bourdieu 1977a, 1977b; Bourdieu & Passeron 1977). Bourdieu and Passeron (1977) describe a system of dispositions (habitus) which link class structure to a set of practices associated with different class cultures. Habitus includes the elements of perceptions, understanding, and style which bond and mark members of particular cultural groups and separate them from members of other cultural groups (Feinberg & Soltis 1992). According to Bourdieu, schools function as the primary institution for affirming and reproducing the social legitimacy of the habits, objects, and symbols of the dominant class culture. Children from higher social classes enter school familiar with these sociocultural arrangements. The cultural properties acquired from home differentially facilitate students' adjustment to school, thereby transforming cultural resources into what Bourdieu calls cultural capital (Lareau 1989).

It is important to note that while Bourdieu's concept of capital parallels the notion of a resource profitable for both individual and collective purposes located in the concept of human capital (Schultz 1963) and social capital (Coleman 1988), the principles of conflict theory and cultural reproduction distance cultural capital from the functionalist imperatives and implications of human and social capital. The concept of cultural capital underscores *differences in class cultures* and the role of social institutions (schools) in differentially rewarding class cultures. In sharp contrast, the concept of social capital emphasizes the role of organizational (school) relationships in establishing *social ties between members* who share similar attitudes, norms, and values instrumental in promoting a strong sense of obligation, shared expectations, and trust. Conceived as a bridge between rational (economic) theory and social organization theory, the principle of social capital exists, according to Coleman (1988) in relations among people (social structure) in ways that facilitate collective, purposeful action (e.g., Catholic school communities).

Cultural capital provides the necessary theoretical framework to examine cultural patterns associated with social class and to analyze how these patterns provide advantages in social institutions. By exploring the interinstitutional linkages among schooling, family life, and individuals, cultural capital furnishes the theoretical lenses necessary to understand why social class influences family-school relations (Lareau 1989).

Although Bourdieu does not examine the question of parent involvement in schooling, his analyses contribute to the research on the importance of class and culture in parents' interactions with schools (see Baker & Stevenson 1986; Connell et al. 1982; Ogbu 1974; McPherson 1972; Wilcox 1978). More recent research, however, applies the concept of cultural capital to studies of parent involvement to understand how social class provides parents with unequal resources and dispositions in the educational experiences of their children. Annette Lareau (1989) asserts that higher social class provides parents with more resources to intervene in schooling and to bind families into tighter connections with social institutions than are available to working-class families. These resources are derived from their education, income and material resources, occupational status, style of work, and social networks. Consequently, even if all parents are encouraged to be involved in their children's education, all do not have an equal chance to participate in the ways teachers want. Specifically, the Lareau study suggests that: (1) more years of schooling provide parents with a greater capacity to understand the instructional language used by teachers and, more generally, the competence to help their children with schoolwork; (2) higher social status allows parents to approach teachers as social equals or superiors and provides a sense of confidence in the educational setting; (3) higher incomes make it easier for parents to purchase more educational resources and to obtain child care services and transportation to attend school events; (4) upper-middle-class jobs more closely resemble the interconnection between work and home that teachers envision for students and their schoolwork; and (5) upper-middle-class parents are more likely to be members of social networks which provide information on school processes and practices.

Although the Lareau study provides powerful evidence for the importance of considering the influence of social class and culture on family-school interactions, it deliberately excludes the effects of institutional characteristics of schools on these relations. Consequently, little is known about how the effects of school organization may alter or mediate the influence of social class or cultural capital on family-school interactions. At the same time, researchers have examined the effect of certain organizational factors on family-school relations, e.g., the effect of functional community (Coleman & Hoffer 1987); the effect of affirmative choice (Erickson 1982; Metz 1986); the effect of teacher practices and attitudes (Becker & Epstein 1982; Epstein & Becker 1982; Epstein 1983); the effect of school charter (Baker, Oswald, & Stevenson 1988; Stevenson & Baker 1988); however, they have excluded the concept of cultural capital from their analyses.

## MEDIATING CONDITIONS: ORGANIZATIONAL CHARACTERISTICS

This study extends the organizational focus of community, choice, and teachers' practices/attitudes by refracting these images through the lenses of family background (cultural capital). The intent here rests with providing a model for family-school interactions which emphasizes the active and dynamic relationship between family characteristics and school organization.[1] This perspective allows us to examine the characteristics of schooling that may influence the experiences and expectations of families, thereby mediating the influence of social class on the nature and quality of family-school relationships.

This book argues that there are three key institutional characteristics of schools which may influence the ways in which families from different social classes interact with schools: *community, choice,* and *commitment* (defined as teacher/school-initiated programs which reflect a significant organizational commitment to family-school partnership). In the literature on effective schools and schools of choice, the social relations derived from a sense of community is repeatedly referenced as an organizational dimension of schooling which establishes a particular cultural ethos and renders deep and sustaining effects on the character and content of family-school interactions (e.g., see Grant 1985; Hallinger & Murphy 1986; Rutter et al. 1979). The promotional influence of school sector on the interlocking core components of school community (shared values, sense of membership and like-mindedness, and regular occasions of face-to-face interaction) is underscored in the research on the degree of communal association in magnet and Catholic schools (see Bryk, Lee & Holland 1993; Coleman & Hoffer 1987; Metz 1986). The voluminous effective schools research and the additional work which examines the effect of school programs designed to promote a family-school partnership (see Comer 1980; Davies, Burch & Johnson 1992; Epstein 1992) further testify to the critical and potential mediating role rendered by this organizational characteristic.

The multiple case-study design of this book reflects and displays my interest in examining the influence of each of these organizational aspects of schooling on the ways in which families with different amounts of cultural capital interact with schools. The case studies of a Catholic elementary school, a magnet elementary school, and a public neighborhood elementary school reflect the conceptual argument related to the intersection of school organization and cultural capital on the character and content of family-school interactions. The next section explores each of these organizational characteristics more deeply and relates the selection of the cases to the central argument of the book.

To understand patterns of family-school interactions and how they differ across social class,[2] this study focuses primarily on: (a) elements of cultural capital activated in family-school relations; (b) the effects of these elements on the nature and quality of interactions between families and schools;[3] and (c) mediating conditions (school organization) that affect family-school relations.

## COMMUNITY

The concept of community has a rich and extensive research literature which is centuries old. Sociologists in the nineteenth century (and earlier philosophers as well) distinguished *community* from *society* by noting differences in the level of social cohesion, familiarity, and generational changes. In stark contrast to mass society, communities were identified by their self-sufficiency and structural (economic, educational, religious, and recreational) consistency and interdependence.

In a seminal work on education and community, Newmann and Oliver (1968) trace the historical conceptions of community from Tonnies' distinctions between Gemeinschaft (community) and Gesellschaft (society) to more contemporary sociological definitions. The differences that Tonnies (1963) underscores relate to the nature of relationships within communities and societies, which range from more natural and organic to more mechanical or rational (Newmann & Oliver 1968). Thus, relationships within a community are rooted in familiarity and interdependence whereas societal relationships reflect formal, contractual relations found in legal and commercial institutions and bureaucratic organizations and are characterized by independence and logic.

Contemporary notions of community (e.g., Bronfenbrenner, Moen, & Garbarino 1984; Coleman & Hoffer 1987; Newmann & Oliver 1968; Scherer 1972) argue that the community of residence in society today does not reflect the community of psychological meaning for most families (Steinberg 1989). These observers distinguish between a concept associated with physical or geographical boundaries and a concept of community grounded in social structures and social relations. For example, Newmann and Oliver (1968) include the following criteria in their definition, each of which is viewed as a continuum and indicative of greater or lesser degrees of community: (1) membership is valued as an end in itself, not merely as a means to other ends; (2) members share commitment to a common purpose; and (3) members have enduring and extensive personal contact with each other. The sense of solidarity, membership, and mutual support that results from community is thought to impact both the individual in terms of personal development and integration and the larger society in terms of social cohesion and stability (Raywid 1988b).

A distinct component of the notion of community is a social network or a social system of formal and informal organizations and opportunities for information exchange and face-to-face interactions among individuals (Cochran & Brassard 1979; Steinberg 1989). Members who are considered a part of a functional social network are characterized by well-known roles and contexts (neighborhood, relatives, work- or school-mates, people in agencies or organizations, etc.) and are distinguished from a more peripheral social circle (Cochran & Henderson 1986).

The notion of a school as a community embraces both the communal associations and personal relationships, which are sustained by a school's symbolic and personal dimensions and the more associative relationships, which are driven by the need to accomplish structured activities and maintain particular work relations (Bryk & Driscoll 1988). The vision of the school as a community portrays adults and students linked to one another by a common mission and by a network of supportive personal relations that strengthen their commitment to the organization (Bryk & Driscoll 1988). Three core components comprise this communal school organization (Bryk & Driscoll 1988): (1) a system of shared values among members of the organization which include the "norms of schooling" (Bird & Little 1986); (2) a common agenda of activities which include those formal and informal events which enable school participants to engage in face-to-face interactions, promote social ties, and encourage communal association; and (3) a pattern of social relations which embodies collaboration and extensive involvement and is highlighted by the collegiality shared among the adults in the school and the expanded role of the teacher.

The impact of community on the degree of social integration between families and schools is examined by Coleman and Hoffer (1987) in their study of private and public schools. The researchers argue that the type and strength of community in schools differentially affect the critical social connections which bond families and schools in the joint enterprise of education.

This concept of community refers to two types: functional and value. *Functional communities* are characterized by structural consistency between generations in which social norms and sanctions arise out of the social structure itself, and both reinforce and perpetuate that structure (Coleman & Hoffer 1987). Functional communities exhibit a high degree of uniformity and cohesion within geographical, social, economic, and ideological boundaries. *Value communities* describe a collection of people who share similar values about education and childrearing but who are not a functional community; they are strangers from various neighborhoods, backgrounds, and occupations united around an educational organization—their children's school.

*Catholic Schools*: Families of Catholic school students may constitute both value and functional communities. Besides value consistency, these families (may) attend the same religious services and know one another. These functional communities, however, are more circumscribed than the ones described earlier; they encompass only a religious institution and ignore other social or economic institutions.

*Magnet Schools:* Parents of children who attend a magnet school may constitute a value community if they exhibit a high degree of value consistency—e.g., commitment to a particular educational philosophy—but are mainly strangers drawn from a wide collection of city neighborhoods; they have little contact with one another outside school corridors.

*Neighborhood Schools*: Many public, neighborhood elementary schools reflect geographical communities but lack the value consistency or interinstitutional linkages of either the value or functional communities. While neighborhood schools a century ago served residential areas that were functional communities, social and technological changes have transformed many of these communities from enclaves of shared values and daily face-to-face talk to somewhat disparate sets of interests and weak affiliations.[4]

The research on organizational features which promote school community points to an array of structural and compositional features, including school size, sector, diversity of student body, and student selectivity (Bryk & Driscoll 1988). The empirical research in this area has focused primarily on the characteristics of "effective" schools in the Catholic and private school sectors (e.g., Bryk & Holland 1984; Cookson & Persell 1985; Peshkin 1986). The explicit mission or ethos of Catholic and private schools, combined with a comparatively smaller size and more homogeneous student body, have been considered key elements associated with creating the foundational elements of community (e.g., shared goals, personal ties) within schools. Little research has focused on organizational elements in public-sector or public-sector choice schools which may promote or constrain the development of community in these schools.

## CHOICE

Choice refers to the affirmative decision parents make when they send their children to a school other than the public elementary school in their neighborhood.[5] It is assumed that enhanced choice (when it is exercised) creates communities of shared values that inspire the loyalty and commitment of parents and teachers (Chubb & Moe 1990; Elmore 1987; Erickson 1982; McNeil 1987; Metz 1986; Raywid 1988a). Research on public schools of choice indicates that parent satisfaction rates tend to be unusually high and often exceed approval ratings in comparable local schools (Raywid 1988b). Erickson (1982) suggests that both students and parents may feel more committed to school life when their enrollment at a particular school is voluntary. The act of choosing may make parents aware of benefits that would otherwise go unnoticed (Erickson 1982). Additionally, the opportunity to choose may generate a sense of power that itself enhances commitment (Erickson 1982). The effects of purchasing educational services through the payment of tuition may engender an even greater sense of commitment and affiliation. Thus, private choice parents and students might approach schooling with greater effort and thought than their nonchoice public school counterparts.

These processes and conditions associated with the concept of choice correspond to two mechanisms which encourage organizations to be responsive to their clients: exit and voice (Hirschman 1970). "Exit" refers to the act of shifting from one provider to another or from one school to another school. If a parent dissatisfied with the education her daughter is receiving in a Catholic elementary school transfers her child to a public elementary school, she is exercising the exit option. The option reminds schools that the interests and concerns of parents must be responded to in order to sustain the commitment and loyalty of these "clients."

The concept of "voice" is considered here as a mechanism families may invoke for encouraging schools to be responsive. Voice refers to protest, discussion, negotiation, voting, and other forms of political or "client" participation to obtain one's goals (Hirschman 1970). Voice is most often used by individual parents to obtain services for their children or collectively to alter local school and school district practices (Levin 1989). Voice can be exercised within a formal forum of decision making (e.g., a school board meeting) or in a spontaneous, informal exchange with a school official. The degree to which parents have access to this mechanism and the nature of school response to its employment is an area of focus in this study.

## COMMITMENT

Commitment is defined as the array of programs, policies, and procedures schools design to develop and sustain parent participation. These programs may be teacher-initiated, principal-initiated, or schoolwide strategies developed by a group or organization such as the PTA or school-site council. They may range from strategies designed to promote home learning activities for parents, e.g., Family Math, to school-based governance and decision making opportunities. Commitment extends from the most explicit, mandated programs requiring parents' time to the more subtle, implicit support for parent volunteerism and recognition.

The research on the effect of school programs (organizational commitment) designed to involve parents in their children's education is both broad and somewhat incomplete. Most studies point to the promising results of school/teacher-initiated efforts designed to assist parents in engaging in educational activities at home and the positive impact of school-based parent volunteer activities for families and schools alike (see section above). School-based projects such as Family Math, Schools Reaching Out, and the Yale Child Study Center programs have recorded strong and positive responses from both families and schools (Kreinberg & Thompson 1986; Davies, Burch, & Johnson 1992; Comer 1980).[6] At the same time, studies indicate that parents respond in different ways to involvement efforts and requests. For example, the important influence of family structure is evidenced in the participation patterns of single mothers and mothers who work outside the home. These mothers are less likely than other parents to attend school meetings or school-based workshops

(Espinoza 1988) but are as or more likely to help their children at home with school work (Epstein 1990; Herrick & Epstein 1991). Other research identifies the critical role of racial and ethnic backgrounds on the ways in which parents interact with their children and schools. This research includes African-American families (Scott-Jones 1987); Hispanic families (Delgado-Gaitan 1992); and Chinese-American families (Sung 1987). In sum, while studies suggest that parents whose children's school or teacher encourages involvement (home or at school) are much more likely to engage in those interactive types of activities than other parents, the evidence underscores the important influence of family background and organization on family-school interactions.

With the conceptual focus on cultural capital as an element of family background which influences patterns of parent interactions with schools, this study considers the relative and reciprocal influence of an organizational (programmatic) commitment to parent involvement in mediating the effects of social class on patterns of parent involvement. The possibility exists that the type, intensity, and conduct of a programmatic commitment to involving parents in school and home learning activities may level some of the effects of social class differences. Alternatively, the programs and policies designed to encourage broad and inclusive participation among parents may actually exacerbate social class differences rather than advance the educational opportunities for all.

## INTERACTIONS BETWEEN FAMILIES AND SCHOOLS

The nature of family-school relations is both broad and complex. In descriptive analyses of parent involvement, researchers often construct schematic charts which depict parents acting in roles ranging from "advisers" and "advocates" to "home-based tutors" and "traditional audience" (see Brandt 1979; Brown & Haycock 1984; Crespo & Louque 1984; Criscuolo 1986; Romero 1982; Wolfendale 1983). Other researchers diagram the location of potential parent action to include the home and the school and within those broad categories identify activities as either advisory or collaborative (McLaughlin & Shields 1986). The partnership model of family-school involvement in students' education outlined by Epstein (1987) includes five distinct strands: (1) basic obligations of families to create healthy and nurturing home conditions; (2) basic obligations of schools to communicate with families about school practices and programs; (3) volunteer roles for parents which assist teachers and administrators in supporting academic, sports, and other activities; (4) family involvement in skill-building and educational enrichment activities at home which support classroom learning; and (5) parent participation in school decision making and governance through school site councils and other organized policy-making and advocacy groups. The emphasis throughout this and other models is on the separable and identifiable activities which comprise school, community, and parent activities (Epstein 1992; Epstein & Dauber 1988).

To be sure, these descriptive role titles are useful for painting in broad brush some of the activities and responsibilities of parents in the education of their children. This book, however, considers parent involvement within a less restrictive framework of parents' experiences and perceptions in the context of schooling. The focus rests with the nature of parents' and teachers' requests of each other (e.g., information, attendance, time, participation, cooperation, etc.) and with the nature and quality of their responses. For example, teachers might request parents to help with homework, attend meetings and school events, employ a tutor, and reinforce reading skills as well as to ensure that their child is dressed, fed, and on time. Parents' requests of teachers may range from the vague and general—ensuring their child receives a "good education"— to the more directed and precise—advancement to a new reading group, extra support and direction, regular progress reports, classroom volunteer and observation opportunities, approval of curricular materials, and flexible appointment hours. Both parents and teachers might request the respect of the other but may have very different conceptions of this term, depending upon whether they view families and schools as separate, parallel institutions or mutually supporting, overlapping enterprises. The point here is to avoid a checklist or time sheet approach which merely records the number of interactions; my interest rests with the explanations parents and teachers give for what they do or what they fail to do and in the value or meaning these interactions (or their absences) represent.

## AIMS AND ORGANIZATION OF THE BOOK

This book bridges two relevant, yet traditionally disconnected discussions related to school organization and the influence of social class on patterns of parent participation. The research blends an organizational study with issues of social stratification by examining the impact of community, choice, and commitment (programmatic) on family-school interactions. Discussion and analyses are drawn from case studies of three elementary schools: a Catholic school, a magnet school, and a public neighborhood school. The intent rests with describing the elements of social class which affect the ways in which parents participate in their children's schooling, examining how these elements influence the nature and quality of family-school interactions, and explaining the processes through which school organization mediates the influence of social class on family-school interactions.

Chapter 2 examines the implications of the generational, organizational, and philosophical chasms which fracture relationships between families and a Catholic parish school. The importance of nonacademic school programs is highlighted by demonstrating the ways in which these extracurricular activities unify the disparate sets of parents within the parameters of space and time. Chapter 3 examines the case of the Carlton Magnet School by identifying the ways in which the school community is constructed. School-based social networks between socially and economically differentiated school parents are promoted by extensive communication channels, required participation, and school choice. Chapter 4 provides a template against which to compare the nature of community and family-school interactions in the previous chapters on public- and private-sector choice schools. The situation at Western School reflects a critical absence of social cohesion and communication despite a multifaceted parent volunteer program. The chapter argues against traditional, piecemeal, programmatic approaches to enhancing parent participation in schools and asserts the need to examine the organizational processes and structures which contribute to elements of a school community. The nature and function of community in each of the three schools and the organizational arrangements are revisited in chapter 5. The analysis focuses on refining the concept of school community and its implications for mediating the influence of social class on family-school interactions. The final chapter contributes to the ongoing discourse among school officials, policy makers, and researchers regarding parent involvement and school organization. Policy recommendations are proposed which are aimed at achieving two separate but complementary goals: (1) building community among parents; and (2) building connections between parents and school staff. The objectives lie with promoting better communication, understanding, and trust between families and schools in order to enhance the experiences and expectations of both parents and school staff.

## NOTES

1. It is neither the design nor the intent of this study to examine the assertions embedded in the research on social class differences in family life as they relate to particular childrearing practices (see Bronfenbrenner 1966; Heath 1982; Kohn 1969; Rubin 1976; Wright & Wright 1976). This study is concerned with the ways in which class culture facilitates or impedes parents' management of the process of schooling. While examining the educational values of parents across social class, this book does not include analyses of social class differences associated with linguistic patterns and occupational socialization, which are important influences on the educational outcomes of students. This book focuses on the factors which influence parents in their negotiation of the schooling process and not on the broad and complex question of differential educational outcomes by social class.

2. In this study social class is defined by an individual's occupational status, education, and income level.

3. This study focuses on the influence of social class on parent participation in schooling and is not designed to examine the influence of social class on students' achievement.

4. It is certainly true, however, that some neighborhood schools, particularly those that serve middle- and upper-middle-class families who can establish residence in neighborhoods with "good" schools reflect elements of both value and functional communities. The point here is that in general, these influences are less prevalent and less pervasive than in either public/choice or nonpublic schools.

5. This concept of choice does not overlook the issue of choice as exercised by families with the financial means and information to establish residence in neighborhoods served by "good" or "desirable" public schools. However, the primary focus of this study rests with the set of explicit and implicit understandings, expectations, and assumptions which influence patterns of parent participation in those schools which are recognized by all participants as "schools of choice." Public, neighborhood elementary schools do not reflect the level of choice embodied in magnet schools or private schools; the issue of choice is solely that of some individual families.

6. Family Math is a program designed to involve parents in home activities which reinforce mathematical concepts and applications. The strategies and techniques used in the program emphasize the fun and enjoyment of the learning activities and are shared with parents through a series of workshops which emphasize the wide and natural application of mathematics. The Schools Reaching Out program is designed to promote parent-school linkages in low-income communities. The program includes a community portrait project to celebrate the school and its local community's historical, social, and cultural traditions; regular home visits to school families; a parent's center furnished to provide parents with an array of social and educational materials; and staff development to strengthen family-school partnership techniques. The Yale Child Study Center program was developed by Dr. James Comer in 1968 to address the psychological, social, and academic competencies of children. The Comer program includes a governance and management team (with parent representatives); a parent participation program; a mental health child study team; and a professional development program for school staff.

# 2

## St. Martin's School

### INTRODUCTION

Speed by or simply turn away for a second and you may miss it. St. Martin's Parish School[1] sits back a comfortable, quiet distance from the street and is marked by only a modest, painted wooden sign. The school's benign physical presence contrasts sharply with the handful of Protestant churches and public schools which dot the street for nearly a mile; their edifices boldly face the bustling traffic moving past them.

Turning in from the street, you come upon the parish hall, rectory, church, and thrift store which front the zigzag driveway. The school sits on the back edge of the property. A long, narrow, grassy field marks the western border of campus. On the far side of this field, a chain-link fence, topped with barbed wire, separates school property from a set of single-story, lower-income apartment buildings. The cinder block school building is flanked by an asphalt playground and on the eastern side, by another grassy field. A bit ragged and bumpy, the field bears the scars of children's punishing feet and drought conditions. In the field there's a row of shady trees, swings, and tire tubes hanging long from heavy wooden beams. A gold plaque with a school-inscribed "Thank You" identifies the names of families who donated the swings. A six-foot-tall wooden fence runs the length of the field, marking the backline of both the school and their middle-class neighbors' backyards.

Double decker, clear glass windows allow children on skates or standing on the exterior benches to peer inside the classrooms. Outstretched wooden eaves form a protective overhang and natural walkway around the perimeter of the building. A bank of newer portable (now permanent) classrooms stretch across the end of this central rectangular building, forming a T-shape and joining the kindergarten and extended day program with the first through eighth grade classrooms.

Inside the classrooms there are rigid rows of steel desks and small plastic chairs; in some classes, the desks are clustered in groups of two. Typically, the teacher's larger, gray steel desk sits strategically in the back corner, piled high with books and papers. There is a sense of the ordinary, the ubiquitous classroom setting: tall wooden cabinets for paper, posters, jackets and lunchboxes; shelves of social studies textbooks; a long, green chalkboard in the front topped with colorful alphabet cards; desktop globes; world maps; pictures of astronauts and planets; a "superstar" bulletin board with students' poetry; a small sink and counter in the corner; and the American flag.

Other articles signal a difference, a visual reminder that certain religious beliefs and values find prominent and official expression here; St. Martin's is, after all, a Catholic school. A wooden crucifix hangs above the chalkboard in every classroom; a statue of the Blessed Virgin Mary is placed upon a tabletop. At least one, sometimes two, bulletin boards depict a biblical or distinctly Catholic theme: "Turn Away From Sin and Be Faithful"; "Lord, Make Me A Channel of Your Peace"; "Let Your Face Shine on Jesus and the Shadow Will Fall Behind You"; "My Spirit Finds Joy in God My Savior." Some of the artwork blends spiritual messages with geopolitical instruction: a map of the Middle East with a superimposed picture of the Blessed Mother bears the caption "Lord, Watch Over Our Troops As We Pray For Peace."

The school office in the front corner of the central building has two large rectangular windows which are far too high for children to peer through. A faded sticker on one window warns: Students Will Not Be Admitted Unless An Immunization Record is Presented and Immunizations Are Up-To-Date. Inside, against the wall on the right, stands a six-foot tall glass case stuffed full of trophies adorned with miniature basketball and volleyball players, track athletes, and baton twirlers. A gold plaque identifies the trophy case as a gift from the 1965–66 Parent's Club.

A Xerox copy machine, a pair of old Steelcase typewriter tables, and a cluster of gray metal file cabinets fill the cramped work space on the other side of the waist-high counter. The door of the principal's office is clearly visible to the right. Just outside the principal's office, above the clock and to the left of an antiquated intercom panel, hangs a large wood crucifix.

## STUDENTS

St. Martin's School has one classroom of thirty-six students in each grade from kindergarten through eighth. This past year, the school reached capacity enrollment at 317 students. The student population is predominantly Catholic (77 percent versus 23 percent non-Catholic) and white (75 percent versus 13 percent Asian, 8 percent Hispanic, 4 percent Black). Most of the children live with two parent families (84 percent) in homes in the nearby suburban communities. A small but growing number of students (8 percent of total) travel thirty minutes from an affluent community in the nearby foothills to attend St. Martin's.

## FAMILIES

Of the 240 families that send their children to St. Martin's School, 111 of these are listed as parishioners. Some of these families attend Mass regularly but up to a half of the families attend only occasionally or infrequently. The vast majority of the families at St. Martin's are two-income families in which mothers work at least part-time. There are wealthy families from the foothill community and struggling ones from nearby lower-income apartments. Most, however, are self-described middle- to upper-middle-income families. Many are college graduates and pay a mortgage on a home valued at $300,000 (upper-middle class) to $150,000 (middle class). In their free time, these families enjoy skiing and travel (higher end) or camping and organized sports (lower end).

## FACULTY

The full-time faculty at St. Martin's numbers eleven, all of whom are female. In addition to the nine grade-level teachers, there is a physical education teacher, a music instructor, and a resource specialist. A counselor from Catholic Services serves St. Martin's as part of her diocese responsibilities. The lay principal, who is also female, has been at St. Martin's for five years. Most of the faculty members have taught at least ten years, almost exclusively in Catholic schools, and have been at this school for at least five years. Although all the teachers are certified by the state, they earn on average 70 percent of their public school counterparts' salary.[2] Neither the teachers nor the principal live in the local community.

## SCHOOL PHILOSOPHY

The St. Martin's School Parent/Student Handbook states the school's philosophy as follows:

> The goal of St. Martin's School is to educate the whole child, keeping an appropriate balance of spiritual, intellectual, cultural, social, emotional, and physical development. We recognize that the parents are the prime educators of their children and that the function of the school is to extend and support this process. It is our aim to implement a program that will recognize and address the individual needs and dignity of each child because all are children of God and ". . . have a dignity of their own. They are important not only for what they will do in the future, but for what they are here and now" (*Sharing the Light of Faith*, #181). We perceive the importance of our role in helping to build a faith community devoted to the knowledge, love and service of God and each other. "All those involved in a Catholic school—parents, pastors, teachers, administrators, and students—must earnestly desire to make it a community of faith which is indeed 'living, conscious, and active'" (*To Teach as Jesus Did*, National Conference of Catholic Bishops).

## POLICIES AND RULES

### Admissions

The order of priority for acceptance to St. Martin's is as follows: (1) brothers and sisters of students who are presently enrolled at St. Martin's; (2) Catholics who are members of St. Martin's Parish (a parish member is defined as a person registered in the parish and using the offertory envelopes); (3) transferring Catholics who become members of St. Martin's Parish and whose children currently attend parochial school; (4) Catholics who are members of parishes other than St. Martin's; and (5) non-Catholics.

### Tuition and Fees

Upon admission to St. Martin's, parents are required to sign a registration contract which stipulates the tuition charge, payment schedule, and opportunities for credits. The registration fee per child is $80. Tuition charges for one child are $1,480, for two $2,270, for three or more $2660. A $150 credit is granted to "sustaining parishioners whose participation enhances the overall life of the Parish." Those families who regularly attend Mass and contribute to Sunday collections are regarded as "sustaining parishioners."

All school parents are automatically considered "parent club members." However, contributing parent club members receive a $150 credit against tuition costs. In order to qualify, parents must earn ten points during the school year by participating in fund-raising and volunteer activities. Additionally, each family is responsible for eight hours of work in the parish thrift shop each year. Normally, this involves two four-hour shifts sometime during the year. Those who choose not to contribute their time are assessed $100.

### Financial Aid

Financially needy parents who need assistance in the form of grants or loans so that their children can attend St. Martin's can apply any time the need arises. About 10 percent of St. Martin's students receive some form of financial aid.

### Code of Conduct

Students who attend St. Martin's are expected to adhere to specific behavioral guidelines outlined in the Student/Parent Handbook. Highlighted in bold print, students are urged to "**conduct themselves according to the principles of Christian behavior.**" In order to "respect the rights and privileges of all other members," students must be honest, cooperative, respectful, courteous, responsible, and comply with school rules. Inappropriate conduct such as fighting, using obscene language, smoking, drinking, or defacing property is grounds for suspension. Serious or repeated violations of these rules can lead to expulsion.

The handbook also outlines conditions for transferring a student when "parents are consistently uncooperative and conduct themselves in a manner that is disruptive of the harmonious relationships in the school." Specific reasons for recommended transfers include "parental interference in matters of school administration and abusive language toward principal, pastor, or teachers . . ."

## GOVERNANCE

### School Board

Although St. Martin's School operates under general governing procedures established by the Catholic School Department, essential administration activities are directed by the principal and members of the school board. The board makes recommendations concerning the budget and educational policies, which are defined and implemented by the principal and faculty. Board members include representatives of the Parent's Club and members of the parish. A teacher representative, the principal, and the pastor are ex officio members of the board. The handbook states that any parishioner or parent "who has a positive attitude toward the philosophy of Catholic schools" is eligible to serve on the board.

### Parent's Club

Every St. Martin's parent is automatically a member of the Parent's Club. The fund-raising activities and fees generated by the Parent's Club amount to 6 percent of the school budget each year.[3] Members also contribute in-kind support by maintaining school grounds and equipment. Parent's Club members assist in the school library and help serve at the hot lunch program. The handbook urges parents to attend monthly meetings: "St. Martin's School is truly your school. The Parent's Club is one important way you exercise that ownership."

## ORGANIZATION OF FAMILY LIFE: IMPLICATIONS FOR SCHOOL INVOLVEMENT

### Family Profiles

The parents from St. Martin's School interviewed for this book[4] range from upper-middle class to lower-middle class.[5] Their residences vary in size and value from a sprawling two-story house with a swimming pool, to a small, poorly ventilated duplex off a noisy street. At least one parent in six of the ten families I spoke with holds a college degree. Although most of the families interviewed are two-parent working families, some of these include mothers who work part-time outside their home, while other mothers work full-time. I also interviewed two single parents, both of whom are female and work full-time outside the home but differ sharply in socioeconomic status. While some of the families interviewed are Catholic and others are Protestant, all claim some church affiliation; some are regular churchgoers, others are occasional or infrequent participants. All the parents have at least one child enrolled in the third or fourth grade at St. Martin's School.[6]

The following composite portraits represent families from each of the three social class groups: upper-middle income, middle class, and lower-middle class.

*The McDonnells.* The McDonnells have lived in their large, two-story home for seven years.[7] The neighborhood is quiet and comfortable, with manicured, landscaped, well-maintained yards, interrupted occasionally by a large speed boat parked in the side driveway. The homes in their former neighborhood were older and far more modest; in this neighborhood homes sell for as much as $260,000.

Both parents graduated from college after attending Catholic high schools and elementary schools. Mrs. McDonnell is a certified public accountant and works three-fourths time for a quasi-government agency. Her husband has a master's degree in social work and is a licensed therapist in private practice. They gave up their membership at a racquet club because they were not spending enough time there to make it worthwhile. Mrs. McDonnell belongs to a choir group but spends a lot of her free time attending her three children's volleyball and basketball games at St. Martin's. Her son also plays Little League baseball. The McDonnells are Catholic but usually attend Mass at a different church because they prefer the pastor there.

*The Campbells.* The Campbells have lived in their home since they moved to this community twelve years ago, shortly after they were married. Other St. Martin's families live nearby in similarly modest, one-story, three-bedroom homes. Some of the houses are rentals and look a bit worn and neglected. The frontyards and driveways in the neighborhood are dotted with bicycles, skateboards, and minivans and suggest an established lifestyle and parallel routines for most of these young middle-class families. Since graduating from high school, Mrs. Campbell has worked intermittently and mostly part-time as a secretary. Her new secretarial job at a real estate company allows her to leave each day at 3:00. Mr. Campbell, who earned his college degree in business, is a sales representative for a small medical supply company. The Campbells enjoy camping on an occasional weekend and for a week or so during the summer. With their three children involved in soccer and softball, the Campbells spend many afternoons and early evenings at St. Martin's. They attend Mass far less regularly than they do games and practices; a "blended" family (he was raised Catholic; she was not), they go to church "less than once in a while."

Table I  St. Martin's School

| FAMILY | EDUCATION* | OCCUPATION | MARITAL STATUS | RELIGIOUS AFFILIATION |
|---|---|---|---|---|
| 1 | Father: B.S.<br>Mother: H.S. | Sales rep, medical supply company<br>College student (full-time) | Married | Catholic |
| 2 | Mother: B.S., M.B.A. | Financial analyst | Separated | Presbyterian |
| 3 | Father: B.S., M.A.<br>Mother: B.S. | Licensed therapist<br>Certified public accountant | Married | Catholic |
| 4 | Father: B.S., J.D.<br>Mother: B.S., J.D. | Government attorney<br>Government attorney (formerly) | Married | Episcopalian |
| 5 | Mother: B.S. | Marketing director | Divorced | Catholic |
| 6 | Father: B.S.<br>Mother: H.S. | Sales rep<br>Secretary | Married | Catholic |
| 7 | Father: H.S.<br>Mother: H.S. | Construction worker<br>Government clerk/analyst (part-time) | Married | Catholic |
| 8 | Father: H.S.<br>Mother: H.S. | Unemployed (disabled)<br>Nursing student (full-time) | Married | Catholic |
| 9 | Mother: H.S. | Occupational skills trainer | Divorced | Baptist |
| 10 | Father: H.S., A.A.<br>Mother: H.S. | Sheet metal maintenance<br>Day care, house-keeping (hospital) | Married | Christian |

* J.D.—Law degree
M.A.—Master of Arts degree
B.S.—Bachelor of Science degree

A.A.—Associate of Arts degree
H.S.—High School diploma

*The Duncans.* The Duncans have been married thirteen years and have five children, ages eleven to sixteen months. For the past three years, they rented a 3 bedroom home that is a little cramped and run-down but costs only $450 a month. Mrs. Duncan hopes that they will soon be able to move into a nicer rental home in the same neighborhood.

After meeting in high school and marrying shortly after graduation, the Duncans squeezed in one or two semesters of community college but soon started a family and began working full-time. An "army brat," Mrs. Duncan has lived in the community her entire thirty-one years and is a graduate of St. Martin's School. She currently holds two jobs; during the weekdays she operates a home day care program with her mother and on weekends and one night a week, works in the housekeeping unit at a hospital about twenty minutes from home. The hospital job provides much-needed health benefits for the family; one child is asthmatic. Mr. Duncan works full-time for a sheet metal company in the maintenance department. The Duncans enjoy camping and the outdoors but have not taken any kind of a family vacation in over four years. The three oldest children often go fishing for the day with their father and grandfather in the foothill streams about an hour away from home. Most time is spent at work or at home, as Mrs. Duncan observed, "doing things that are required around here." Mr. Duncan coaches boys' basketball and his wife bakes cupcakes in order to earn enough points for a tuition reduction. Although the Duncans were raised as Catholics, they are now members of a Christian church and attend those services regularly.

## PARENTAL VALUES AND EDUCATION

### Reasons for Selecting St. Martin's School

Many observers might expect parents to choose a Catholic school for the religious instruction, in order to reinforce Christian values and to introduce their children to Church doctrine. While many of the parents expressed these desires, the motivating factors in selecting St. Martin's were far more complex and varied. On why parents select her school, the principal noted with some regret:

> I wish the reasons they send their children here was for the value-centered education and moral training. But that isn't the first reason. The first reason they send their children here is for academic excellence, and then the close family feeling. And about third or fourth on their list would be religious training.

Across social class, parents expressed interest in obtaining an education for their children which offers a package of these highly valued elements. These comments from a middle-class family were typical:

> [We picked it] for the foundation of faith, plus, and probably just as important, we thought and we still do, they're better off educationally. They're

exposed to ideas that they're not going to be exposed to in a public school. Plus, their peer group at the Catholic school—I mean you have to go to keep up with everybody.

Other parents relied upon their own experiences as a template for the kind of education their children should have, and could have, if they attended St. Martin's. In this case, an upper-middle-class mother who attended Catholic schools and graduated from a Catholic university relates:

> I wanted my kids to be spiritually grounded. I wanted them to have that basic connection. That was one reason I decided to send them to a Catholic school. The second reason was I wanted more of a community atmosphere. I didn't want them going to this great big school where there were two or three classrooms at each grade and where they may or may not run into a good teacher.

Notably, some parents, particularly nonpracticing Catholics or Protestants, consider the religious education at St. Martin's an almost incidental matter. One parent, an attorney who was raised Catholic, responded with some uncertainty and ambivalence when asked whether or not he had an interest in a Catholic or Christian education for his children:

> Ummm, I don't think so specifically. We were not opposed to it and I don't think that's a bad idea. The fact that the kids are going to take half an hour, twenty minutes, forty minutes or whatever you give them every day in religious education, is not a deterrent.

Many parents selected St. Martin's after considering their alternative, the neighborhood public school. A common perception that public schools are riddled with crime, drugs, and incompetent teachers convinced them of the wisdom of their choice:

> I felt I had more control or a little more say or they were more closely watched, each one individually, as far as they were progressing and what they were doing. Of course I've never been to public schools. This may be just my perception. There's an awful amount of drugs going around, even at that level. I felt it would more easily be controlled at a private school setting than a public school setting. (upper-middle-class mother)

> [We chose it] for the fact that there is discipline. I think that in the public schools they have taken away the ability to discipline from the teachers. I think the teachers are there as babysitters, especially nowadays. And knowing as many public school teachers as I do, basically, that's how they feel. They can't do their jobs unless they're in the elementary grades and they can kind of work with them. (middle-class father)

For another parent, a recently divorced mother of two small boys, the idea of discipline and value congruency offered her solace.

> Knowing that I was going to be a single mom, I really was looking for a more structured environment. I just figured, I needed all the help that I could get and that I needed something more conforming than something against me. (upper-middle class)

## Parents' Expectations and the Value of Education

Not surprisingly, St. Martin's parents value education. They have made an affirmative decision to send their children to a school other than their public neighborhood school, and they are paying for it. Making that choice distinguishes these parents from public school parents, at least objectively. They are, by definition, a self-selected group of individuals.

Given this context, the consistency with which St. Martin's parents endorse the value of education is hardly surprising, nor is their expectation that their children will graduate from college. Parents with college degrees were rather matter-of-fact when the question of educational goals was raised. This comment is typical:

> When I was growing up, it was never a question of if we would go to college; it was a question of where we would go to college and I've tried to do the same thing with my kids. (upper-middle-class mother)

For lower-middle-class parents, the desire for academic success and achievement is tempered by financial concerns and constraints. When these parents were asked how much schooling they would like their children to complete, many gushed with enthusiasm and pride as they reported that their child wanted to be a doctor or marine biologist. There was a sense of unrestricted hope and optimism—that everything would work out somehow. As one parent who is low income told me:

> [I want them to get] as much as they want. I don't want to push them into anything they don't want to do. It's their life. When they grow up, they've got to decide on what kind of lifestyle. I'd love to see them all be doctors or lawyers. As much as they want.

St. Martin's parents embrace education as a vehicle for economic and social advancement and are certain that their educational credentials have contributed to the professional success and material rewards that they now enjoy. The social and economic benefits associated with educational achievement have convinced them that doing well in school and earning a college degree is a worthy goal. Consider this comment from a mother who has returned to night school in order to finish her nursing degree:

One of my educators said education is an investment. What you invest in it you always get out of it. And I will always remember that to the nth degree. My parents were never investors. I don't have the money to invest, but I'm giving it my effort to do it that way. (lower-middle class)

When parents were asked what influenced their thinking about education, almost all recalled the role their parents played in their own schooling. These experiences seem to provide a framework for thinking about their own actions and beliefs in the education of their children. This response was typical:

[I'm influenced by] the way I grew up, probably. My parents' involvement and knowing how much it meant to me. Knowing that they cared and that it really mattered to them what I did. I always felt like part of the community where I went. And my mom and dad were both very involved in Parent's Club and in the parish when we were kids. You don't know that there is any difference. (upper-middle class)

Other parents' memories of childhood were more painful and regrettable. These parents wanted more for their children and expressed a determination to ensure a better childhood than they themselves had experienced. Their commitment to overcoming any challenges, particularly financial needs and constraints, was resolute. A single parent who is lower-middle class explained that her schooling was disjointed and abbreviated due to her family's constant moving.

[My parents] did farmworker type things. They went to different farms, picked different things to make money. We lived in tents or little old dinky houses where we all slept together. If it wasn't for her [mother], we probably wouldn't be together. She kept us out of drugs.

Another mother expressed regret and a corresponding resolve:

I had one parent, but she worked. I didn't have a person there. I did, I had my grandmother. But she was old. She was my great-grandmother. She wasn't fun. She wasn't involved. You can't at age seventy. You can only swing the rope; you can't jump it. You can't do everything then. I'm pretty young so I figure, let's go with it. We can have a ball. (middle class)

Later in the conversation she observed:

I think if I had had two parents, full-time and the push, that extra drive, that I might have gone to college . . . and I just want them to have that.

When parents were asked what they thought was the most important outcome of schooling, some suggested that reading, writing, and arithmetic were critical tools, "because if you have the basics down, you can just about do the rest." Most other parents, however, reflected on the larger implications of learning and credentialing, noting qualities which transcend the boundaries of school and carry into the experiences of adulthood. These comments were typical:

> I'm hoping that they can get a real good handle on the basic tools that they'll need to be able to think, solve problems, to be able to get along in life. Exposure to different values and ideas. I guess what I'm looking for is so they can really think for themselves. (upper-middle-class mother)

> [School] is a tool to make them think. Not just to look and see something but to wonder about it. And then a value system. That's why we want them to go away (to college). In terms of what an education should do for them, hopefully, they're going to be bored with what they've done and with what they've accomplished here and want to go—leave the stream and get into the ocean. (middle-class father)

> I want them to be well-rounded—knowing where to find an answer, having a thought process of figuring out what could be next. And socially well-rounded, well-balanced in every way and being able to handle every situation and having some kind of decision-making ability; figure out how to get where they want to go. (upper-middle-class father)

> The desire for learning. That's what I want them to have out of school. (lower-middle-class mother)

## SCHOOL PARTICIPATION AND SOCIAL CLASS

### Cultural Capital

The idea that all parents, once they understand the importance of active involvement in their children's education, have an equal chance to participate in the ways teachers want them to, has been undercut by recent research on the influence of class and culture on parents' interactions with schools. Lareau (1989) identifies essential elements (education, income and material resources, social status, style of work, and social networks) associated with social class that critically influence the ways parents involve themselves in their children's schooling.

While the experiences and expectations of St. Martin's parents certainly indicate that patterns of participation are derived from social class differences, parents' work lives (as distinct from their particular "style of work") and the organization of the school community seem to mediate the influence of some of these factors.

The following sections explore the interaction between parents' work lives and the rhythms and routines of family life on patterns of parent participation in schooling. After this discussion, I examine the influence of St. Martin's community and the ethic of Christian values on the nature and quality of family-school interactions. First, How do parents at St. Martin's participate in their children's schooling? How do they describe their role? What factors limit or constrain the nature of their involvement?

## Patterns of School Participation

The repertoire of actions and decisions considered under the rubric of "parent involvement" in most school settings is fairly routine, uniform, and predictable. Social scripts provide parents with a language and a framework for interacting with school officials. Over time, parents learn and adopt the institutionalized roles which define meaningful and appropriate behavior. They learn to think of themselves as "supporters," "helpers," and "fund-raisers."

St. Martin School and its parents are no exception. Most parents consider helping with homework and attending meetings as the universe of parent roles. Other important roles include driving on field trips, cheering at sports events, and attending fund-raisers. The majority of parents, however, place greater emphasis on activities which are enriching and supportive in terms of children's learning and achievement. One parent said the key to parent participation is simply, "the ability to listen. If I can't listen to my child, I don't feel that I could participate adequately."

Notably, none of the St. Martin's parents mentioned the more custodial aspects of parent involvement—making sure that their children are fed, dressed, rested, and arrive at school on time. These seem to be taken for granted, and as such, are unspoken responsibilities. Most St. Martin parents described their patterns of involvement as managing, supervising, and assisting their children with school activities. This mother asserted:

> If I don't show any support or belief in what they're doing in school, it's not going to really . . . it's like when you send your kids to Catholic schools but you never take them to church. It's just another subject. It doesn't really take. So in that sense, I think [parent involvement] is really essential both ways. (upper-middle-class mother)

A lower-middle-class, single parent who complained that her own reading and comprehension are somewhat weak, nonetheless checks her son's homework every night. In the past, she made multiplication flash cards and asked him to read road signs to her as they drove around town. How does she see her role?

> I try to help him and assist him. The teacher has thirty-three students and I have one. And I can back her up by continuing it here at home through the homework.

Several other parents echoed the general theme of partnership with teachers in the joint enterprise of the teaching and learning. Parents repeatedly referenced their particularistic concerns and teachers' universalistic interests (Lightfoot 1978). Rather than allow these different perspectives to create distrust and disagreement, there is an implicit agreement that these patterns are part of the package in a school in which thirty-six children is the standard classroom size.

The following comments exemplify this perspective. The first parent is a high school graduate who works as a part-time accounting clerk for the state government; the second is a former attorney with the U.S. Justice Department, now a stay-at-home mother. Each mother expressed a similar interest in and commitment to their children's learning:

> I think I put in on an individual basis as much as the teacher does during one day. Individualized attention for each student at St. Martin's is probably fifteen minutes a day over a five hour day. They can only give each student fifteen minutes. And I feel that I give them at least two hours of quality time. And you break that down between three of them and it's just about thirty-five, forty-five minutes that each one of them gets—a playdough time, a reading time, and science time or book report time. And that's every day. (middle-class mother)

> I watch their educational progress like a hawk. I have no teaching credentials. They have a professional teacher there but she's got thirty-six kids. She does her job and I come home and I give her a kid who is motivated and who knows he's going to have to toe the line and let her work with him. I guess I'm an overachiever that way. I make my kids do more than the teacher requires. (upper-middle-class mother)

This last comment was echoed by other parents who said that they expect more from their children than their children's teachers do:

> I don't think [the teachers] expect as much out of the kids as we do, as my husband and I do. And if it's not done neatly, they have to do it again. The teachers know, okay, at this age, that's how they do it. But we want perfect kids, I mean at least academically. Academically, we expect a lot from them. (middle-class mother)

The middle- and upper-middle-class parents at St. Martin's emphasized repeatedly the importance of modeling appropriate study habits and high standards of performance. A mother who is finishing her bachelor of science degree at the University of California observed:

> We're avid readers and I enjoy math and the sciences. I do what I can do here at home. The fact that I'm in school now has really helped because they see

me studying and they see me struggling and everybody comes home with their tests and homework. I think that helps them see that your education is important and you need to keep up with it. St. Martin's is big on teaching study habits. I try to be supportive of what the teachers are doing. (upper-middle class)

Another parent noted that she and her husband are introducing American literary classics, such as *The Adventures of Huckleberry Finn*, *Little Women*, and *Treasure Island*, to their sons. She made it clear that they were careful to avoid exposing their children to the popular Nintendo video games, which they view as harmful to their children's educational development:

My children will be different and they are different now. They stand out from a lot of folks. They know that education is important to us. We have books in our house. We sit down and practice reading at bedtime. They know that's important to us. All of this gives an environment where my kids know that learning is important. (upper-middle-class mother)

There are strong indications that income and material resources allow some parents to do more than others. Lower-income parents at St. Martin's School noted some of their concerns and constraints, such as the need to work full-time at jobs which prevent them from volunteering in the classroom or driving on field trips, or the lack of money to buy their kids more books. As one parent said:

If I was wealthy, my kids would have lessons—tap dancing, piano, whatever they want. But I can't afford that, nor do I have the time. If I didn't have to work, I could do these things and be able to financially afford it. My main goal is to show my children as much as I can. My children were the first ones to see the new exhibit of the dinosaurs at the California Academy of Sciences. The first day, opening day, they had to get there.

Another parent, a single mother, noted:

My main problem is financially I'm not able to really participate. My son gets the brunt of it because I don't have the money that some of those parents do. "I want to go, Mom," my son says. I can't do it. So that's a real problem. Most people in private schools, their parents have sufficient funds to do those things. At one time I did. But all of a sudden it went, right from underneath you.

One parent whose husband is disabled and unable to work talked openly about their financial difficulties.

I think with anybody it's the economic factor. You want so much for your children. You'd die for your children, and because of the multiple sclerosis, it puts a real damper on everything. But we're doing as well as we can in giving the children as much as they really want and just letting them learn whatever they want to learn.

These differences in social class and the implications for parent involvement were noted by an upper-middle-class parent who acknowledged that her financial position offers certain rewards and opportunities that are unavailable to other families. She teaches French at St. Martin's on a part-time basis, volunteers in the classroom, and assists at the hot lunch program. She observed:

> My husband brings in a wonderful salary. It's not wonderful by some terms. But it's perfectly adequate for us to live well, for us to take care of my children, and for me to have time to take care of my family and some of the needs in the community.

In sum, certain opportunities extend beyond the means of lower-income parents. Typically, they do not take trips to San Francisco or go to the Sierra Mountains for summer vacations. Parents are not free to volunteer in the classroom or drive on field trips, and their children do not attend summer camp. Nevertheless, lower-income parents seem willing and able to make extraordinary financial sacrifices to provide their children with certain "basic extras" such as a set of encyclopedias (on discount), membership in Book-of-the-Month Club, or, in another case, a tutor for a son who suffers from a reading disability. Moreover, the differences in income and material resources between families at St. Martin's are dwarfed by overarching and pervasive *similarities* which transcend social class. This symmetry is grounded in the nature of family organization in response to both parents working outside the home. Lower-middle-class parents may not be able to volunteer in the classroom or drive on field trips, but neither are their middle- or upper-middle-class counterparts; just about everybody works.

## Work and Family Environments

The intersection of work and family lives produces patterns of stress and corresponding rhythms of accommodation and adaptation which direct families in their relationships with schools. Thus, while other research suggests that the style, routine, and purpose of parents' work affects family-school relationships in significant and particular ways (Lareau 1989), this data from a self-selected group of Catholic school parents point to the need to examine the ways in which parents adapt to their work lives, however variable the type or nature of their work. Differences in the interconnectedness between home and work identified in working-class and upper-middle-class families, such as parents' response to homework and their ability to alter work schedules to attend school activities, seem less salient here; rather, similarities in family patterns and values are reproduced in strikingly similar ways in another context—family-school interactions. The argument that an ecological perspective[8] is necessary to understand the effects of work and family lives on parent-school interactions is not new. The aim here is to give greater voice to congruency across social class and contexts and to acknowledge the relationship between the ways families organize time and their patterns of interactions with schools.

A high level of stress and the tensions of their frenetically paced lifestyles suffused the voices of St. Martin's parents as they considered the demands of balancing work with their involvement in their children's lives. Across social class, parents identified work as the primary impediment to participating more fully in their children's education. Parents referred to inflexible work arrangements (including those parents with professional occupations), a general weariness, and a lack of discretionary time as barriers to both home and school-based involvement.

**Q.** Are you participating the way you would like?

**A.** No, because I work. I don't have the time to do it. It's hard even spending time working on the homework with the kids at night. I'd read to them a lot more, and go exploring a lot more, and go to the science center and things like that more if I had the time. Why don't you support me so I can do those things? (said to her husband) (The speaker is a full-time certified public accountant/upper-middle class.)

**A.** I kill myself at work. I usually work at night when the children are asleep. They don't know that I'm at work. I come home. I see them for breakfast. I come home. I have dinner with them. I mean I might look 100 years old by the age of 40 because of the lifestyle I use. I'm telling you, this is my life. (full-time licensed vocational nurse/lower-middle class)

**A.** Just my time because I travel. My schedule is real sporadic. . . . [Last night] I had to give this dinner. I didn't get home until 11:30. . . . I got up at 7:00 this morning and drove to Reno and back today. So I'm tired. Could I have participated last night? No. Could I even have taken him to school this morning? No. (full-time regional marketing manager; single parent/upper-middle class)

Another mother offered this dim view:

I think some teachers know some kids more than their parents do, especially two working full-time parents . . . at the dinner table, mom and dad are talking and the kids might throw a few words in. I don't know any dinner table anymore that asks them: How was your day today? I don't know anybody who does that. We sit down every night and eat together. Six nights of the week. And even though we say it's a family dinner, my husband and I are normally talking. And the kids might throw a few things in: "Where are we going tomorrow night, Mom?" But they really don't get to say how their day was. (part-time income tax processor/middle class)

Perhaps no other activity associated with schooling provides a more explicit, established linkage between home and school than homework. St. Martin's parents willingly embrace the value of homework; I found no evidence of parents who reject this interconnection between work done at school and work completed at home. Across social class and regardless of occupation, there was an unquestioned acceptance that homework is inseparable from the experience of schooling.

As one parent noted simply, "Homework comes first."

> My kids come home. They have a snack. They do homework. The television doesn't come on and nobody goes out to play until homework is done. (upper-middle-class mother)

Nevertheless, many parents suggested that homework can have destructive and destabilizing effects on family life. In the context of family rhythms and routines, homework establishes the pace and priority of after-school and evening activities:

> They spend 6½ hours a day at school. Then they come home. They have no time to relax. No time with the family. They're just back into the school work, and I don't believe in that. I really don't. It takes too much time. I guess I must be the number one parent complainer because I really get on the teachers for it because there's no time to be a normal family. That's why I love summertime so much. You know, I get to be with the kids. (lower-middle-class mother)

> They really don't want to do it at 4:00 in the afternoon. They're burned out. They want TV. They want a snack. They want to eat. They want to go out and play with their friends and I said, I'm not going to aggravate myself. So in the evenings I would just take a pencil and go through [word list flashcards]. Whether it took fifteen minutes or not, it just wasn't worth it to me [to do words right after school]. (lower-middle-class mother)

Due to the fact that many of the parents interviewed are college graduates (ten out of a total of eighteen parents interviewed), it is not surprising that only one parent mentioned a lack of education as an impediment to helping with homework. This mother of five children, who did not continue her education beyond high school, commented:

> Homework, homework, homework. I help them an awful lot when it comes to homework. I really do. . . . I try to help them as much as possible with homework. I'm not a real scholared person as far as education goes. But I'm sure I can help them as much as possible until they're in calculus. (lower-middle class)

Another parent said she supports the idea of homework but resents certain assignments which require excessive parent input and supervision:

> When they send a lot of homework home that parents have to be involved with, it makes me mad because I feel like I'm paying them this much money to teach my kids. I work all day. I come home and they're all fighting and clamoring to get my attention one over the other because none of them have seen me all day. They're all hungry. I have to feed them. They're all exhausted. They want to relax and watch some TV. Then we have bath time. We have homework time. If I'm lucky. And sometimes I have meetings to go to. I don't have time to do this stuff at home. I don't mind doing homework, but I resent helping them teach. I'd probably still resent it if I were at home because I feel like I'm paying you to teach them. When I teach my kids something, I want to do it my way and go do something fun like take a picnic to the zoo. (upper-middle-class mother)

Regardless of whether or not parents' own work continues at home, afternoons and evenings seem to follow rigid time grids, with basketball practices, soccer games, meetings, and meals somehow squeezed into particular temporal slots. If parents don't carry files or timesheets home, there are other tasks: cleaning up the kitchen, organizing bath times, returning phone calls, and reading the newspaper.

Certainly, the idea of homework seems to correspond with these parents' interest in education and their commitment to supporting their children's academic achievement. However, many parents indicated that actually allocating their (scarce) discretionary time to working out math problems or helping to write a book report was burdensome: checking homework is okay; doing it is not.

For many parents, the exigencies of work and family life demand deliberate rationing of their limited time and energy. School-based activities, like the crab feed, St. Patrick's Day dance, and Parent's Club meetings, are considered by many parents extras which they cannot afford. While some parents expressed regret and made apologies, most seemed comfortable in collapsing their energies around the "family core unit." For these parents, parent involvement is more broadly defined than attending meetings; it's attending to their kids and spouses.

> If you've worked all day, or if two parents are working all day, then to go and whatever. . . . I think sometimes it's the battle of the working family. Where is your time? Or do you have the energy to go? That's my thing. I'm like too tired. I feel like I'm being a better parent if I just stay with them than if I go. (upper-middle-class mother)

One parent justified her decision to limit participation by recalling her own parents' intense level of involvement at their Catholic school. She pointed out the possible negative effects of parent involvement when participation takes place away from home. Her own memories of absent parents provides a framework within which to measure and tailor her particular patterns of participation with her own children.

> They were never home. They were always doing something for the church. I always brought the largest amount of papers in for the paper drive. I had the largest amount of rags. Oh, I won every damn prize in the world. We had candy apple sales. We had all this stuff. . . . That's why I disagree with the Catholic schools. They want you to get so involved that people would rather be out of their house than in the house looking at their family. That's where we draw back, and we do more things here as a family. (lower-middle-class mother)

Some parents acknowledged that more and more parents seem to be staying home rather than attending school fund-raising or social events, with obvious implications:

> I think with both parents working now it's real hard to have any community. You see the involvement in the school going down because people are more willing to pay money if you don't want to go to Parent's Club meetings. And each year, more and more families are just paying the money because they just don't have the time to work their points and that type of thing. People just don't have the time. They'd rather give a donation of $10 than go work at a crab feed on a Saturday night because their weekends are really important to them, and they have other things to do. (middle-class mother)

It is important to note the absence of fathers in these discussions, although five participated in the interviews along with their wives. Regardless of maternal employment status, most mothers in this study assume the primary educative role in the family, at least by the terms measured here. Mothers contact teachers, make sure homework is completed, and sign permission slips. This role is rarely undertaken by fathers, except under conditions of paternal employment that provide ample flexibility—such as a sales job which utilizes the family home as the office. In those cases, fathers may assume the responsibility for picking up children after school or taking them to games and practices. Most fathers in this study view their role as supportive; that is, they support the school financially; they support their children by attending volleyball and basketball games; and they support their wives by agreeing with them that the children need to study and finish their homework.[9]

An extensive examination of these role differences and the influence of employment patterns, particularly maternal ones, on the organization of family life and family-school interactions exceeds the aims of this study. Nevertheless, its salience validates the critical need to explore family processes and routines of family functioning to better understand these interinstitutional linkages.

## SCHOOL COMMUNITY:
## IMPLICATIONS FOR FAMILY-SCHOOL INTERACTIONS

The competing priorities of work, family, and school impose certain decision-making imperatives on families. Some parents at St. Martin's School have resolved to redirect their time and energy to family-based activities and to forego some of the traditional social and fund-raising activities at their school. Beyond the need to achieve balance and peace in their lives, this collective action, or inaction, is driven by the fundamental nature of school community at St. Martin's.

The following sections examine the organizational, religious, and philosophical cleavages which undergird the school community at St. Martin's. The discussion focuses on institutional and individual responses to diversity and explores the implications of these actions for family-school relationships. First, what is the nature and quality of community at St. Martin's School?

## PARISH AND SCHOOL

Although born together and conceived as mutually reinforcing units for the Catholic community, St. Martin's parish and school now reflect a somewhat uneasy alliance. Socio-demographic changes in the community and weak leadership within the parish have influenced this relationship.

When the parish and school were established in the early 1960s, the community was new and brimming with young, middle-class families. The connections among families, church, and school were natural and immediate. Several teachers at St. Martin's recalled "the old days":

> The whole community, the whole neighborhood was new, and the school was really a stenciled part of the whole community experience. (teacher)

When the nuns left the school in 1972, some parishioners felt the school had lost its central mission of religious education; they resented supporting a school without that core. Other parishioners fought to keep the school open. There were fund-raisers; petitions were sent to the bishop and diocese officials. Amidst this conflict and controversy, the school remained open, but other demographic changes were beginning to buffet the parish-school community.

In the late 1960s and early 1970s, an economic downturn at the local aerospace manufacturing plant forced some families to leave the area. Other families simply "grew up"—the youngest of the children graduated from eighth grade. Families retained their ties to the parish but were financially, and perhaps emotionally, disconnected from the school. It is these families, whose children are now grown and have moved out of the community, who today constitute a major portion of the church-going parish community.[10]

As the community matured and experienced other demographic shifts, the new school parents were drawn from an increasingly heterogeneous community. These families were more geographically dispersed; many were members of parishes other than St. Martin's or were nonpracticing Catholics. A large proportion were employed in the community but lived outside of it. Perhaps most significantly, an increasing number of the school families were non-Catholics. The school population had changed from a predominantly Catholic parish group to a decidedly mixed one. As these St. Martin's teachers and parents observed, this transformation had a profound impact on the formerly functional community:

> I think maybe the parish as a whole doesn't feel quite the same commitment to the school as it once did because when the school first started the parish was new and all the families, they were younger and had children. And now we have a lot of older people who are very active in the parish, but it was their children who went here. So they don't have that immediate involvement with the school as we had when the school and the parish and the community were all new together. So I think there's been a distancing of the parish members at large from the school that wasn't there before. (teacher)

> When I went to this school, it was a neighborhood school, basically. And so you saw the children elsewhere, in your neighborhood. Not all of them, necessarily, but you'd see a handful of them on your block. So you'd see them outside of your school. It was really easy to play with them and establish relationships there. And more of them were members of the parish, very active members of the parish so that the parents all knew each other better than I think we have now. (teacher and a graduate of St. Martin's School)

> When I went to school there everybody was Catholic. Everybody in the whole school was Catholic. We went to school. We went to church there. We knew everybody. It is different now. It's a different makeup of people. (lower-middle-class mother and a graduate of St. Martin's School)

In addition to these demographic shifts, the St. Martin's community was also impacted by the steep increase in the number of young mothers who joined the workforce in the late 1970s and 1980s. Whether working part-time or full-time, maternal employment translated into fewer opportunities for the kind of face-to-face interactions with neighbors and friends that several St. Martin's teachers and parents (all of them former students) described as typical during their childhood. Mothers are less likely to be home in the afternoons or available to work in the lunch program, or to find time to chat with a parent or teacher when they pick up the children after school. With discretionary time truncated, more and more families have less time to spread over a greater number of responsibilities and commitments. Parents and teachers suggested that more typical today are the two-parent working families with children enrolled in the school's extended day care program, which provides child care until 6:00 P.M.[11]

A former St. Martin's student herself, this mother offered a retrospective observation:

> I guess it's because then, all the mothers were so involved in the kids' schooling and the sports. You knew everybody's mom. Now it's just different people from all over the place because everyone's got to work. You don't really meet the families like when we were younger. You could be more involved with those people's family. Now you can't because everybody has so much to do, so much to do. (lower-middle-class mother)

Despite these vast changes in the constitutive elements of St. Martin's community, it seems reasonable to suggest that a strong parish organization could overcome some of these constraints by reconstructing the community around its spiritual and communal needs. However, for many Catholic parents at St. Martin's, participation in parish activities, let alone regular attendance at Sunday Mass, assumes a far less significant place in their lives than it did when they were growing up. Most perceive church attendance and parish involvement as only tangentially related to their children's religious instruction. Indeed, many parents remarked candidly that they were parish members for reasons other than community worship or spiritual guidance. Their reasons for commitment to the parish seemed to include as much financial reasoning as spiritual reckoning. Many explained that they were "as active as we have to be" to qualify for the $150 tuition discount allowed to parish members. Some parents suggested that their busy weekend schedules make regular church attendance difficult. Others were comfortable with the fact that they were raising their children "in a way that is moral and just."

> It doesn't take going to church every Sunday to make you a good person. It's just the life that you live and the way you raise your family. (low-income father)

> It's hard to get them up and get them there. And then at their age, I don't want to do it just because they think it's the thing to do and it becomes a habit. If they're not going to absorb anything. So I don't think that we're deficient in bringing them into faith per se. I think it's superfluous to go just to go. (middle-class father)

This exchange typifies the rather casual attitude many parents expressed when they reflected on their patterns of church attendance.

| | |
|---|---|
| **Q.** | Are you part of the parish? |
| **Wife:** | Yea, you have to be [laughs]. It affects your tuition if you aren't. |
| **Q.** | Are you Catholic? |

| | |
|---|---|
| **Wife:** | I am. He's Methodist. One of those marriages [laughs]. |
| **Q.** | Do you go to church as a family? |
| **Wife:** | We only go all together usually, unless she's gone [her daughter]. |
| **Husband:** | It's not every weekend but it's not . . . |
| **Q.** | Would you say occasionally? |
| **Wife:** | Yea, and it's a little bit more than that. |
| **Husband:** | Fifty percent, probably. |
| **Wife:** | It's mostly because we're travelling. That's when we miss. And we travel occasionally. So it affects how much we're at church. |

Still other parish members attend Mass at a different Catholic church because they prefer the pastor there. Thus, rather than actively embracing parents, recent pastors have shown a perceived lack of interest in reaching out to newer, younger school parents, which further exacerbates the chasm between school and parish. Some parents blamed a lack of parish leadership for the disconnection between parish and school. The following statements were some of the reponses when asked their impression of the relationship between the two:

It's terrible. The priest who is on leave now would like to close that school right now. Would love to close it. It's just a bother to him. I can't believe in this day and age when there are so many assaults on the faith that that priest leaves the school alone the way he does. (upper-middle-class mother)

It's really polarized because our previous pastor could not handle children. He admittedly said, I cannot deal with kids. And as far as he's concerned, the school could burn down and it would be no big loss to him . . . it's a huge parish with a very substantial debt. So they're more concerned with bringing money in to keep the parish going and they have a large group. I think the parents that are involved in the parish are there because if they aren't, they're going to have to pay more tuition. As soon as their kids graduate, they're gone. And they wonder why they have such a turnover in their parish. (upper-middle-class father)

Several of the St. Martin's School teachers provided insightful comments when they were asked about the relationship between the parish and school. Many echoed parents' comments about the financial incentive attached to parish membership and parents' corresponding irregular participation in parish activities, including Sunday Mass. Another teacher suggested a mutually beneficial, conspiracy of silence between the school and parish, rooted in financial imperatives.

**Q.** Do you think most of the families here are parishioners?
**A.** We know they aren't. The school receives lots of money from the parish. Now, why would the parish do that? The parish would do that because the Catholic school is producing Catholics who are going to come and pay more money. Now, it looks like we're not doing that. We are educating a

whole bunch of people who are going to Lutheran Church or something. You see? So we want to please them. They don't want to know something that's not true.

She continued, perhaps speaking for herself as well as other parents:

> **A.** I barely make enough money to send my kid here. However, they're going to take $150 off if I say I'm a contributing parishioner so by God I'm going to check that. And once a month, I'm going to put a dollar in the Church. So now all of the demographics will match. That happens. I don't know if that happens here but my guess is yes because we're as normal as anybody else. (teacher)

The efforts to maintain a symmetry between the parish and school are not all so benign. Some teachers described a kind of subtle organizational imperative designed to preserve the foundational elements of a parish-school community. These teachers spoke guardedly about the special efforts they are sometimes asked to make to keep parish family members in the school:

> I know we have kept children in this school who really should not be here, who would be better served somewhere else or who are so thoroughly disruptive that it's not fair to the other children to have to cope with that kind of distraction. I think we have put up with an awful lot of that, consistently, because the parents were members of the parish, because the parents had been supportive in one way or another to the school or to the parish and so we consider it a Christian obligation to work with these children when we're not really. When everybody else is suffering as a result. (teacher)

Many of the school staff were once parish members, but several recently moved out of the community and are new members of their local Catholic parish.[12] Nevertheless, the school staff expressed strong concerns regarding their perceptions of a growing chasm between parish and school. The teachers suggested that this division weakens the degree of the parish's financial and symbolic support for the school, with detrimental consequences for the academic program.[13] However, many teachers were also aware of a gradual unraveling of the ties binding the larger school community. With increasing diversity, much of it born out of the necessity to ensure financial support for the school, new enduring challenges have emerged:

> There is with some parents, this mentality: I'm not in the parish; I'm in the school. They don't understand it's one in the same. The parish and the church and the school. There isn't the parish and the school. Sure, we have that and that's our fault. We need to do some education because we've taken those people because we want their tuition. So now we have to be patient with them and we have to educate them, call them to be. (teacher)

If the need to "educate" parents seems absurd to some observers, it should not. It is reflective of changes within the parish community which have altered the St. Martin's School community in profound and meaningful ways. The consequences of the division between parish and school are immediately obvious. The structural consistency which Coleman and Hoffer (1987) describe in their study of Catholic school communities surely existed here as recently as fifteen years ago but has subtly and substantively shifted over time. The social context in which parents with shared values knew one another and interacted naturally, frequently, and cross-generationally, fractured with the geographical separation of home and work communities, maternal employment patterns, and an increasingly diverse religious population. The face-to-face talk which provided additional resources for parents to monitor the school and their children and to sustain these congruent values is today more intermittent and unpredictable. Indeed, the bridge between parish and school, which created the fluidity for a functional school community, has been slowly severed in the unceasing currents of change.

## CATHOLICS AND NON-CATHOLICS

The principal reported that 14 percent of the school parent population is non-Catholic (23 percent of the student population), but most parents' perception is that the number is far higher. This may be due to the fact that as many as 50 percent of the Catholic families are not active members of the parish. To be sure, actual numbers probably mask a range of different levels of parish involvement among families. When I asked teachers for their assessments of the makeup of school parents across lines of religious affiliation, they estimated that about one-third of the school parents are participating Catholics[14] (although one teacher thought that this year the number might be closer to 50 percent in her classroom), with one-third nonparticipating Catholics and one-third non-Catholic. One teacher noted that a simple way to test this was to ask students from self-identified "participating" Catholic families whether or not they had received the sacraments of baptism and communion:

> They come in and say we're practicing Catholics, but they haven't been baptized. They haven't been to communion. Where did you practice? [laughs]

For most families, Catholic and non-Catholic alike, this mixing of religious faiths has few negative ramifications. For so-called participating Catholics, the school's strong and obvious commitment to Catholic education alleviates any fears of a diluted religious program due to the integrated student body. Nonpracticing Catholics are comfortable with the introduction of Church doctrine for their children. In turn, non-Catholics, many of whom selected St. Martin's School for its reputedly solid academic program, are alternately unbothered or relieved that their children are receiving a Christian-based education.[15] These opinions were typical:

> I was raised Catholic but I don't go to Catholic Church. I go to a Christian Church. We bump heads on a few issues but it's not anything too drastic. . . . I never really separated the religions. (middle-class father)

> We're Christian. We love the Lord. We believe in Jesus, and that was all. And I know being raised in the Catholic Church they believe the same things. It's just a different format. That's the way I see it. People believe different ways because they have different needs. (lower-middle-class mother)

> They're all Catholics, but I don't think my particular brand of Catholicism is much like most of them. Some, a few. But there are a lot of people who send their kids to Catholic schools because they have very definite ideas about the ways things should be. I can't handle that. (upper-middle-class father)

> Some of the things they teach, as a Baptist, I don't believe in. But that's fine. [My son] will make that choice later. What they're giving him is the basics. And that doesn't bother me at all. Anything that deviates from that is a belief anyway, part of a belief anyway. The main things I want is a belief in God, Jesus, the Holy Spirit. (lower-middle-class mother)

Even the principal and staff claim to find value and meaning in the heterogeneous school population, if for very different reasons:

> We have a 14 percent non-Catholic rate. Yes, we do lose some of that closeness. But I think the advantages outweigh that. It is nice when you're all in one nice, close-knit community and everybody knows everybody else. Everybody has the same background and values. But then I think you become extremely insular and you're not open to new ideas. My own belief is I like the much wider draw, and I think it's a lot better for the kids to be exposed to so many different ideas and values. (principal)

> I'm certainly not opposed to teaching non-Catholics. First of all, we use them as much as they use us. Our school would not survive financially if it weren't for them, without the tuition. If we didn't have them, we would have less students and we wouldn't stay open. Secondly, it gives me an opportunity to evangelize. So it's not a bad thing. (teacher)

In sum, few teachers or parents view the diversity of religious faiths represented at St. Martin's as detrimental to either the core mission of the school or the sense of community. Instead, most seem eager to cast any divisions in terms of parish versus school and to identify this conflict, at least in some part, as a generational cleavage—the "old parents" versus the "new parents." Although the cleavage between parish-school parents and other school parents has created what one parent termed "two separate worlds," it has also produced a residual of unity, if not community, around the loose collection of disparate families. There is a strong sense of the "insiders" and the "outsiders" which seems to bind the broken factions into more tightly wrapped units. The next section examines the implications of this conflict on the nature of school community and family-school relationships.

## CONFLICT, CLIQUES, AND COMMUNITY

While the separation between parish and school can be traced to the broad demographic changes identified earlier, the conflict between these groups stems from the collective choices of non-Catholics and nonparticipating Catholics. In large part, school parents who are also participating parish members are viewed by the other school parents as "insiders." These families tend to be, but are not necessarily, established community members. The "other" school parents tend to differentiate themselves from this group, to consider themselves less connected—politically and physically—to school and parish activities. These parents also recognize the resentment they have engendered among parishioners who are former school parents and may disapprove of either non-Catholics or nonparticipating Catholics attending St. Martin's School. Several parents offered these observations on this subject in response to my questions:

> **Q.** Do you think there is much overlap between the parish and the school? Is there a sense of community across the two?
> **A.** There's a friction there. There's a lot of people who send their kids to school who don't follow up by taking them to church. And of course, there's some resentment there by various factions in the community. So there's resentment by people at the Church—parishioners—whose kids are not school-age anymore. And you want to say, hey, you guys are the senior citizens in this church with the more conservative ideas. Who do you think are going to be the next members of this church when you're gone? (upper-middle-class mother)

Another parent commented:

> It's more like because we're at the school we know people in the parish. That's more my sense. And this parish wants parents from the school to volunteer for things so we've met a few people doing that. But then we always felt like outsiders and it's like gosh, they asked us to come why are they treating us so bad.

> **Q.** Why did you feel like outsiders?
> **A.** Because we weren't part of the parish. We were part of the parish but not in the parish community. You know what I mean? It seems like the parish community was the group of older people who Father had gathered

around himself and worked with and that he knew and that he cared to
have communications with and then there was everybody else. And I
don't know if that was just him. And the new priest that they have now,
we just haven't been around to get to know him so I don't know. (upper-
middle-class mother)

The conflict between parish and school involves territorial disputes, as well:

We have a real problem with the parish hall. I like to call it the gym. They call
it the parish hall. They don't want to let the school use the parish hall and the
Parent's Club is trying to work around that. The parish wants to charge the
school every time they use it. They [the school] really need the facility but
they're saying it's a parish facility, not a school facility. There's a lot of strife
going on about that right now so we'll see if the Parent's Club has enough
clout. (middle-class mother)

Perhaps no other single organization or activity more accurately reflects
the messy entanglement of competing interests and loyalties than the St. Martin's School Parent's Club. Here, the tangible consequences of simmering conflicts between "outsider" school families and "insider" school families play out
in patterns of membership, authority, and decision making. The Parent's Club
is the primary fund-raising arm of the school, as well as the source of the volunteer corps which builds, cleans, and refurbishes school grounds and facili-
ties. It is here that, despite a brief period of "outsider" control, the established
parish-school families dominate decision making.

It is instructive to note that no other central topics were raised with more
consistency and passion than the related issues of the Parent's Club, cliques,
and school fund-raising activities. The consequence of creating a community
of diverse backgrounds and interests seems to be to form cliques or enclaves of
like-minded individuals. The explicit acknowledgement of these differences,
indeed the promotion and maintenance of these divisions, creates the opportunity for control and confrontation, however subtle and polite. Thus, the formation of cliques becomes a natural response to the parish-school cleavages; the
Parent's Club acts as the stage on which these divisions confront and tussle:

Not all the families belong to the parish. And over the last couple of years
there's . . . I mean, we try real hard to say this is our community; this is our
family. But you don't always get that feeling. You go in there and you feel
like, okay, what side of the road are you on today? And that's at a lot of the
Parent's Club functions. (middle-class mother; parish member)

Another mother added:

I went to a couple of Parent Club meetings. It was okay. To tell you the truth,
the parents are cliquish, most of them. And I just don't want to deal with that.
So I let them do their little cliquey job and I'll do my job.

**Q.** Do they know one another from the parish?

**A.** All the way through school, from being in the Church. Parishioners. That's the only reason the Parent's Club is hard because they are a family and you become an outsider if you don't participate in the Church. (lower-middle-class mother)

The pattern of remarks by parents on the topic of the Parent's Club suggests that rather than build community, the organization discourages even casual socializing, except for a limited number of parents who are also active parishioners. In that sense, while serving certain instrumental purposes, the club is more successful in fueling division and discontent among a wide number of school families.

This exchange between upper-middle-class parents who are not parishioners but who are very actively involved in their children's education (in terms of classroom volunteer activities and home-based learning), is particularly revealing:

**Wife:** It's worse than the Officer's Wives Club. It really is. There's a lot of power politics that goes on in the Parent's Club. That's where a lot of parents' egos go and just . . . I have the least contact with them as possible. I would rather go to the principal and say, what do you need? I will do what the teacher wants. I will write the check for whatever money they want and just leave . . . there's a ton of power politics going on there. It's ridiculous.

**Husband:** On the other hand, although I don't agree with the way they do it, necessarily, it does serve a useful purpose for St. Martin's because you need to get some parental participation to help that school go along and to raise money. And if nothing else, they do that.

**Wife:** But they don't build community.

**Husband:** Oh, I didn't say they build community. They raise money. There's a difference.

**Wife:** They do not build community. They cause a lot more problems at times.

Many families indicated that the persistent rancor of the Parent's Club has altered their attitudes and actions toward involvement in school activities. Rather than attend fund-raising events or help to plan the annual spaghetti dinner, many parents selectively participate in a limited number of activities and focus more attention on family responsibilities and obligations. According to one mother:

We have five families on this street now that go to St. Martin's. And they pay their Parent's Club money now. I can honestly say probably choose to pay the money instead of time.

Because? [Interviewer]

> **A.** Just the cliquishness. If you don't do it their way, it's really a difficult
> school. I think, that aspect of it. You just keep hoping every year that it
> will change. That they'll get new parents in there, new blood and new
> ideas and more people who will be adaptable. That's what we're hoping
> because I have a lot of years left there, a lot. (middle-class mother; parish-
> ioner)

Another parent/parishioner, who was treasurer of the Parent's Club for two
years during a brief "outsider" administration, has bitter memories of her
involvement:

> That's where we heard all the vicious scuttlebutt and all about the conflicts.
> And this year we made a conscious decision to back off and not do anything,
> except for the mandatory, because we didn't have the energy for it. Hearing
> both sides of the story. They call you at night and they bitch, bitch. And then
> the other one calls and bitches about the person you just got off the phone
> with. (middle-class mother)

Many parents do not seem to "have the energy for it." When asked if anything keeps them from participating the way they would like, almost all the parents, parishioner and nonparishioner alike, mentioned "cliques." This response
was typical:

> The cliquishness. I would love to be involved. I do have a lot of time. I stay
> home with my son. Before I used to bring him there. Do things in the office,
> redo the bulletin boards, run paperwork. . . . It's [St. Martin's] really close.
> My mother-in-law picks him up when I can't. So there's a lot of opportunity
> for me to do things, but I'm going to save it. Catholic high school I hear is a
> real bear. They expect even a lot more of you. (middle-class mother; part-time
> data processor)

The consequences of these parents' collective actions have implications
which are both corrosive and enduring to the nature of the school community
at St. Martin's. First, the perception that an increasingly insular group domi-
nates the central fund-raising arm of the school has created a level of animosity
which discourages broad-based support for activities such as crab feeds and
spaghetti dinners, which attempt to blend fund-raising with socializing. A con-
tinual erosion of support for these activities obviously diminishes the financial
contributions the club can make to the school.

Perhaps far more critical, the cleavages born out of generational divisions,
philosophical/religious differences, and petty, partisan demands have ruptured
the St. Martin's community. There is little sense of traditional Catholic community here in which the parish lies at the heart of the functional community,

providing spiritual nourishment and social sustenance across generations. The punishing demands of work and the family and the corresponding constraints bounding time and space have widened these chasms.

These interviews create the striking impression that when considering the nature of school community at St. Martin's, many parents reject notions of cohesion and consensus that most observers would expect in a Catholic school community. There is a sense of their separateness and individuality, rather than of their collectivity and mutual interdependence—a sense of distinctive beliefs rather than shared values.

These themes were echoed when I asked parents if they socialized with other school parents. Almost all of them responded negatively and suggested that if they socialized with other adults, it was often with family members or "old friends." It is hardly surprising then that doubt and uncertainty color the remarks of these parents when they are asked to consider whether or not other school parents are people like themselves:

> I think some of their value systems are different than ours, definitely. Yea, they're different. As far as having and meeting some really close friends there, we haven't developed any close friends. A high percentage of them are more concerned about being upwardly mobile than we would ever consider giving any time to. It's not as much a priority with us as it is with a lot of them. (middle-class father; parishioner)

> I don't know if they share my same values. I'm sure there are a few parents who have the same values for their children. But as a whole, I don't really communicate that much with other parents so I guess I don't really know. (lower-middle-class mother; nonparishioner)

Another parent, who is an accountant, suggested that while many of the St. Martin's mothers work, they typically hold jobs in retail sales rather than in professional occupations. Her husband complained that he can never find anyone who enjoys "stimulating discussions about philosophy or politics." Most only seem interested in professional football or basketball, he said. His wife continued:

> There are some people like us but there's really nobody over there that we've gotten to be social buddies with. There really aren't a whole lot of people like us. We don't enjoy the parish that much. It's a real mixture of types over there. There aren't a lot of educated, professional people like we are. (upper-middle-class mother; parishioner)

When asked whether she's like other parents at St. Martin's, this mother suggested that although most families at the school have more material wealth their values are probably similar to her values:

A quarter of them. I'll take that one-quarter. And the other ones . . . I'd say were lower-middle class. A lot of the people there are upper to middle. They just go there. It is structured. They want their kids to have a good education. There is the extension program for the working. And there are a lot of single parents there. There's a lot.

**Q.** How about values? [Interviewer]
**A.** We all have the same values, I think.

From these comments, it appears that these families are talking about several different, separate school communities. Middle-class families perceive the majority of St. Martin's school families to be more concerned about "being upwardly mobile" than they themselves are. At the same time, upper-middle-class parents see themselves as a minority group in a school community of working-class families. This striking contradiction and the parallel assumptions of parents who perceive themselves as distinct from other families, either in terms of values or social class, underscores the fact that most school families know very little about one another. Why?

When parents' fragmented and frenetic lives leave little room for discretionary time to spend at school functions, there are fewer opportunities for casual or spontaneous face-to-face exchanges with other parents. When institutional divisions further distance parents, the situation is exacerbated. Without these exchanges, it is difficult to know many faces or names, except perhaps of the parents of their children's friends. Without sustained and continuous interactions, little can be known beyond an occupation or address—the stuff of carpool lists.

If one activity provides the seeds for sustained social interactions at St. Martin's, it is school sports. Nearly all the parents interviewed indicated that their children—and by necessity, they themselves—were actively involved in the tightly organized and highly competitive worlds of volleyball, basketball, football, and softball. With an average of three practices a week and a game on Saturdays, these events provide the time and place for casual, if perhaps abbreviated, social exchanges between families from different backgrounds and school experiences. Parents exchange information about teachers' reputations, ability-grouping, and science fair projects. It is also an opportunity to discuss issues ranging from Parent's Club fund-raisers and the school board's decision to allow students to wear shorts, to the condition of the lunch room.

The significance of the school sports program cannot be exaggerated, neither in terms of its importance to individual families, nor as an instrument for socializing and constructing community among families. A single incident helps underscore its importance. When a parent complained that her daughter was not getting enough playing time on the volleyball team, the school board designated the upcoming monthly meeting to discuss school athletic policy (the issue of whether or not all team members should receive roughly equal playing time or, alternatively, that only the most talented should play the majority of the time). Parents' reactions were overwhelming. The meeting room was packed and overflowing with agitated and vocal parents. The principal doubted that that level of response could be matched again—even if the school board held a meeting to discuss abolishing religion.

Despite the integral role of school sports, the St. Martin's School community reflects only limited dimensions of the constitutive elements of community: interaction and mutual dependence, the intention of longevity and permanence, expressive ties, communication, common and mutual sentiments, shared beliefs, and an ethic of individual concern and sympathy (Raywid 1988b). There is a sense of community there, but it is neither absolute nor aggregative; it is neither rooted nor ephemeral. Rather, the nature of community embraced and fostered at St. Martin's is grounded in an alliance of accommodation and differentiation. That is, there is an implicit understanding among families and school staff that internally, the St. Martin's community may be differentiated but externally, against the backdrop of a larger community of school parents, set apart. The contours of individual differences across class, occupation, neighborhood, and religious faith, are leveled at the intersection of private choice. These parents' collective actions—to enroll their children in a Catholic school—assume public dimensions by providing the link to bind these disparate families to a "school community." The nature of this "common ground" and the role of the principal in nurturing its growth are explored in the next sections.

## "COMMON GROUND"

The literature on school choice is replete with evidence which suggests providing parents with educational options for their children engenders commitment, social cohesion, and community (for a review, see Raywid 1988). In a comparative study of private and public schools, Erickson (1982) argues further that the consequence of obligating parents to a tangible "investment" in their children's education is that "most parents will probably not invest in a school (if given a choice) unless they expect something extra in exchange for the costs. If they get something extra, or think they get it, they may feel obliged (committed) to reciprocate in some way."

Parents at St. Martin's pay directly for the educational services their children receive. Individually, tuition expenses may be viewed as a necessary sacrifice to obtain highly valued services. However, collectively, a willingness to pay for education seems to purchase a sense of commitment and the satisfaction of membership in a group which is decidedly separate from other school parents. Tuition is the badge, the currency of commitment, that provides parents with a manifest sense of belonging to this community. There is an unfounded belief that "if they care enough to pay, they must value education more than parents who simply send their kids to the neighborhood school." The point here is that rather than being internally derived from a homogeneous collection of necessarily like-minded school families, the sense of community is externally driven. The school is a repository for parents with differing interests and beliefs, whose commonality is their separateness from public school families, not their consensus on the school's central mission. In the absence of a parish-driven school community, the ethos is foundational, elemental. As these comments indicate, the dividend paid to parents for their decision to exercise choice seems both profitable and rewarding:

> There is automatically a matter of selectivity in a Catholic school because every parent is paying to have their kid educated in a certain way which ipso facto means education is important. Whatever community you build, you've got that on the foundation. A lot of these other parents in your neighborhood schools are sending the kid to school because the state says you have to go to school. They are automatically selecting out a group which has something in common to start off with. (upper-middle-class mother)

> If they're paying the money, in a lot of cases, making a lot of sacrifices to pay the money, it's pretty obvious the education is a priority with them. So there's going to be more involvement and concern. In a lot of public schools, some of the parents, for whatever the reasons, because they haven't had any education themselves or they, finances, or whatever, they view school as a babysitter.

> Q. There's not that feeling at St. Martin's because?
> A. If we're paying the money, we would obviously think it's important that they be there. And you're going to do anything you can to keep your kid there. (middle-class father)
> A. There's more common ground. There's more a common reason for the children being there. In a public school, maybe 10 percent of the kids are Catholic and maybe of those, one-tenth of those go to church. But in a Catholic school, you have more of a common focal point. Not everybody is there for a Catholic education. A lot of people are there just for a Christian education; a lot of people are there just for a private education, and they think it's a good school. But mostly, they're there because it's a Catholic school, and they're interested in that tradition. So that gives them more of a common ground than you have in a public school, not as much variety as you have in a public school. (upper-middle-class mother)
> A. I think there's more of a commitment. I think there may be more of a commitment on the family's part, like we're paying for this, so let's make it right. (upper-middle-class mother)

## THE PRINCIPAL GARDENER

Although typically framed under the mantle of school "climate," the effective schools research highlights the influence of the principal in establishing "what people in a community share that makes them a community rather than a group of disparate individuals" (Grant 1985). There is no example more vivid and vocal than that of the St. Martin's School principal. To be sure, the "common ground" which parents describe is tended and cultivated by this school principal using the tools of humor and laughter, an uncanny ability to recall names, and a deep sense of caring. From Back-to-School Night in September to the final Weekly Bulletin in June, she invokes a language which reverberates with the themes of community, commitment, and school family. During parent-teacher conferences, which are held in the parish hall, the principal glides easily around the room, warmly greeting mothers, fathers, and their children by name, often inquiring about a sick relative or a parent's new job. She employs both instrumental and symbolic channels to share these messages; her articles appear in the local newspaper each week, the parish bulletin each Sunday, as well as in the Weekly School Bulletin. She shares her own personal news in the school bulletins, including items about a daughter's upcoming wedding and her mother's move to another city, and frames announcements about other faculty members or parents in terms of "our family rejoices because . . ." with the aim, she told me, "toward community-building and community with shared values." Parents seem to be listening:

> She knows all the siblings, even the ones who aren't in school yet. She knows the family. She knows who your kids are. She knows every single kid's name in that school! I think when a parent sees that the principal, the head of the school, takes an interest in their child, their child's name, their child's brothers' and sisters' name, that that kind of gives the parents the impression that the school cares, and so if the school cares, the parents are going to care too. You're not a nameless face. You're not a one of 1,000 kids somewhere. You're not a student number when you're at St. Martin's. You're an individual kid. You're a family, and they know you. (upper-middle-class mother)

> She makes an all out effort. She really makes you feel good. That's what I really like. That's the warmth that I need or that family that I need. I know that I might never have a problem, but I always have her as the liaison for anything. (lower-middle-class father)

> As a school, I do feel a unity. I really feel like it's a school family, especially with the teachers and the faculty there. They'll listen to any problem that I have. They're always open to suggestions, and any gripes or complaints. And they're always very willing, especially the principal. She's such a wonderful person. She's always very willing to help you out in any way, any way possible. (lower-middle-class mother)

As parent after parent raised the topic of the principal, and described her wit, intelligence, and friendliness, a consensus emerged in direct proportion to the agreement around a dramatically different issue—parish-school conflicts and cliques. The principal's popularity seems to neutralize the discordant voices which rumble just below the surface of the "common ground." Her leadership acts as a kind of leveler across this set of disparate families. She seems to thrive in her role:

> [Parents] can disagree with me all they want, as long as they never raise their voice. I have full respect for them. No matter what my field, each one of them is an important piece of the puzzle, because just as we need all kinds of kids, we need all kinds of parents. And of course, I just like people. Oh, you couldn't do this job if you didn't like people. (principal)

Her tireless promotion of an ethic of caring and compassion unifies St. Martin's school community, soothing any parents' doubts that they have chosen wrongly:

> There's a real sense of Christian community. Everything has to be fair at St. Martin's almost to the point where sometimes it drives you nuts because life isn't fair, you know? But there's a real sense that you've got to treat all these kids the same and you can't single out a child. (upper-middle-class mother)

> I don't think as many children slip through the cracks. I think they grab them before they get through the crack, or they're well aware that this one is going, and it's like everybody is scrambling to do what they have to do. If there is a family problem, everybody on the faculty is trying to work and help and do the things that will be beneficial. (upper-middle-class mother)

Another parent, whose child attended both public and private schools before enrolling at St. Martin's, said the other principals were not as helpful or compassionate:

> They just weren't there when I asked for something. I think that if I asked for help [at St. Martin's], which I have asked for through the principal, that there [would be] an immediate reply, whether it was: "Well, Mr. Jones I don't know if I can give you an answer today, but there may be some help for you." And there always has been. And it's not that I'm asking for a helping hand. It's just that because of the disability, the need is there. If we would come into a windfall, in the back of my mind and in the back of my heart, I know the sort of things that I'm going to take care of, and St. Martin's would be the first on the list with some gratitude. (lower-middle-class father)

The principal promotes a feeling of inclusion, regardless of parents' particular socioeconomic positions. Although school uniforms help parents who cannot afford to outfit their kids in $60 jeans, the price of "fitting in" sometimes exacts other costs—such as tuition, athletic uniforms, or cheerleader outfits. If these items exceed parents' means, the principal steps in and provides them. Her actions are grounded, she says, by a particular set of Christian values:

I know if a family hits a bad spot in their life, and they will come in and say, "Look, I cannot pay for the rest of the year." And I simply tell them not to worry about it. Because besides being an educator, I'm a Catholic educator, and I truly believe the money will come from somewhere and you know it always does. And I'm certainly not going to boot a kid out just because his father lost his job or because they found out his mother needed major surgery and both grandparents died or something. Unfortunately, these things happen. That's reality. (principal)

If parents' impressions are any gauge, the principal has successfully enacted the style of leadership she envisions for herself. There's no slick, studied appeal or contradiction here, only a deeply personal, visceral response to the challenges of school leadership. On this subject, the principal has the final word:

My job is here, to be here to serve the people. I mainly perceive my job as an instructional leader. And to be here as the educational leader for the kids but also as a sort of adviser, counselor, whatever—sort of everything. I also do toilets and windows. Our custodian doesn't come in until noon. Any plugged toilets in the morning, I take care of, and I'm quite good at it too. [laughs]

Although the principal has gathered around her a staff with largely consistent and parallel beliefs to her own, the nature of interactions between parents and teachers are markedly different than those reported between parents and the principal. These relationships reflect the distinctly different roles of principals and teachers, but they also highlight the competing perspectives which color the experiences and expectations of teachers and parents. The next section explores the nature of parent-teacher relationships at St. Martin's by examining the value and meaning these two groups attach to one another's actions.

## RELATIONSHIPS BETWEEN PARENTS AND TEACHERS

### Parents' Expectations

Recent research suggests that parents' educational and occupational status influences the way in which they interact with teachers (Lareau 1989; Wilcox 1978). Lareau asserts that parents who hold professional occupations and/or have an equivalent educational background as teachers are more assertive, comfortable, and controlling with educators than are parents without this equivalent or superior social and educational status. In a private school setting, however, other variables may mediate this relationship between parents and teachers.

Parents at St. Martin's have voluntarily elected to send their children to a private school and commit certain resources—money and time—to gain admission to the school. The "badge of membership" includes a package of expectations of which both parents and faculty are cognizant. These expectations undergird relations between parents and teachers in this school of choice and serve to level or flatten other incongruities associated with educational and occupational status. Thus, although several of the parents interviewed (eight out of eighteen) did not graduate from college and hold jobs which are not equivalent in occupational status to teaching, there were no indications of deferral, discomfort, or unwillingness to challenge teachers.[16] Rather, the fact that they had "literally bought into the system" seemed to purchase status and equality and a sense of entitlement:

> I am a paying customer, and I expect to be treated like one. I'm paying for a service, and I would expect a little bit more than going into a public school. I am involved here and I make sure that my tuition is paid for on the tenth of every month. I'm not late. And I expect to be treated the same way as far as when I have a question. Don't be: "I'm busy right now; Could I get back to you later?" A little bit of respect, that's all I'm asking. I give them that much respect, so I expect the same. (middle-class mother; data processor)

> Do I feel entitled to have more access or say or something? Sure. I think economics does that whether you're paying rent or a mortgage or tuition. Sure . . . I do think I have an ear. I've never been told that, because you're paying this tuition you have this right that allows you to do thus and so, but I take that on. I take it. (upper-middle-class mother; financial adviser)

Some parents suggested the school has clear incentives to be more responsive to their concerns and interests than a public school. Why do parents think that?

> Because you're paying for it. And they know if you're not there to pay for it, at some time they're going to lose you. (lower-middle-class father; disabled and unable to work)

> When someone hands you money, you don't forget it. You're saying, "here." Whether it's going into a general fund or to become your paycheck, or it's going to buy books, you remember that face. (middle-class mother; data processor)

> I bet they are more responsive because of that. I've never thought about it before. I don't think they are conscious of it, but I sure would be if people were paying me $3000 a year to send my kids there. Rather than I'm here because the law says these kids have to have an education. (upper-middle-class father; licensed therapist)

Other parents were not sure that the level of school responsiveness reflects a client-provider relationship. Other families rejected the notion that they were somehow entitled and reframed the issue in terms of their individual decisions to exercise choice:

> I'm paying just to be able to let my child learn in that environment as opposed to another environment. I think this is a better environment, and I'm willing to pay for the privilege of letting him enter that environment. So the payment is not that we expect necessarily more out of the education, per se, but more in the value kind of sense. We will be sending them to be taught by people who share the same kind of value system. (upper-middle-class mother; attorney)

## What Teachers Think Parents Expect

While the message from parents may be somewhat mixed and murky on the issue of entitlement, their expectations of teachers are transmitted with apparent regularity and clarity. Parents have incredibly high expectations of them, teachers asserted, due in part to the fact that parents pay directly for the educational services their children receive:

> It alters their expectations of us because they chose us and they have purchased this package, and they feel that they have a certain amount of say in what goes on because they are paying for it. They seem to demand or expect a lot of personal attention because they are paying for this. (teacher)

> They do expect to have a lot of say in how things are done and because they have to earn so much money to help pay bills, they figure that that entitles them to a lot of say in how that money is spent and what they have to do to earn it. (teacher)

> For the most part, they are going to take more interest in what's going on because they have chosen it, and they are paying money for it, and they are making somewhat of a sacrifice and for different people, it's an even greater sacrifice, depending on their income level. So they probably will be more vocal about it and will want more input. (teacher)

As parents and teachers discussed their expectations for one another, both expressed frustration and weariness, but teachers were far more vocal and dispirited. This could be related to the fact that parents deal with only one teacher at a time, while teachers must interact with thirty-six different sets of parents. Nevertheless, the vastly different levels of satisfaction between the two groups seem larger than these ratios. For the most part, the parents seem content with the status quo; they are extremely satisfied with the academic program at St. Martin's, despite occasional disagreements or misunderstandings with teachers. On the other hand, as teachers considered the level and nature of parents' expectations, there was a growing sense of resentment, although they kept assuring me (and perhaps themselves) that they were very happy at St. Martin's School and did not mean to sound "negative."

How does the staff perceive parents' expectations? The principal recalled the time she turned around halfway home to retrieve something at school that she had forgotten. The phone was ringing when she walked into her office. The parent on the other end said, "Where were you?" It was 6:00 P.M.

> They expect me to walk on water during a drought [laughs]. I think they expect me to always be here. And by "always be here," I literally mean that. I do get here before 7:00 in the morning, and I usually stay until about 5:30 or 6:00 at night, unless I have a meeting that night; then I don't go home. (principal)

> [They expect] everything. I think they have incredible expectations. Not for me personally, but for the field of teaching. And they have an incredible lack of understanding. I've had people say, "God, it must be nice to go home at 3:00." I mean, it's not 3:00 when I go home. I'm only beginning! I don't understand what their expectation is except that we can do no wrong. We are allowed to do no wrong. (teacher)

> I think some parents might bring their children here with the expectations that we're going to solve all their problems. (teacher)

Although many of the issues that separate teachers and parents can be attributed to ambiguous roles and conflicting expectations which bridge public and private schools alike, the critical difference between these two groups at St. Martin's is anchored in the religious charter of the school. In sharp contrast to the heterogeneous student and family population, the faculty at St. Martin's reflects a coherence and consistency across gender, educational backgrounds, and religious affiliation. They are all Catholic and attend church regularly. The principal likes to say about the faculty that "we are family people too." They are an obviously close-knit group who enjoy occasional "TGIF" get-togethers when their schedules permit. Beyond social compatibility, these teachers share similar pedagogical philosophies, which find expression in the tenets of Catholic education. Their decision to teach at St. Martin's reflects a shared belief in these values and a willingness to incur heavy costs, in terms of diminished salary and benefits, to exercise this choice. Unlike the variety of reasons parents offered for their decision, teachers offered only one, echoed in only slightly differing tones:

**Q.** Can you tell me why you teach in a Catholic school?
**A.** Because I cannot separate teaching from Christian values. There's no way I could teach without bringing in Christian values. How do you teach history without doing that? How do you teach economics without social justice? How do you tell them you must cooperate with each other if there's

no basis. You do it because, if you're a humanist, that's the best that we do. Try that with a twelve-year-old, and he'll say, "Hey, getting my own way is the best that I can do and without getting caught." But if I say this is a historical character named Jesus Christ, and He is our role model and you can't deny the existence of the world, all of that, you are valid then. You are credible then. (teacher)

The teachers' deep sense of commitment to the tenets of Catholic education is a flash point of opposition to those parents who send their children to St. Martin's for the rigorous academic program alone. Several staff members, including the principal, discussed the difficulty of teaching children Catholic or Christian ethics when there is little reinforcement of these same values in the home. For the staff, this gulf between school and home is exemplified by parents who do not attend Mass regularly. These differences also find expression in academic matters. To some teachers, it is a difference between *growth* and *grades*. Parents expect good grades, and if their child is not at the top of the class, there is a sense of failure and disappointment projected onto the child. Teachers have different goals, ones which emphasize personal growth, achievement, and honest work. They complain that parents place far too much emphasis on competition, both in the classroom and on the playing field, with an attitude that suggests the following: if my kid's not first string and out there the whole time, he's a nobody.

## Teachers' Expectations

As teachers reflected on the demands imposed on them by parents, they asked for a partnership. Their expectations of parents, they said, were simple and traditional—reading to their children, helping with homework, attending conferences and back-to-school nights. Most suggested that parents' increasingly fractured lives were leading more and more parents to bracket their roles in their children's education into smaller, manageable units, leaving teachers with larger chunks of responsibility for the education of their students. With more children starting preschool at age three or four, these teachers worried that parents were completely dismissing their primary educative role by reducing learning situations to their most organized, school-like forms. Many suggested that it is a constant battle to remind parents that learning exceeds the boundaries of a classroom or the bindings of a book. These teachers observed:

I see a lot of parents of young children assuming that they're not learning at home, that they have to be in school, in a formal environment to learn and for small children, that's just not true. When I test for incoming students, I am constantly amazed at the number of parents who say, "Oh, they didn't do that at their preschool," and I think, Where were you? What were you doing with your child? I see myself as a bridge with the parents to remind them that they can do a lot with their children and need to follow through at home a lot on what we're doing because it's not an isolated little cubby hole where they are for four hours or five hours a day.

Another teacher pointed to broader societal changes which have changed dramatically the rhythms and routines of family functioning. The pace of life has generally quickened, she noted, and patterns of maternal employment have permanently altered the role of women:

> I think the number one billing is the women are working. The women are in the workforce and there's no one at home. A woman is doing two jobs already, and there is simply not enough time. You can't be at work all day and be in the classroom helping or even have a lot of energy left. And I'm seeing that so, so much.

One teacher who said she asks parents to commit fifteen minutes a day to reading with their children, observed:

> I've had parents who said to me, "I'm just too busy when I get home. I'm too tired. I have to do dinner. I have to do this . . ."

The teachers' message was unequivocal: a two-income family may enjoy more material comforts, but the cost in diminished discretionary time weakens parents' ability to play a primary role in their children's educational lives. The trade-off is a wholly unsatisfactory one for teachers:

> My students come in and they have a swimming pool and they go to Disneyland and they do this and that, but mother is absolutely exhausted because she has to work in order to maintain this lifestyle. I really think that the biggest problem is that we have so many two-income families where the mother's job or the father's allows so little flexibility, they just don't have the time or energy.

Another common complaint registered by teachers parallels the concern about parents' time usage patterns by suggesting that students' lives are unnecessarily fragmented across various extracurricular activities. Repeatedly, these teachers argued that if the pace and scale of leisure activities were diminished, there would be more interest and commitment to supporting educational activities in the home and at the school. When one teacher was asked what things prevent parents from participating the way she would like them to, she responded immediately:

> The multitude of activities for children—going to soccer, and dance class and all of this. I think maybe all our society in general, the more leisure time we get, the more we try to fill it up and so we're doing so many things. We're just maxed out in terms of stress and in terms of what we think we have time for.

Another teacher, when asked what are some ways she would like to see parents participate in their children's schooling, suggested:

> I would like to see them model for their child, in other words, read. Do they read at home, or do they say, "come on, you've got your dancing and flute lessons and then we've got to get over to soccer." So they're sending a message that conflicts with the message that I'm sending. I would like to see them help their kids with their homework and know what the homework was, not do it for them. There's a real big difference.

While the issue of homework was raised consistently in conversations with teachers, it was unclear whether the value of homework lies in its intrinsic contributions to learning, as a vehicle for parent involvement in schooling, a combination of both, or neither. It was also unclear whether teachers designed homework activities with the explicit intention of parental involvement or whether this was merely a byproduct of students' individual needs. A stronger possibility may be that homework is just an unquestioned ritual of schooling which both parents and teachers seem to embrace, despite the attendant conflicts.

## Intersection of Divergent Lives

Distinctive images can be drawn from these interviews. First, teachers echoed the voices of parents as both groups described the challenges of balancing work and family entanglements in their increasingly complex lives. Although many seemed weary and worn, most parents expressed satisfaction with the ways in which they are able to manage these competing demands. They feel comfortable expressing concerns and are comfortable with the responses that they receive from the school. From their perspectives, an alliance exists between themselves and the staff which is basically stable and resilient.

In contrast, teachers expressed bitter resentment at both the unrealistic demands they believe parents impose and the corresponding lack of response they perceive from their "partners in education." It is not a lack of commitment; it is more often a difference in attitudes. For teachers, the intersection of these conflicts centers on the issues of homework (parents' lack of involvement in it), grades (parents' excessive emphasis on it), and students' personal growth (parents' lack of appreciation of it).

Teachers also suggested that parents were neglecting their primary educative role. While stopping short of blaming either parent in a dual-income household, many of the teachers indicted parents whom they consider absent when it comes to monitoring and reinforcing the educational and religious values teachers work to promote. From their perspective, parents' increased income and material resources balanced out to a net loss; parents' hectic work lives meant additional distractions and constraints, and added little to the educational or social lives of the children.

## SUMMARY

Despite differences in social class and status, parents at St. Martin's School participate in strikingly similar ways in the educational lives of their children. Although parents with more income and material resources may draw from deeper reservoirs, universally shared stresses and strains associated with balancing frenetic work and family lives seem to produce a fairly uniform set of responses. Thus, rather than differentials in income, occupation, and education prompting varied patterns of participation, we see widely shared patterns of adapted family routines.

St. Martin's school community represents a self-selected group of parents with expressed dedication and commitment to education. This common ground, however, belies a generational, organizational, and philosophical chasm which divides the school community. With humor, political savvy, and instinctive leadership, the principal engenders a sense of gratitude and connection (if not community) between school families. Her conscious and deliberate extension of Christian ethics effectively neutralizes disparities in social status and income which could exclude or isolate some parents. Additionally, the intense and pervasive interest in school sports unifies the disparate set of families within the parameters of space and time and provides a predictable and accessible social network for parents to exchange information and rumor regarding school activities.

The issues around choice find explicit articulation at St. Martin's School in the sense of entitlement many families associate with tuition. To the degree that parents translate this belief into a set of expectations for teachers, there are direct negative implications for relations between teachers and parents. These conflicts coalesce around the issues of homework and grades and suggest that teachers and parents have somewhat different social and educational goals for children.

## NOTES

1. All school names used in the case studies are pseudonyms.

2. The principal regards paying her teachers a "just wage" her greatest challenge over the next several years. Her comment: "we've got to pay them something halfway decent—which is just where it is—halfway."

3. In 1989, Parent's Club funds paid for the conversion of the snack bar to a learning center, carpeting for the kindergarten and library, and repairs for the thrift shop. Additional funds were raised to pay for new desks in the first and second grade classrooms.

4. A total of ten families from St. Martin's School were interviewed for this study. Of this total, nine families were interviewed in their homes; one was interviewed in her office. All interviews were audiotaped with the permission of the subjects.

5. These categories reflect composite definitions of social class and in many cases, respondents' self-identifications with a particular category. Composite measures include income, occupation, education, and material resources.

6. While no attempt was made to select a statistically representative sample, these cases reflect the range of backgrounds and family structures represented among the population of families at St. Martin's School.

7. All names used here are pseudonyms.

8. An ecological perspective suggests that behavior is neither totally context-specific nor totally an expression of enduring personality traits.

9. Sometimes this concept of support brings fathers to the school for events such as back-to-school night, but rarely, if at all, into the classroom. At St. Martin's, parent-teacher conferences are held during the late afternoon and evening hours to accommodate working families. Observation and teacher reports indicate that over half of these conferences are attended by both parents.

10. Currently, only 111 of the 1,700 registered parish families have children enrolled at St. Martin's School.

11. The principal reported that 110 of the 316 students at St. Martin's are enrolled in the extended day care program. This translates into about 80 families (one-third of all St. Martin's school families).

12. Currently, four members of the faculty are parish members.

13. The parish's contribution to the school's total income amounts to about 6 percent, a figure close to the revenues raised by school registration fees.

14. "Participating" Catholic here refers to a Catholic who attends Mass on Sundays on a regular basis and observes the Church's holy sacraments.

15. Only one parent expressed some concern about the influence of non-Catholics on the education program at St. Martin's: "There are a lot of people who send their kids there who are not Catholic. . . . When I ask them how they like it, they go, 'Well, except for the Catholic part, it's great.' Now, I take a little bit of offense at that because the reason I'm sending my son there is for the Catholic part. And if he's going to sit with thirty kids who aren't Catholic and who say this is dumb, I think that's defeating the purpose." (upper-middle-class mother)

16. These occupations include construction foreman, licensed vocational nurse, data processor, secretary, and maintenance worker. Most of the parents with college degrees (ten out of the eighteen parents interviewed) hold professional occupations, including accountant, financial adviser, and attorney, or work in sales and marketing.

# 3

## *Carlton School*

### INTRODUCTION

Carlton School sits a block away from a busy four-lane boulevard. A neglected field of dusty dirt mounds and dry, untended weeds provides a buffer zone from the noise of the traffic three hundred yards away. Built over twenty-five years ago, Carlton School was one of the area's first development projects. Over the last ten years, new residential developments have filled in the surrounding pockets of open land, providing units of single-family dwellings currently valued at between $125,000 and $150,000. These spacious three- and four-bedroom homes with well-manicured lawns contrast sharply with the far more modest two-bedroom duplexes and run-down rental homes that border the school on the eastern side. On the opposite side, bumping up against the school's asphalt basketball courts and generously sized, grassy athletic field, a small treeless park is nestled adjacent to the school grounds.

The entrance to Carlton School is marked by rectangular-shaped tinted windows and tall glass-framed doors which open to an atrium. A number of stickers affixed to the glass windows alert persons who pass through the doors that "All Volunteers And Visitors Must Get An Office Pass!" There is a sticker which thanks people for "Helping Us Keep Carlton A Safe Place For The Children, Staff, And Parents Who Study And Work Here," and another which announces that Carlton is a "Tobacco Free School." Inside, the set of four heavy doors on the right open to the cafeteria/auditorium, and to the left is the main office. Beyond the atrium, a bank of classrooms forms the central core of the campus. The one-story, concrete-block building suggests standard 1960s elementary school architecture, with tinted windows that stretch from the benches to the ceiling. A set of portable classrooms sits on the back edge of campus, demarcating the zones of classroom instruction and physical competition; just outside these classroom doors, an ample, grassy playing field extends for hundreds of yards in each direction.

The school office features a rather familiar standard arrangement. A long, hip-high counter divides the room between an open waiting area and the school secretary's wood desk, black metal file cabinets, and a single Touch-tone telephone. The principal's office door is just beyond the work space. A large room off to the left is used by the faculty for assembling, copying, and organizing classroom materials. The nurse's office is directly across from the secretary's work area. There is a pervasive sense of calm and efficiency here, as teachers occasionally walk through to check their cubbyhole boxes or to use the copying machine in the workroom.

The classrooms at Carlton are similarly ordinary. Rows of paired desks (or single file ones) are arranged facing the green-shaded chalkboards. Green alphabet cards depicting printed and cursive letters border the tops of the chalkboards. The primary grade classrooms (grades 1–3) typically have reading corners—small metal and plastic chairs clustered in a circle with books neatly arranged in shelves that mark the borders between the classroom areas. Bulletin boards feature the history of Black Americans, early American/California settlers, and assorted artwork projects. Just outside each classroom, on the bottom corner of the tinted window nearest the door, is a sticker which warns "We Report Suspicious Activity."

Carlton School changed from a neighborhood school to a magnet school almost overnight. As a result of a class action suit brought by the NAACP in 1979 on behalf of the parents of Carlton School, the school board elected to create a magnet school to alter the 98 percent minority enrollment (mostly Black) to a ratio which more accurately reflected the minority/majority balance in the district at large.[1] Two years later, the district added another magnet elementary school. Three more magnet schools were added in 1988–89, and two in 1989–90, all of which emphasize a particular curricular theme pedagogy such as math and science, literary arts, or basic studies.

There are now three basic elementary magnet schools in the district.[2] The district is divided into three sections; of the fifty-six elementary schools in the district, sixteen schools feed into Carlton.

## STUDENTS

Carlton School has two classrooms of 30–33 students in each grade from first through sixth. Typically, school enrollment is about 340–345 students. According to the most recent district figures (1992), the school population is 49 percent white, 23 percent Black, 14 percent Hispanic, 10.5 percent Asian, and about 3.5 percent Native American Indian. About one-third of the students live in the neighborhood; the other two-thirds of the children ride a bus each morning from their neighborhood/feeder school or are driven in a car to Carlton.

## FAMILIES

About 230 families send their children to Carlton School. Most of the students are from two-income families in which mothers work at least part-time, but there are also a large number of single-parent families. Although the vast majority of Carlton families are middle to lower-middle class, a small number are upper-middle class. Many of the parents of Carlton students attended community college after high school and hold technical/skilled or semiprofessional jobs. Most of the parents who are middle class to upper-middle class pay a mortgage on a home valued at between $125,000 and $185,000.[3] In their free time, typical Carlton families enjoy camping, fishing, soccer, and other team sports for the kids. Many families belong to a church and attend services regularly.

## FACULTY

The full-time faculty at Carlton numbers thirteen (twelve grade-level teachers plus a music teacher), of whom ten are female. The principal, who is male, has been at Carlton for four years. Most of the teachers have taught in public schools for at least fifteen years and have been at Carlton for ten or more. (At least three of the faculty members have taught at Carlton for over twenty years.) Neither the teachers nor the principal live in the local community.

## SCHOOL PHILOSOPHY

As part of the school district's magnet school program, Carlton offers a particular educational program option for parents and students, which is designed to attract a student population reflective of the racial-ethnic makeup of the larger district student population. Carlton offers a "basic school" program which emphasizes academic excellence in reading, math, science, and language arts (grammar, spelling, and handwriting). Students also participate in art, music, and physical education.

In the Carlton Parent Handbook, the basic school program is suggested as an alternative for those parents and students who "feel a need for a structured learning environment." The handbook notes that no special services such as remedial classes, limited English assistance, or special education programs are provided. With required parent participation, regular homework, dress standards, and a three-way contract between parents, students, and teachers, the program is designed to "help students achieve academic excellence, effective study habits, and a sense of responsibility."

## RULES AND POLICIES

The code of conduct at Carlton extends to parents as well as to students and teachers and is made explicit in the contract each is required to sign every year. Parents are expected to "encourage," "support," and "review" their children's learning and academic progress. They are expected to support district and classroom rules, get their children to school on time and in bed by 9:00 P.M., and provide a quiet time and place for study. In addition, parents are required to contribute forty hours of volunteer time to the school. If parents fail to complete these hours by the end of the school year, their children can be expelled and returned to their neighborhood school.

The contract requires students to follow classroom rules, do their best work at all times, complete assigned work neatly, and attend school every day (unless they are ill). In addition to these rather noble and traditional goals of student behavior, students are also expected to fulfill two other requirements uncommon in public schools—to adhere to a dress code and participate in "class meetings."

In the parent's handbook, the section on the dress code warns students to wear clothing which "does not draw undue attention to the wearer." Such articles as baseball hats, tank tops, thong-type shoes, and "bare midriff" blouses are prohibited. Shorts are allowed only if the weather is predicted to be ninety degrees or above; even then, the shorts must be hemmed and at least midthigh length.

As explained in the parent handbook, students who fail to meet their responsibilities are expected to accept the "logical consequences" for their behavior as identified by the recommendations made during "class meetings." These meetings are conducted on a regular basis in all classrooms to resolve concerns that students themselves identify. Each week, students list any problems, conflicts, or concerns they have on an "agenda" sheet. These items are discussed during the regularly scheduled class meetings. Solutions are offered and voted on by the students, with the aim of promoting conflict resolution through student initiative and responsibility.

Homework is a central element of the basic school philosophy. Consequently, the rules governing it are specific, explicit, and rigidly enforced. Homework must be turned in; late homework receives a grade of zero. Homework delivered by parents is not accepted. If students do not turn in their homework or it is incomplete, they are required to attend study hall, which is held during the last twenty minutes of the lunch period.

## ADMISSIONS

Admissions to Carlton are conducted through a lottery. After a name is pulled, the student's academic report is reviewed by a committee comprised of Carlton teachers. "Favorable profiles" are admitted. For potential first graders, this assessment is based on reading and math readiness (e.g., the ability to recognize letters, numerals 0–10, etc.), fine motor development, and general work habits. For the other placements, students must demonstrate similar grade-appropriate competencies. The principal reviews any "questionables" tagged by Carlton teachers. A large number of recorded "poor" performances in academic subjects, unexcused absences, and behavioral problems are valid reasons for nonacceptance. Since Carlton does not offer compensatory (Chapter

1) or bilingual education, students who require these programs can be denied admission.[4]

During the lottery, students are assigned a priority number and accepted in order according to the ethnic/racial slots available at that time. At Carlton, there are sixty-six admission slots in the first grade, but typically only six or seven in grades two through three, and even fewer in the intermediate grades. Almost all students who enter Carlton in the lower grades continue there until graduation.

## GOVERNANCE

As part of the city's unified school district, Carlton is governed by decisions of the seven-member board of education and district superintendent. In addition, the Director of Integrated Education/Magnet Schools and her staff help coordinate and supervise admissions policy, transportation, public relations, curriculum and staff development, and program development for the magnet school programs.

The Carlton PTA listed 270 members last year; attendance at regular monthly meetings usually numbers about 30–40 parents and a handful of teachers. Typical of many schools, the PTA serves a critical fund-raising function at Carlton. Successful events such as the annual fall carnival, the winter bazaar (a Christmas gift show in which parents donate handcrafted items), the "Panther Breakfast," and monthly treat sales generate over $10,000 in revenues annually. The PTA sponsors entertainment and educational assemblies for the school and helps defray some of the classroom expenses teachers would normally incur. Last year, for example, each teacher received $100; new cabinets were built in the intermediate grades with PTA funds. Every three years, the PTA sponsors the Carlton Jog-A-Thon, a major fund-raiser which typically generates over $30,000 for the school.

As participants in the state School Improvement Program (SIP), the Carlton School Site Council governs the disbursement of funds used for "school enrichment" services. The SIP council, which consists of the principal and a handful of selected teachers and parents, meets quarterly to allocate the SIP funds. Typically, 95 percent of these funds are used to help pay for teacher aides, with the remaining funds used for teacher in-service programs. These funds account for less than 5 percent of the total school budget.

## ORGANIZATION OF FAMILY LIFE:
## THE CONSEQUENCES FOR SCHOOL INVOLVEMENT

### Family Profiles[5]

The Carlton parents interviewed for this study range from upper-middle-class to low-income parents who receive public assistance.[6] Their residences vary in size and value from a luxurious two-story home in an exclusive neighborhood, to a tiny rental home with cracked ceilings and paint-chipped walls. While parents in only two of the ten families I spoke with are college graduates and hold bachelor's degrees, many of the parents attended the local community college. Most of the families are two-parent working families, although the majority of these include mothers who work only part-time outside their home. I also interviewed two single parents, both of whom are female. One is a college graduate who works part-time as a hospital nurse; the other is unemployed and receives government assistance. Seven of the ten families are members of a church and regularly attend church services. They are all parents of at least one child enrolled in the third or fourth grade at Carlton School.

The following composites portray families from each of three social class groups predominant at Carlton: middle class, lower-middle class, and low income.[7]

## The Watsons

The Watsons live in a comfortable, three-bedroom home in a neat, quiet middle-class neighborhood. Mrs. Watson refers to it as the "Leave it to Beaver" neighborhood because people know and care about one another. In their former neighborhood, where they lived up until five years ago, the homes were far more modest and their neighbors more transient. Homes here are valued at around $160,000.

After graduation from local high schools, the Watsons attended community college while they worked part-time. They earned their associate of arts degrees and were married two years later. Mrs. Watson has worked part-time for the last twelve years as a bookkeeper in a medical office. Her husband works in construction for a commercial builder.

On most summer evenings and weekends, the Watsons enjoy swimming in their built-in backyard swimming pool. When they get the time, they drive to Mr. Watson's family-owned lakeside cabin about two hours away, where they and their two sons enjoy fishing and winter skiing. Both of the boys are also soccer and Little League baseball players, so many weekends and weekday nights are taken up with games and practices. The Watsons are members of a Protestant church and attend services regularly.

## The Marshalls

The Marshalls have lived in their home for twelve years, ever since they married, and say they are "stuck here because we can't afford to move." (The homes were priced around $40,000 then and are valued at about $60,000 today.) Their neighborhood is dotted with small, two- and three-bedroom houses on tiny, sparsely landscaped lots. Several of the homes have chest-high chain-link fences around the perimeter of their dusty, dried up lawns. The Marshalls live here with their four kids ages thirteen through six.

Table II  Carlton Magnet School

| FAMILY | EDUCATION* | OCCUPATION | MARITAL STATUS | NUMBER OF CHILDREN |
|---|---|---|---|---|
| 1 | Father: B.S.<br>Mother: H.S. | High school teacher/coach<br>Administrative assistant | Married | 4 |
| 2 | Father: H.S.<br>Mother: H.S. | Construction worker<br>School secretary | Married | 2 |
| 3 | Mother: B.S. | Nurse (part-time) | Divorced | 2 |
| 4 | Father: H.S., A.A.<br>Mother: H.S. | Owner, tree trimming business<br>Community college student (part-time) | Married | 2 |
| 5 | Father: H.S., A.A.<br>Mother: H.S. | Surveyor, community college instructor (part-time)<br>School clerk (part-time) | Married | 3 |
| 6 | Father: H.S.<br>Mother: H.S. | Owner, carpet cleaning business<br>Beautician (part-time) | Married | 4 |
| 7 | Father: H.S., A.A.<br>Mother: H.S., A.A. | Occupational therapy technician<br>Preschool teacher (part-time) | Married | 4 |
| 8 | Father: H.S., A.A.<br>Mother: H.S. | Computer technician<br>Homemaker | Married | 7 |
| 9 | Father: H.S.<br>Mother: H.S. | Shipping clerk<br>Medical billing clerk | Married | 2 |
| 10 | Mother: --- | Unemployed | Divorced | 3 |

* B.S.—Bachelor of Science degree        H.S.—High School diploma
A.A.—Associate of Arts degree        --- —Left high school at age 16

After attending community college for about a year, Mrs. Marshall married and shortly thereafter started her family. When her children were younger, she had a licensed day care program in her home to earn extra money. For the past three years she has worked part-time at a local preschool. Mr. Marshall works for a cable television company in the shipping department. He has never attended college.

The Marshalls love to go camping but rarely find the time or opportunity. Instead, they say that going out to dinner "at some place really cheap" is their "major treat," which they manage to do, "more than we should, probably once every three weeks." Last year the family collected newspapers for recycling so they could buy a season pass to a local marine amusement park. Although Mrs. Marshall was raised Catholic, the family attends another Christian church regularly, including midweek Bible study classes.

## Mrs. Boyle

Mrs. Boyle lives in the house she grew up in thirty-two years ago. It is a small three-bedroom home in a lower-income neighborhood a twenty minute bus ride away from Carlton School. The home is sparsely furnished and the paint is cracked and peeling off the family room walls; there is a 35-inch color television set and a VCR in the far corner of the room. Mrs. Boyle lives here with her three children ages ten, seven, and three.

Mrs. Boyle dropped out of high school when she was sixteen, attended continuation school for less than a year, and then left home. She returned four years later and has lived in this house off and on since then. She was divorced three years ago from a husband who abused drugs and alcohol. Although Mrs. Boyle trained to be a grocery checker at the county employment skills center, she could only get a job paying $5 an hour as a bagger. She is presently unemployed and collects AFDC.

Mrs. Boyle and her children enjoy playing Nintendo games together. They are not members of a church.

## Parental Values and Education

Many observers might expect parents at Carlton to choose the school based upon its particular pedagogical emphasis and strengths and to weigh these against other schooling alternatives before making their selection. However, as accumulating research on school choice indicates, a number of factors—including the level of parents' education, participation in particular social networks, or a general feeling of alienation—influence the decisions of parents with respect to school choice (Archibald 1988; Nault & Uchitelle 1982). Archibald, for example, reports that "college-educated" parents are much more likely to participate in magnet schools than other less-schooled parents and that parents from "higher-education neighborhoods" are likely to have better knowledge of specific pedagogical alternatives and to incorporate these criteria in their choice decisions. Parents with fewer years of education may have a general awareness of the magnet school program or a particular school's reputation, but little more.

Does this framework describe the participation and decision-making patterns of Carlton parents? In the following section, the context of choice is explored by examining the explanations parents gave for selecting Carlton School. What did parents know about Carlton before they chose? What information did they have and from what sources? How did they gain access to these resources? What influenced their decision? The answers to these questions provide a framework for considering the serendipitous nature of choice and its implications for building a community of school families across social class and neighborhood.

## Reasons for Selecting Carlton

The school district's Coordinator for Magnet Schools Public Relations and Recruitment is expected to make parents aware of the magnet school options available to them. For the past three years, these efforts have included a magnet schools fair at which parents can pick up applications and discuss their options with principals and teachers. (Translators are available.) A brochure about the magnet/alternative school program is mailed to every public school parent (those with a child currently enrolled in a district public school for whom the district has a current address). In addition, the district targets the Hispanic and Black community newspapers and includes an advertisement in the community supplement section in the city's largest newspaper.

Despite these efforts, the ways in which most parents learned about Carlton School suggests the serendipitous nature of choice. If a pattern emerged from this study, it was one of chance circumstances, desperation, or plain good luck. As one middle-class parent responded when asked why she decided to send her daughter to Carlton: "Well, it just kind of happened by accident." She and her husband had bought a house in a neighborhood with a school nearby. After expressing her concern about the large number of non-English-speaking children in her daughter's first grade class, the teacher suggested she check out Carlton School:

> At that point I had absolutely no idea. I did not know what the school was about. She just said it was a basic school. So when she suggested it to me, I said okay, sounds good. (high school graduate; homemaker)

Other parents repeated this explanation; kindergarten or first grade teachers at their neighborhood school had provided information on the magnet school in almost whispered tones, lest they create an exodus of children from the feeder neighborhood schools.

Another mother said she had heard from other neighbors that the neighbor-hood school was mostly Black, had lots of fights, and was generally "not a good school." She had intended to enroll her daughter in the Catholic school,

> but nobody told me when registration was so we missed it. Then some ladies told me about Carlton, and we got in so we've been there ever since. (low income)

Another parent grew disenchanted with her son's school after hearing noise and commotion in the cafeteria when she picked him up each day at noon. She was not comfortable with the general atmosphere of the school but could not afford a private school. A neighbor around the block from her house mentioned Carlton School.

Other parents seemed unsure about the circumstances of their decision or had only vague recollections of choices. This quote from a middle-class couple typifies these somewhat casual responses:

> I think basically because we had relatives sending their kids there, right? [asks his wife] We heard it was a real good school. Yea, good discipline and the teachers were . . . sounds like it was more advanced teaching, I think.

One mother heard about Carlton through her baby-sitter. She was relieved to learn there was an alternative to the neighborhood school, where she volunteered one day a week in a kindergarten classroom and found it "the most depressing school I'd ever been in."

Only one parent identified the district's mailer as the source of information about Carlton. Whether or not this is an indication of problems with the district's outreach and recruitment program or simply a uniformly disinterested response to unsolicited mail, is unclear. This upper-middle-class parent describes her decision-making process:

> I didn't really know that much about [the magnet program]. He was going to be going into first grade and I opened this pamphlet and said, "Oh gee, this sounds interesting." He could either go to that elementary school or I could sign him up for this one. But I really didn't know that much about it. I thought, well, I'll go ahead and send in his name in case I want to do this. After that, some other good friends of ours, I just mentioned it, and she said that's where her kids go to school. And she just raved about it.

When the faculty was asked why they thought parents chose Carlton, they suggested that the choice was made for a myriad of reasons. The staff agreed that parents' decisions have little to do with the curriculum emphasis on "the basics." Most parents, it seems, are attracted to Carlton for reasons unrelated to the school philosophy. The principal explained:

You know, I'll tell you, I'm not sure it's the basic philosophy. I think it's safety, cleanliness, a good reputation for academics. I think if we had those elements we could have any philosophy. (principal)

One year in my class I heard a lot of them came here to be safe. Came here to get away from those people at certain schools. And then other times, not at all. They came for the education, the structure, the discipline. . . . They all have their own reasons. And we're not changing our program, but they all seem to be happy with it. (teacher)

Several teachers suggested that their students vary tremendously in academic abilities and social backgrounds and that contrary to some impressions, "We don't get the cream of the crop." As this teacher explained:

Mostly we get children whose parents are not happy with their neighborhood schools. That's the bottom line. They don't feel safe. The children aren't safe and they don't feel their children are doing well in school. They're not getting good study habits or any of those things, so they'll send them here to us. But that does not mean that we get children who are exceptionally bright. We don't. We get parents who want to be involved, and children who know their parents are involved.

If there is a difference between these magnet school parents and other parents who send their children to neighborhood schools, it is far more subtle than some observers would predict. For the most part, these parents could not be characterized as sophisticated or informed consumers of educational services. Rather than investigating their alternatives systematically, most parents learned of Carlton almost accidentally, indeed, often incidentally. Consequently, their knowledge about magnet schools and the basic philosophy is somewhat murky. They may have clear ideas about what they like about Carlton, but they are a bit fuzzy on the magnet school program objective (district desegregation) and the school's curriculum focus.[8] This middle-class mother, who learned about Carlton from her daughter's first grade neighborhood school teacher, "explains":

Carlton is basic, and it's not quite a magnet. I think the difference is that they just stress the three Rs—reading, writing and arithmetic—with a lot of homework and parent involvement. Whereas the magnets have, I guess some are qualified as science magnets, art magnets, things like that. There's a little bit of difference but I'm not sure what it is.

Another parent, who heard about Carlton through some church friends whose children were enrolled there, said her first impression was confounded by mixed messages from two different groups—parents who wanted their kids in a basic school to straighten them out and those who thought their kids were "so super wonderful, absolutely superior" that they were in a basic school. Her concerns about the neighborhood junior high convinced her to make the switch to Carlton in the hope of linking into the magnet junior high school.

For many parents, Carlton represents an alternative to their neighborhood school (rather than the last option before private schooling); that is, if their children were not enrolled here, they would be attending the neighborhood school. The strongest attractions, echoed throughout these interviews with parents and teachers, rests with the school's reputation for strong academics, safety, and structure—all rather generic qualities of "good" schools.[9] For these parents, their choice has been rewarded generously:

> It's been a really nice experience for everyone. Basically, it's a safe place. I feel confident because I know my daughter is safe there. And I also know that she is learning, and she is really building some good habits about learning. (middle-class mother)

> I like Carlton because of the learning. I felt that she was safer there than at the neighborhood school because they did have the discipline where the kids, they couldn't, there was no fighting, arguing, hitting or pushing or anything. Or they would be put on report. You get so many marks and they won't let you go back to the school. So I felt safe, not always worried about fights. (middle-class father)

> I can't say enough good things. Not only the responsibility it's taught my child; I feel safer with him going there. I feel if there's a problem . . . they can learn to deal with problems in a mature, structured way, instead of fighting and learning to be mouthy, using muscle. They learn diplomacy, I guess is the word. I like that whole idea. (lower-middle-class mother)

The impression that Carlton School offers a solid academic program tied to higher expectations for both students and parents prompted many parents to characterize Carlton as a "private school program for public school kids." Several low-income parents echoed the sentiments of a mother of three young children who suggested that Carlton is "like sending [them] to a private school and not having to pay the money." The notions of responsibility, good study habits, and lots of learning resonate with these parents' conceptions of what a school can and ought to be. They are supremely pleased with their choice. How "typical" are these middle- and lower-middle-class parents? Are Carlton parents somehow different in terms of their educational goals for their children? Does Carlton School match their expectations or simply help define them?

## Parents' Expectations

Research which has pinpointed particular parental values and practices (with respect to childrearing) associated with social class (Bronfenbrenner 1966;

Kohn 1969; Wright & Wright 1976; Rubin 1976) has implications for school choice; parents with higher socio-economic status prefer more child-centered, developmental approaches and less formally structured environments and within choice arrangements are more likely to choose nontraditional schools (Archibald 1988). Compared to parents with lower-income levels, middle-class professional parents tend to be less concerned with "the basics" in elementary school, taking these for granted. These parents tend to emphasize independence, interpersonal skills, and self-esteem (Archibald 1988).

A rigorous examination of these assertions is beyond the aims of this study. Rather, the effort here rests with identifying the "educational value context" of the parents who have chosen Carlton School for their children. This context was mined by asking parents to discuss the important outcomes of schooling, their goals for their children's education, and the ways in which they participate in their kids' education.

When asked what they wanted their children to gain from their education or to name the most important outcomes of schooling, many parents invoked terms like "fairly basic," "a real good education," and simply, "knowledge." Some parents coupled a foundation of basic skills with the need to learn responsibility and dependability. Thus, along with viewing the adoption of "basic skills" as preparation for work lives, many parents identified these elements as building blocks for decision making in adulthood.

While it is difficult to ascertain the consistency or compatibility of social class categories across research studies, the collective responses of these parents to questions of educational values argue against classifying Carlton parents as atypical or extraordinary. Consider these perspectives:

> I just want them to know things. It goes back to the basics as far as I want them to know how to read and know their math because there are things, like multiplication, that you just have to memorize. . . . I want them to get the basics and then they can do all the other stuff because I want them to learn to do the computers and I want them, if they want to, to learn to dance. But they have to have the basics first. (lower-middle-class mother)

> Besides knowledge? I'm not quite following you. I would have to go along with basic knowledge. If you have a good concept of math, a good concept of reading, of writing, of history, those basic things, I feel that gives you that really good foundation for whatever you want to go into, for whatever you do. I think if your basic language escapes you in those early learning years, that reflects on you. I think that reflects on your self-esteem. So I think the basic education is the most important thing. (lower-middle-class mother)

Several parents specified their preference that their children learn skills which enable them to cope successfully in life, rather than merely compile a successful academic record. These parents seemed to envision competencies and abilities which may not be measured in report cards:

**Q.** What do you want your children to get out of their schooling?

**A.** The ability to function in society . . . to make an informed decision. I'm not the kind of parent who wants straight As and all that stuff. They both read very well, comprehend what they read. We're quite lucky. (middle-class father)

**A.** To enjoy it. If they could just enjoy picking up a book and reading it. I want my children to be: I'm glad I can do this. This has been a great thing. This is interesting. If they [teachers] could bring out the good things and really build on that and not frustrate them but try to bring out, I keep saying, bring out the best. (middle-class mother)

**A.** My philosophy is if they can just be well-adjusted adults and lead happy lives doing something they feel is fulfilling. Just getting along with people. Being able to live in the world and being able to live with other kinds of people. That's it pretty much. I don't care if they're Albert Einsteins or anything although they seem to do extremely well so that makes it easy for me. (upper-middle-class mother)

**A.** I want them to be able to survive in the world; to be able to be intelligent human beings; to be whatever they want; to do whatever they want. If they don't get an education now, they won't be able to do anything. (middle-class father)

Although all the parents interviewed expressed an interest and desire in sending their children to college, these goals were shaded in slightly varying tones and conditions. For those parents who are college graduates themselves (three of the four upper-middle-class parents), there is an unquestioned expectation that their children will graduate from college. In fact, for some parents, it is more than an expectation; as one parent put it when asked whether sending her children to college was a goal: "No, it's a requirement." Another college-educated parent, whose oldest is in seventh grade, noted that she and her husband discuss college with their children frequently in the hope that "early brainwashing" will lead them to follow their parents' advice to attend college.

Although the majority of parents I interviewed are not university graduates, these families expressed similar desires for their children to obtain a college degree. These hopes are anchored in the parents' unwavering belief that a college degree has value in the job market and that economic success will come a bit easier for their children if they possess this credential. Some parents expressed regret that they had not obtained a college degree themselves, while others suggested that they were "fairly successful without going to college." Interestingly, there was not a hint of the "requirement" to attend college that permeated the discussion with the college-educated parents, just simply a hopeful intention to fulfill their children's dreams.

**Q.** How much schooling would you like your children to get?

**A.** As much as possible. If you ask me, that's really up to them. I hope I can influence both of them in that direction where they will be compelled to accomplish as much as they can. I already know my oldest one is driven. She's very competitive. I hope that sticks. (middle-class mother)

**A.** It doesn't seem like you're going to get very far in this world without . . . you just don't graduate from high school and make it anymore. I don't really care what kind of work they do. I want them to be happy, but I want them to be able to take care of their families. I want the girls to be able to support themselves, their families if they need to, and to be confident in themselves. I'm afraid that for most people that would mean college. (lower-middle class)

Another parent, who is unemployed and receives government assistance, expressed similar desires for her daughter to graduate from college and "make her own money so she can support herself." She recalled with pain and regret her decision to drop out of high school:

I think it would've been smarter if I had thought if I wanted to make money and support myself, I should have been straight out of high school and college. My cousin did that and she's an attorney now and makes a lot, a lot of money. And now she's got no money problems. I've got money problems. (low income)

For many of these parents, college courses have been something to squeeze in between raising a family and earning a living. Although some have brothers and sisters who are college graduates, and two of the mothers who are middle-class completed a year or more of college at a four-year institution, most of these parents sought a community college experience for practical/occupational purposes. They would like their children to enjoy broader opportunities:

I would like them to be interested in learning forever. I used to make fun of [my husband]. I call him the professional student because he never really got a degree, but he's always going to school. He's always taking classes. He's always learning. He seems to always be involved with a college or whatever. And I didn't go to college but I like to read and I like to learn.

**Q.** Is that more important than if somebody actually finishes college?

**A.** I don't know about that anymore. It seems like to get a good, better job, they need four years in something. I would like to see them go to college. (middle class)

Her husband continued:

**A.** I have not gotten a four-year degree and that is something that I will accomplish before I die. I would like to see them if they start young in college, to finish and get a degree. If nothing else, just that they finish it.

These parents peg their educational goals to their children's academic performance in elementary school and junior high school. Consequently, some parents' hope and optimism are tempered by suggestions that for their children who were struggling in school, a trade or technical school might provide the best opportunities for them after high school. For lower-middle-class- and low-income parents, hopes for college degrees are further dampened by financial realities and constraints:

We hope, we plan for our kids to go to college. They'll be going to college from here, going to the community colleges because there's so many [children], there's not going to be money to go anywhere. (mother; lower-middle class)

I want them all to graduate from college. I hope. I hope they will. [My son] wants to go to UCLA. How much does that cost? I'm thinking, go to [the nearby university] and stay at home and save money. That's the whole thing. There's not a whole lot of money. We'll just do it. I don't know how we'll do it. (mother; lower-middle class)

What has influenced these parents' beliefs about schooling? Perhaps predictably, parents have been influenced by their own parents, by the values which were expressed in their homes when they were young children. One mother, for example, noted that the family routines she followed as a child are mirrored in her young family. Her husband is a high school teacher and coach. For her, the fact that "school is just our main event of the week and Saturday and Sunday are just days in between school to get ready for school on Mondays," is normal and natural. Other parents, however, suggested that their own work experiences have influenced their views regarding the importance of education and the market value of a college degree. Thus, while some parents' educational goals for their children reflect the values their parents imparted, others are rooted in their own experiences in the workplace.[10]

**Q.** What has influenced your ideas about education?
**A.** My parents. My parents really had a lot of determination that we all get an education. They felt that was one of the most important things. Something that no one could ever take away from you. I think your parents are your model. (mother; middle class)
**A.** My parents' influence in my life. My parents were always interested. When I brought my report card home we went over it. We discussed it. I saw they were interested. They were concerned. My mom went to all the

open houses, helped me with my homework. She was concerned. She was involved. (mother; middle class)

**A.** I've never thought about this. I guess one thing where it comes from is seeing my husband so equipped. In his work, he is so respected. The doctors want him in on the family conferences. He's just treated so well but he doesn't get the pay. So I just can see the importance of the education. When these kids get older and decide not to [attend college]. Hey, just get the degree. You will get better money, wherever you go. (lower-middle class)

## Patterns of School Participation

Many observers might expect parents who enroll their children in a school which requires parental participation to view their involvement in schooling in somewhat more active terms. It might be posited, for example, that these parents are a self-selected group, different in their outlook on and commitment to their children's education than other parents who opt for neighborhood schools. Is this the case with Carlton parents?

Reflective of the social scripts which provide parents with a language for social interactions in schools, these parents identified rather routine, established activities when they were asked to define their role in their children's schooling. Nevertheless, there emerged from these conversations different perspectives, or lenses, through which parents view and catalog their behavior. Many parents consider their role *in relation to* the teacher's or the school's. These parents tend to invoke the language of manufacturing or coproduction— using such terms as "partnership," "joint effort," and "technical stuff." While these parents tend to separate the social worlds of school and home (either explicitly or implicitly), they express a literal commitment to the partnership with schools in the interest of their children's learning and academic success:

> I feel like I'm a help. I'm an aide. But I'm not the main teacher. I'm a teacher here at home. The real hands-on kind of learning we've definitely done here at home. (mother; lower-middle class)

> If [parents] have something to say, I think you ought to work together. The main goal is education. It's not your pride or my ego or whatever. It's supposed to be a joint effort. It's not just you or just me. (mother; middle class)

The product of this partnership between parents and teachers is a routinized, taken-for-granted activity called homework. Through homework, this rather imprecise joint effort finds explicit and easily identifiable goals and roles for parents and teachers alike. Tasks such as helping with multiplication tables, checking the spelling list, and listening to their children read, help parents identify their appropriate roles vis-a-vis teachers. Parents fulfill this niche with faith and, often, with some stress and difficulty:

I think I need to stay up-to-date on everything that she comes home with. I'm already finding out that I'm behind. I really need to keep up with anything that comes out new. It's going to be a real challenge. I think that's really what they want. (mother; middle class)

I feel like I'm their second teacher sometimes because there is so much work. (mother; middle class)

Homework is much more of a headache to me now than it was when I was a child. I don't remember my parents hovering over me. It seems to me that parents are involved making sure homework is done and understanding it. There's been many times when I've looked at the homework and said, I don't know either. Your best guess is good. If you have trouble, I'll talk to your teacher. (mother; lower-middle class)

Many parents complained about the amount of homework assigned at Carlton, particularly in the fourth grade. Indeed, if any conflict exists between parents and teachers, it is over the amount of time spent on homework. Both groups expressed strong and vocal opinions. Parents feel homework is excessive; teachers view it as an important tool for learning skills and self-discipline. Parents counter that homework disrupts family routines; teachers suggest better time management. Consider the two divergent perspectives:

By the time you have three children, then every night you're answering questions. My husband is gone a lot with coaching in the evening. It's kind of a zoo around here in the evening, trying to get everyone fed, and they all go to the different spots with three of them doing homework. And it's like, "Mom, can you help me with this; Mom, can you show me?" And it's like you're jumping from first grade to fourth grade to sixth grade, and everybody needs your expert advice on how to do this and that. (mother; upper-middle class)

I teach them. The parent gives them the support they need at home. If they need help with their homework, they give it to them. They give them a place to study. They give them a time to study. Make sure nothing interferes with their study. I mean you don't take the kid to Mervyn's to shop until 9:00 at night and then send me a letter and say, "I'm sorry but my child had to go shopping with me last night and didn't do the homework." (teacher)

Homework is good but there's a limit. There's a limit. These kids need to do some exercise too and they've been in school. I give these people my children for all these hours and it's like, it's our turn now. I want them to play. So that's my issue. There's too much homework. And some stuff is just stuff that's not important. Busy work homework really gets me. (mother; lower-middle class)

When parents perceive that their own abilities are insufficient to help their children with the homework, they tend to feel frustrated, defeated, and angry.

Sometimes these feelings lead to a gradual disengagement from their children's schoolwork (particularly after the primary grades); other times it leads to reconfiguring their roles. Given the frames in which they and teachers portray their roles, these consequences are not surprising, nor are they trivial. Consider the perspectives of these parents:

**Q.** How do you see your role in your kids' education?

**A.** There's some overlapping but all the technical stuff of actual teaching I pretty much leave to the teacher. I could teach my children first grade stuff. Probably, I could teach them second grade stuff. After that, I start to not know the material. I could teach them to read and count and do the basics. But the teachers, they're a lot more well up on the subjects. So I'm sort of a backer-upper and a cheerleader and a nagger, and a support person and sometimes a mediator. (mother; low income)

**A.** I just look at myself as an overseer, to see that they get their work done. I worry about when they get a little older having to help them with their homework. Right now, it's pretty easy. But I wasn't exactly, I didn't exactly fly through high school. Last year our daughter was bringing home some homework, and we were showing her how to do it. She just wasn't getting it because her teacher at school was showing her one way, and we were showing her a different way. Of course, we were showing her a long, drawn out way. So we just had to go into the teacher to understand ourselves how she wanted it, how she was coming about getting this answer. It was just making us angry. Everybody just had a lot of anger and frustration. (father; middle class)

Although the "relational" perspective predominated the views of parents as they defined a role in their children's education, other parents framed involvement within the broad responsibility of parenting. Although these parents express an interest in participating in their children's education and acknowledge the value of school involvement, they tend to define this involvement in terms of a general awareness of their children's lives and a strong interest in their well-being. Rather than specific, identifiable activities, these parents frame their roles in more abstract terms:

**Q.** How would you define parent involvement?

**A.** I think more than between parent and school, it's between parent and child. You have to have values and you have to have goals in your family. The kids have to feel you're behind them and will help them with whatever comes up at school, not just their work. You gotta be there. (father; middle class)

**A.** I think it's just being aware of what your child is doing in school—whether it be schoolwork or activities or their friends or whatever . . . I think you have to be involved in what your child, in whatever they're doing. A great part of their day is school, so you'd darn well better know what they're doing at school. (mother; upper-middle class)

Another parent, who last year was an active member of several school committees, including the PTA, casts her role in terms of modeling behavior which has broad implications for her children's development. For her, being involved in the school is unrelated to what teachers might expect or monitor; it reflects a particular set of values which she wants to impart to her daughter:

> I think it's an essential part of education for parents to be involved. I don't think you can have children that will be a success in the future and will be avid students or productive citizens if you don't show that by example. If you're totally indifferent, if you don't care to show up for PTA meetings or be active, then they impersonate that same attitude when they grow up. So I think it's really important that they see a role model in parents. I think it's crucial. (mother; middle class)

## The Participation Requirement

Whether parents frame their patterns of participation in relational terms or adopt a more integrated perspective, none of them "count" these efforts toward the forty-hour participation requirement. Indeed, when Carlton parents discussed their involvement in their children's education, the subject of required participation was never raised; it seemed a topic with little relationship to their roles in their children's schooling. Thus, rather than organizing their involvement around codified activities recognized by the school, parents partition their involvement between the scripted "supporter" and "helper" roles, which are typically centered around their own child's needs, and the activities formally accounted for by Carlton (which are typically focused on schoolwide needs). What are some of these "inventoried" activities?

Parents are alerted in the beginning of the school year regarding the type and number of activities which earn participation hours. For example, assisting teachers with parties, bulletin boards, or cleanup duties will garner points/hours. Working in the library counts. If you bring home-baked goodies such as cookies and cupcakes to school, you get an hour. Attendance at all meetings is rewarded, including the PTA, school site council, and district school board meetings. All fund-raisers, festivals, and holiday pageants buy hours; so do the traditional events such as Back-to-School Night, Open House, and parent-teacher conferences. Teachers may arrange special projects or ask parents to correct homework for credit. Parents who attend the principal's "parenting group" meeting each week earn an hour while discussing such topics as improving self-esteem, balancing punishment with responsibility, and building good study habits.

Carlton is not unique in setting out this requirement for parents; several of the district magnet schools mandate parental participation. Moreover, Carlton did not enforce this forty-hour participation rule until last year. Before then, it was casually acknowledged and produced a varying pattern of compliance. In other words, most parents participated to some degree, but up to one-third of the parents finished somewhere short of forty hours.[11]

What do most parents think about the 40-hour participation requirement? The following views reflect a general consensus on the value and meaning of the participation requirement:

> I'm 100 percent behind it. I really agree. It forces you to pay attention to your children. I think it's easy. I notice in my own life, it's easy to get real wrapped up and real busy. Sometimes you need some discipline from some areas. It's like aerobics: I don't go unless I pay. It keeps you going. (mother; middle class)

> I think it's really good. I think that if a parent's not willing to get involved in his child's education and put time in at the school, then that reflects on the child also. (mother; low income)

> I always do it. I think they should have it. Whatever it is it's a good number. Regardless, it's a fair amount of hours. I don't think they're asking too much at all. (mother; lower-middle class)

The principal provided a bottom-line justification for the requirement:

> I think it's important for the parents. I don't care if they come over here and do the dumbest, I don't know, stack my books on the shelf, just so they're around to see what's going on around here . . . (principal)

The degree to which participation hours translate into activities which are helpful and meaningful to parent and staff alike is limited. While some parents recalled that the classroom duties they had performed for various teachers had helped them to better understand what their children were learning in school, other parents offered a running tally of seemingly unrelated, ancillary activities (sending baked goods, cutting out letters at home, driving on a field trip) in which they had participated. It was unclear what they had "learned" from these experiences. Other parents suggested that the types of activities sanctioned for credit made school officials seem "a bit too number happy." One complained that awarding hours for donating a gallon of punch but not for observing in the classroom was wrongheaded.

The principal identified the following as examples of "meaningful" parent participation activities: Supervision of students at the bus stop, assisting with filing and paperwork in the office, and making of special event buttons at home with a laminating kit. He continued:

> Now the classroom teachers can require and ask those kind of things too— grading papers, cutting out materials. Many parents work in the classroom as aides and help children to read and the kinds of things aides do. (principal)

While teachers enthusiastically endorse the participation requirement and have fostered an "open door" classroom policy to encourage parents' involvement in (or merely observation of) classroom activities, this benefit seems to carry a cost. Several teachers suggested that the parent participation requirement demands a great deal of organization and coordination. Thus, activities may be helpful and meaningful to the extent that teachers design them that way. Here is what several teachers observed:

> I think it's kind of a two-sided thing. When I first came here, it was real exciting to have parents and to have that kind of parental support. I wasn't used to that at my previous teaching positions. I had never had that kind of interest level in any of the other schools. So that was really super, and parents are very helpful. On the other hand, it was a challenge to use them successfully and appropriately. At first I was kind of overwhelmed by the task of finding suitable work for them to do, especially when you have parents in the classroom.
>
> Last year they made it clear that it was not our job as teachers to assure you that you're going to be able to get your forty hours from me because we are here during the day and our first job is of course to take care of the kids. Sometimes it's real difficult to . . . a person will just walk in and say, "I'm here for eight hours." Sometimes you have three or four or five people there for eight hours. It's pretty difficult to continue teaching.
>
> I also have to accommodate non-English-speaking parents. I assume that, like Vietnamese, not only do they not speak English, they don't read our alphabet either. And so they are very limited. So I have to make sure I give them things like math to correct, cutting out letters, stapling papers on background, those kinds of things to do that don't require literacy skills.

The accommodations teachers are encouraged to make to ensure that participation is inclusive, equitable, and meaningful regardless of parents' particular work schedules, language abilities, or status, constitute a rather challenging task. The overwhelming consensus of parents and teachers suggests that the arrangements provide enough varied opportunities for everybody, working parent and non-working parent alike, to participate fully; a parent just has to make the effort. It is noteworthy that the parents who spoke most forcefully about the ease with which these obligations can be met are employed either part-time or are homemakers. Here's a sampling of these dominant opinions:

> When your child is selected from the lottery to be admitted to that school, and you sign the little card agreeing that you're going to put in your forty hours, you're making a commitment, and to fulfill that commitment, you have to make adjustments so that you can do that. So you do it. (mother; middle class; part-time school secretary; makes buttons at home for school events)
>
> They have so many things you can do that it's not hard to do your hours. Even the working person, because there's always tons of stuff to do plus there's

always the baked goods. (mother; lower-middle class; part-time preschool director; works at the winter bazaar, bakes goodies, attends weekly parenting meetings)

We haven't had any problems with it. There's a lot of ways you can get your forty hours. We bake cookies. We send cupcakes. We help with the carnival. They make it pretty darn easy to get your forty hours. You have to be pretty lazy not to get forty hours of help in. You go to a meeting; you get an hour. You help them put chairs away after the meeting; they give you a half an hour. If you can't get forty hours, you're just not putting much effort into it. (father; middle class; part-time fire investigator)

Other parents told of friends who faced multiple difficulties and responsibilities but were still able to "make their forty hours."

I had one friend who was a single mom with health problems working at a demanding job, three or four children, one of them learning disabled. I didn't think she could do it. And she more than did it. And she [wasn't] put out by it. It depends partly on your commitment. You can grade work at home. Sometimes there's phone work to do. Occasionally there's typing sent home. If you can drive once or twice. There's so many different kinds of things. (mother; low income; homemaker)

I don't think there is an excuse. If a person wants to do it. I've come across people who were single, had two jobs, three kids, or what not, and they faithfully put their hours in and never complain. And then there was a lady down the street that was just complaining. They just didn't want to get out of the house and do something. There's really no excuse. If you want to, you can do it. And it's reasonable. (mother; middle class; homemaker)

Several teachers echoed the sentiments of these parents, and compared the frenetic pace that many parents face today with the routines and responsibilities they themselves managed earlier with their own families:

I have no sympathy when parents say, "Well, I'm working." I just say, "Gee, I'm sorry about that. So did I." The thing is if your child's education is important to you, then you will do it. You have to set your priorities. You've got parents here who are working, and some of them are going to complain. But that was your commitment. You signed the contract, and that was on the contract, to do forty hours. If it's too much for you, then maybe this isn't the school for you. Maybe you're not committed to your child's education as much as you thought you were. (teacher)

While most parents and teachers suggested that the wide variety of participation opportunities do not disadvantage any particular group of parents, one teacher who serves on the parent participation committee expressed some concerns and doubts:

> I wish there was some way we could still work out these hours. This has pained us no end . . . trying to find . . . and we want quality hours. And we have gotten to the point of saying maybe reading to students at night and keeping a record of that. We have a lot of parents who are single parents, which is putting another burden. I still have to work out in my mind what kinds of things . . . and I know all parents can't. I don't feel they can participate fully. (teacher)

These parents, who enthusiastically endorse the participation policy, nonetheless offered these concerns for working parents:

> The only thing I find that I don't like about it is, being a working mother, a lot of the ways you can make hours are during the day—working in the library, working in the classrooms. It's hard for a working parent. I'm not saying you can't make the hours. I can make the hours without any problems. But like I said, I might just have to do the setup the night before [the carnival]—kind of the cruddy stuff. (mother; lower-middle class; full-time data processor)

> I think there's things at the school that they really need help with and I'm more than glad to go over there. Once in a while I feel like this stuff is just busywork to fulfill your hours. I try to correct papers so I can do things in the evening. When you work all day it's hard to go over there at night to some things.

Her concerns extend to single mothers:

> For some people it's harder. Maybe a single mother shouldn't be eliminated from going to Carlton because she's got four little kids at home or something and can't work and can't seem to go to everything. Because they'll say, "Well, we have meetings or we have this or that that you can do," but a lot of the stuff is in the evenings and if you work all day and have little kids, it's hard to get back over to the school, and you don't have child care in the evening. (mother; upper-middle class; full-time legal administrator)

There is no clear, articulated rationale for the forty-hour participation requirement. While several school staff members suggested the number was arbitrary, a parent thought it correlated to the roughly forty weeks students attend school each year. The preface to the Parent Handbook refers to the fact that "the support of parents in 'following through' contributes to the success of the program. The school alone is not able to assume total responsibility for the education of the child." The intent or meaning of such generic language as "following through" seems evident: it means anything and everything; in this case, in addition to traditional roles and expectations related to parenting and school involvement, it translates into forty hours of participation in school sanctioned activities. But why forty hours? Why *require* participation?

To be sure, the effect of the forty-hour required participation rule is to separate Carlton parents symbolically and objectively from other nonparticipation public school parents. (This topic is addressed in the following section.) While the program provides the parameters for a sense of social cohesion and solidarity, this effect is a by-product, rather than a primary goal, of the requirement. Instead, two goals seem to be implicit. The first involves a fundamental objective of parent involvement in schools—fund-raising. The requirement ensures that valuable programs and materials are provided with funds raised/contributed by school families. The need is met by a ready and available pool of parents, eager to earn hours by working at the carnival, making crafts for the bazaar, or cooking at the Panther Breakfast. Secondly, a central aim of the basic school program involves broad-based parent participation—assisting with homework, supporting the teacher, enforcing rules, etc. If parents attend all the meetings, events, and activities at school, their knowledge and understanding of the school will reinforce these elemental actions. The implicit assumption is that involvement in school and home-based activities will become an unavoidable, integrated part of their family routines.

To the degree that certain family conditions—single parenthood, inflexible full-time work schedules, unavailability of transportation and/or child care—constrict the opportunities for particular groups of families to participate as fully as others, the requirement constitutes a pernicious and disabling public school policy. There is little evidence, however, to suggest that a differential access to resources derived from social class differences influences the patterns of *home-based* participation.[12] The wide variety of activities parents can fulfill at home (e.g., correcting homework, making signs and buttons, baking cookies) seems to level any effects of social class derived from differences in income or material resources. The primary influence on parents' level of participation at school-based events is the organization of their work lives; that is, whether or not parents work full-time or part-time or enjoy flexible hours seems to dictate the nature and frequency of participation at school-based events. As the case study of St. Martin's school parents illustrated, the organization of work lives is somewhat independent of social class or occupational status. At Carlton Magnet School, an upper-middle-class, college-educated mother who works full-time as an administrator in a law firm identified the same constraints as a high-school-educated, lower-middle-class mother who works full-time as a data processor in a medical office. Parents whose work lives make it difficult to attend school events or to simply volunteer occasionally in their children's classroom are objectively disadvantaged under these arrangements; they may not have access to particular knowledge or to the social networks that these activities promote.

## Parents and Self-Selection

The degree to which Carlton parents represent a self-selected group of parents is difficult to assess definitively, but several clues suggest that they possess few of the characteristics of such self-selected groups as Catholic school parents. There is no tuition at Carlton, no special fees. Transportation is free, easy, and direct; school buses pick up children at their neighborhood school and deposit them at Carlton. The lottery admissions policy established four years ago requires only a mailed application.

Parents' decision to choose Carlton is more telling. Their fuzzy understanding of the magnet school and the basic school philosophy suggests a rather serendipitous, haphazard selection process for most of these parents. Most moved into their current homes and neighborhoods with little knowledge, only expectations, of their neighborhood school. Then a friend, neighbor, or baby-sitter mentioned something about Carlton. Perhaps a kindergarten teacher's casual comment about this option prompted a look-and-see attitude. For most parents, Carlton represents a good alternative to a mediocre, or unsafe, neighborhood school. Their interests in a basic education, safety, and discipline seem far more typical than extraordinary.

If any single element distinguishes Carlton parents from others, it centers on their perception of themselves as members of a separate, elite public school community. Although drawn from widely scattered neighborhoods, the sense of community at Carlton is palpable and pervasive. In absence of the natural familiarity and occasions for face-to-face talk which may be evidenced in geographical communities, Carlton School reflects a constructed community undergirded by a sense of shared values and commitment.

The next section explores the "badges" of organizational commitment and school community at Carlton, including the forty-hour parent participation requirement and the contract which parents must sign. The issues of ownership, elitism, and separatism are examined to better understand the ways in which the organization of schools helps define parents' interests, goals, and their patterns of participation.

## SCHOOL COMMUNITY:
## IMPLICATIONS FOR FAMILY-SCHOOL INTERACTIONS

## School Organization and Community

The impact of the constitutive elements of community— such as communication and shared beliefs—is vividly expressed in the language of Carlton parents. Commitment, identification with a group, and an acceptance of group standards has engendered a pervasive sense of solidarity and mutual support, and a corresponding element of exclusivity and ownership, among these "school choice" parents.

The single most powerful element of school organization responsible for this sense of community is the required participation. Both substantively and symbolically, this requirement binds parents in a sense of solidarity and "family." While the formal accounting of hours is relatively new, the expectation that parents will participate in some way and to some degree is deeply entrenched in the traditions of Carlton School.

As parents discussed the existence and nature of school community at Carlton, nearly all identified the myriad of school events as opportunities for personal exchanges with school families with whom they might otherwise not interact. Thus, while they may live in different neighborhoods, work in various occupations, and share few social networks, the physical arrangement of time and space constructs the opportunity for face-to-face talk. As the occasions accumulate over time, a sense of familiarity and comfort is established, contributing to a sense of connection. The notions of value congruence and social compatibility were echoed repeatedly by parents:

**Q.** Is there a sense of community at Carlton?

**A.** There pretty much is a strong sense of community, partly because we're required to go and work for the school and it grows and the feeling of commitment to your children, to the school. I think that we all feel like we're part of one family. (mother; lower-middle class)

**A.** I know quite a few of the parents. There is a feeling that you know . . . people are not cold. When you go in, you know parents. (mother; middle class)

**A.** Very much so, because the required forty hours of participation brings [parents] together for some major events, like the school carnival, the Wee Bazaar, the Panther Breakfast, which they work and plan for, and then attend. And they work in the classroom, do work for the teacher at home. So I think that the parent population has real heavy identification with this school through that program. (principal)

Several parents pointed out the need to make special efforts to involve both parents and children in school activities, given the fact that sixteen different neighborhood schools feed into Carlton and many students' classmates are not their neighbors:

We try to come up with things for kids to get together simply because of (kids coming from widely scattered neighborhoods). Our kids don't play with kids down the street who go to the same school. So it's really important that we get together and do things together. So I think there's enough sense of community camaraderie. We do enough. We have our carnival and Wee Bazaar and fundraisers. Kids get together. I think individual people make an effort. I know I do. (mother; middle class)

**Q.** How do you get to know them?

**A.** Meetings, sporting events, scouts. I've worked in the class. At some point you either meet them at the school, and then you meet them at a sporting event. Then your children make friends and you meet the parents. It just kind of evolves. I worked in the classrooms and the office a few times. I feel like I know quite a few of them. (mother; middle class)

**A.** I guess partially through the parent involvement. I think I would attend a lot of things anyway but it is required. So I think you tend to have to be over there a little bit more and you work on different projects with people and then you say, "What grade are your kids in?" And then you see them later, "Oh hi, how are you doing?" You get to know the families, even though you don't live near. We don't live anywhere near any of them. I know lots of the parents just through working at the things and through the years and seeing their kids grow up. (mother; upper-middle class)

Many parents said they like Carlton because "the school is so small." In fact, Carlton is an average size elementary school with two classes of 30–33 students each in grade levels first through sixth. This widely embraced assumption about its smallness seems rooted in the fact that once enrolled, kids and parents tend to stay at Carlton; there is very little turnover or transience. Consequently, teachers know siblings' names and parents' occupations *before* the child becomes their student. Parents are enthusiastic about this familiarity:

One thing I like about it real well is its smallness. You find you know the people. You know this parent has this child in this class and you're with the same people. My son has many of the same kids that went to first grade; they've gone all the way up with him. If I go over there, I know the teachers; they know me. They know which sister and brother belong to each other. It's a real close-knit group. And I like that. (mother; upper-middle class)

I like, when you go into that school everybody knows . . . all the teachers know all the students. They know most all the parents. They know everybody by name. You can wander into the office, and she can go call your child for you without asking, "Now, who's your kid? What room is he in?" They all know each other. They all care. (mother; lower-middle class)

It's almost like a little family because the school is so small. The kids all know each other. Quite a few families, we've become good friends with over there. Go to parties, have barbecues together and stuff like that. Our kids play together. They're in Girl Scouts together. And parents look out for other kids too. (father; middle class)

People stay here year after year after year after year, and we do know the families and the parents and it seems that we've compensated for (the feeder system). I don't know how, to tell you the truth. It has a good feeling. It has a great feeling. (teacher)

The sense of familiarity and social cohesion reflects constitutive elements of this school community. Knowing "lots of parents" provides particular benefits to all parents who are members of this community. These relationships are neither tenuous nor temporary; rather, they are stable and predictable sources of information and referral. Reputations of particular teachers, the types of homework he/she assigns, deadlines for applications to the basic middle school, reputations of high schools—access to this kind of information provides an invaluable tool for parents who are engaged (or wish to be) in their children's academic success. The social network established easily and naturally through Carlton's array of school activities provides the channels for shared information, referral, and recommendation. The process creates perfect redundancy; parents have an incentive to attend school events (forty-hour requirement); the more events they attend, the more relationships they form with other parents; subsequent occasions for face-to-face talk provide the opportunity to share information, thus providing additional incentives to attend school events.

Social networks with Carlton parents who possess particular knowledge about schooling may help parents whose social class position does not provide similar resources and who, for example, may be unfamiliar with the language of competency testing and curriculum or in the subtleties of high school admissions strategies. Thus, these school-based networks may mediate the influence of at least some of the elements of social class (e.g., education, social networks) which recent research indicates critically influence the ways parents interact with schools (Lareau 1989). Parents' knowledge of teachers' reputations, for example, illustrates the mediating effect of these processes.

When these parents were asked if they had requested particular teachers at Carlton, most of the parents responded positively. All relied upon other Carlton parents for their information. It is interesting to recall the rather casual, serendipitous nature of these parents' decision to choose Carlton and to contrast those circumstances with these parents' distinctively more active and aware level of decision making as Carlton parents. One parent (middle class) said it was easy to get information about teachers' reputations because, "you develop such a community." Another parent (low income) suggested that Carlton parents "are always trading information," and noted that it was from a Carlton parent that she learned about the gifted and talented program for her daughter. Another parent who works full-time said, "You get to know a teachers' reputation through Carlton activities, talking to parents who have kids in different classes." Many parents suggested that the information was considered accurate because much of it was offered by parents who volunteer in the classroom, or work to fulfill their forty hours in some capacity at the school site.

While the participation requirement is instrumental in providing a mechanism to promote sustained social interactions between parents and school staff, it also marks parents as members of a particular group or *Gemeinschaft* community (Tonnies 1963). That is, rather than being tied together by legal or formal means such as by law or contract (*Gesellschaft* communities), Carlton parents are bound by a perception of shared interests and mutual goals. Just as a willingness to pay for education seems to purchase a sense of mutual commitment and membership for Catholic school parents, the promise to fulfill the participation requirement is the badge that provides Carlton parents with a manifest sense of belonging to this value community (Coleman & Hoffer 1987). The participation requirement acts as a kind of standard which ensures a collection of homogeneous and compatible members.

Choice is a fundamental component in the construction of the value community. The fact that these parents have chosen deliberately, with knowledge of these standards, rather than through coercion, solidifies a sense of commonality around a particular set of values and expectations. The simple act of choosing sensitizes parents to particular benefits that might otherwise go unnoticed and inspires a level of commitment to ensure that the choice is rewarded (Erickson 1982):

> I feel the unity is just the fact that I know that anybody else I meet over there has the same goals I do for our kids. I mean we're all parents. We're all families. We've all got kids in the school. We're united that way because we're interested in it. (father; middle class)

> I could go talk to any of the parents and feel a common tie, even though I don't know them. It isn't that I have to know them or anything. It's just the school and the requirements and the standards. (mother; middle class)

> Q. Do you think most of the other Carlton parents are people like yourselves?
> A. It takes a certain basic responsibility to have your child there. So it draws the same . . . so I think part of the reason that the parents are basically the same values or the same type of people is the participation hours and the different criteria that has to be met to have your child at that school. (mother; lower-middle class)

When parents were asked if they are like other parents at Carlton, many described the population as "mixed" or "balanced" across socioeconomic backgrounds. Most parents suggested that the majority are middle-class people and described this category as "young couples, working, homeowners." In addition, they said there is a sizeable number of "needy" families at Carlton. This general awareness (and accurate assessment) of the mix of families prompted several parents to comment on their perception of commonalities among Carlton families, despite particular differences in social class or religion. These parents seem to underscore the influence of particular organizational elements (tuition or participation requirements) on processes which contribute to a sense of social cohesion and community:

Everybody seems to trust one another. Your kids go to this school. You come from a good family. And I think it's true. I don't have a problem sending my children to any of their friends' home. No matter where. Even if . . . there are some kids who are living in that housing development on the corner. I don't even have a problem with that because I trust the family. The families who are sending their kids to Carlton, you know that their beliefs are like your own. (mother; upper-middle class)

Because you have families who have chosen to go to this school, you sort of set up that you have a lot in common before you ever meet. People with strong values in family and education, willing to go the extra mile. So that's different. We usually feel that most of the time we have a lot of shared values, even though we may come from different parts of the city or different churches or whatever. We know that there's a foundation that we have common goals for our children. (mother; lower-middle class)

**Q.** Do you feel like the other families at Carlton are people like yourselves?
**A.** Yea, they care about their kids. I don't know about the Christian part of it . . . like my friend, she's Mormon, so we're different. There's different beliefs there. But as far as the moral part of it, the family part of it. I feel that a lot of the Carlton people really do care, or they wouldn't be there because you have to put in time. And you have to do it. And I like that. So I feel like we all have a common. . . . We all want the best for our kids. (mother; lower-middle class)
**A.** Yes, I would say so except that I would guess that economically we are probably upper class for Carlton. I know a lot of the families . . . the kids have friends . . . don't have as nice a house, and that type of stuff. As far as value system, they're interested in their kids. They love their kids, and they want them to do well. (mother; upper-middle class)

## A Community Separate and Apart

The formal acceptance of a set of particular standards and expectations contributes to a parallel impression of Carlton parents' separateness from other public school parents and students. That is, the social cohesion experienced by these parents united around a set of articulated aims and expectations has certain consequences; they begin to think of themselves as part of a collective of like-minded individuals, separate and apart from other public school parents. To be sure, there is an objective basis to the elitism: the school's option of forced exit—remanding parents and their children back to their neighborhood schools if they fail to comply with the contract. Although opportunity (racial criteria) and luck dictate who is admitted to Carlton, fulfillment of certain requirements and standards determine students' (and parents') tenure at the school.[13] The result is a not-so-subtle suggestion that Carlton School is not for every family. The principal explains:

> When we get a parent who is telling us they feel their child has been in school for six hours a day and needs some free time, well our school is not for that parent. Or we see . . . putting other activities ahead of homework, ahead of good quality work, and we're getting sloppy work. . . .

Several parents suggested that the demands and expectations set out by the school create standards which ensure that the school screens out parents who don't care as much as Carlton parents do about their children. As one parent said, "You know that the people there care about their kids' education, so you're going to get a better class of people there." These parents also expressed relief and satisfaction with the processes and policies (e.g., homework and agenda) which they suggested help to eliminate children who are difficult or distracting. One parent put it this way:

> I understand the problems with the public school. The nicest thing with Carlton is if you have a problem child, you get him out. It's not that Carlton's academics are tougher; it's just that basically, the distractions are gone. (mother; middle class)

Another parent suggested the benefits of forced exit for teachers and students alike:

> The teachers have the right to say, this kid is really messing up and he doesn't belong in this class; he's not trying. You've given him a chance. And they can send him back to his neighborhood school. It gives the teachers . . . they don't get burned out on just being a disciplinarian. It gives them that room to teach, to experiment with new ideas. It makes their job more enjoyable which spills out of course to the children. (mother; lower-middle class)

Parents acknowledge that Carlton's policies necessarily exclude particular parents and students. Neither by classifying these groups as individuals with particular needs or special problems, or with an unwillingness to participate as required, they dismiss accusations of pernicious elitism. In fact, several parents and teachers pointed to the mixture of social classes and racial minority groups at Carlton as evidence that Carlton is neither elitist nor exclusionary. One parent, who compared the racial composition of Carlton to the United Nations, asserted:

> When you look at my kids' classes, they've got every nationality and size and shape, and I think that's great. It's not that. No one's trying to keep people out because of different nationalities. It's just a matter of, you sign up and get in and as long as you're conforming to their standard. (mother; upper-middle class)

The ability and willingness to conform to particular standards is the yardstick by which Carlton parents measure the suitability of other prospective parents and children. Indeed, these standards not only set the conditions for admission into the school, they help enact the sense of community and social cohesion. It is hardly surprising, then, that Carlton parents have a vested interest in working to maintain a community of conformity to ensure a collection of like-minded families. Their reactions to a proposed kindergarten program which would draw more widely from a "needy" population of neighborhood families is a critical indication of their desire to maintain the standards which they believe contribute to Carlton's academic program and supportive environ ment. While any organizational changes tend to elicit members' concerns, these parents' reactions center on specific issues regarding program dilution, noncompliance with school rules, and diminished expectations:[14]

Q. What do you think about the proposed changes which would create four new kindergarten classes?

A. Everyone ought to have a good education, and it shouldn't just be Carlton, but when they've got Carlton, why should they goof it up? I was talking with some of the other parents. They're going to bring in, I think they call it chapter 2. And they'll be interpreters, and I don't know how it's going to go into the regular basic school program; how it's going to affect the children who are already there. (mother; middle class)

A. At this point, we don't have Chapter 1, so we don't have any provisions for these kids who need extra help so it really wouldn't be fair to them, even though I've heard the district talk about introducing Chapter 1. That disturbs me a little bit because that would really destroy our uniqueness. There really wouldn't be a basic program. (mother; middle class)

A. I think it will end up diluting the program. I understand from the district point of view, but from my personal point of view, I'm disappointed. I don't think it will be as effective. It's the kind of thing the more you have, the less control you have. The bigger the school, the less. . . . Children may get lost in the shuffle. (mother; upper-middle class)

Another parent said he was worried that the district was turning Carlton into a neighborhood school:

Q. What worries you about that?

A. Because I don't think they're going to get people to participate, and they'll have to go ahead and let the students into the class anyway. Basically, there's a lot of people out there looking for a free lunch. (father; middle class)

Several other parents suggested that as long as the district maintained Carlton's standards, they were comfortable with the changes:

I don't see how it could hurt. As long as they stick to the rule. As long as the school administration sticks with the rules and applies it fairly where parents put in forty hours a year at minimum, or if they don't their kid isn't re-enrolled. If they stick with that for the neighborhood kids versus the kids who come from outlying areas, fine. (mother; middle class)

## The Empowering Effects of Community

If there is any doubt about the degree to which Carlton parents are protective of their school community, it should be diminished by the vocal, vigorous, and collective response evidenced three years ago when the district proposed moving the basic program to another school site. Staff and parents' loyalties were realized in a massive demonstration against the proposed move. Parents organized themselves in a letter-writing campaign to the board; dozens attended school board meetings and spoke passionately about the time and effort they had expended over the years to protect and beautify the Carlton campus. The threat to the school seemed at once to demonstrate the existing sense of solidarity and community, as well as to awaken a manifest sense of ownership of the school. The principal recalled:

> When they were going to move us over there and there was talk that maybe that [school's] faculty would take over the basic school, they were up in arms. They were all here. They were downtown. It was just a massive thing. They are very much like a family.

Some parents suggested the incident had enduring effects on their perceptions of the school and their involvement. The shared interest in fighting to protect their children's school was as empowering as it was aggregative. Parents who had never attended a school board meeting attended several; some even spoke to the board. Parents who had never met served on a committee together and learned about one another's family. Parents who knew little about school politics and decision making observed the wrangling firsthand.

For one parent, the experience was particularly important. She emigrated to the United States from an Eastern European country to the United States when she was fourteen years old and had "absolutely no idea" about school when her daughter started kindergarten four years ago; her knowledge was limited to her own high school and brief community college experience. During the several months of debate and conflict over the proposed move, she served on the school committee organized to defeat the district plan. Several committee assignments and school board meetings later, she knows a great deal more about school organization and politics:

> I was operating on the administrative level, really, as a volunteer, but I could take any of their jobs now, really, even though there is so much to learn. I've worked with the staff. I know half that building [district office]. It's been absolutely amazing.

**Q.** How did you go about plugging yourself into the system?
**A.** It just happened. It happened so gradually. It's like gaining weight. One day, you're thin and then three years later you're fat, and you wonder how you got fat. It happened so gradually; you don't know. You kind of learn to live with it. (middle class)

The mutual goals and shared expectations that parents perceive within the community of parents is mirrored in their relations with teachers. There is also a corresponding unity of purpose and collegiality shared among the faculty members, most of whom have taught at Carlton for at least ten years. These pervasive elements of community have implications for the ways in which parents and teachers interact. The next section examines the ways in which the formal organizational elements at Carlton influence relations between parents and teachers and shape the nature of expectations each has for the other.

## Relationships Between Parents and Teachers

The accumulated research on parent involvement in schooling suggests that conflict, distrust, and ambiguity often define the relationships between teachers and parents (Lightfoot 1980, 1978; McPherson 1972; Waller 1932). Boundaries are unclear. Expectations are ill defined and poorly communicated. Disappointment and frustration seem to color most structured interactions.

As Carlton teachers and parents discussed their interactions, some differences or minor criticisms arose, but the tenor of discourse reflected a compatible and congruent relationship. A number of organizational conditions and arrangements seem to account for these cooperative relations. First, the contract that teachers, parents, and students sign every year outlines specific expectations. Secondly, teachers perceive themselves as a community of like-minded, committed professionals who share fundamental ideas about education and teaching with parents. Finally, the established processes for communication between home and school promote understanding, awareness, and cooperation. Each of these elements contribute to an integrated set of roles and relationships which comprise the Carlton School community.

## The Contract

The section of the contract which pertains to parents outlines their responsibilities in five major areas: academic achievement; attendance; citizenship; homework; and parent involvement. (See Appendix G.) Several parents hinted that they do not pay particular attention to specific stipulations and that for the most part, "it's just common sense stuff." Nevertheless, parents and teachers observed that the contract serves both symbolic and instrumental purposes in the same way the participation requirement does. As a condition of admission, the contract signifies another "badge" of community membership. Although it may be signed each year just moments before it is filed and forgotten, it differentiates Carlton parents from most other public school parents.

Substantively and practically, the contract can be used by parents to enforce homework study periods, limit television viewing, and get their children to bed by 9:00 P.M. (stipulated in the contract). While some parents noted that it is not always followed, all agreed that it offers their job of childrearing some leverage and enforcement capacity. Most importantly, the contract seems to avoid confusion and frustration by clearly articulating the expectations of each group. Finally, several parents suggested that the contract symbolizes the commitment each Carlton parent attaches to their children's education. Here are some observations:

> It just lets everybody know that we all have responsibilities in the education process. It's not just the school. It's not just the kid. It's the three—parents, the teachers, and the kids—working together that will make it work, and anyone trying to do it alone is going to have a hard time. (mother; low income)

> I think it's a good idea although we don't stick to it, totally. It's real tough to get your kids in bed every night especially when you do stuff like this [going fishing]. It at least makes the parent aware of what the school expects of him, anyway. If you don't ever commit to something, you may never do it. I think the only thing in there that's really mandatory, that could hurt you as far as years to come, is the participation hours. (father; middle class)

> I like it. It's a sticky subject with a lot of people because some people think that education is free and that you really shouldn't sign anything. But you know, this is an alternative school. You don't need to attend it. If you don't like what we're doing, then you can go elsewhere. I think that it's crucial that the parents stick to their end of the bargain the way the kids do. (mother; middle class)

For school officials, the contract provides the leverage and clarity to justify expulsion procedures against parents and students. It also sets the tone for this school of choice: if you do not follow the rules, you are out. Consequently, the document is more than a piece of paper filed away somewhere; it carries the threat and authority of a forced exit from Carlton. The principal, who said he is a believer in contracts because "when people sign something it has more power then a verbal agreement," considers the Carlton contract meaningful and important:

> It sets out the tenets of basic education pretty clearly and lets the person know what they're buying into. I ask people in the meetings, when we have the orientation meetings for new parents, I want you to please read it, and if you can agree with it, sign it. And if you don't agree with it, don't sign it because you will not accept then, our practices and we're not about to change these prac-

tices. As I say, people are willing to make trade-offs. They may not believe in all of that, but they want their child here. (principal)

Teachers are equally convinced of the contract's merits. From their perspective, the contract encodes what good parenting is all about—maintaining an active, supportive, and encouraging role in children's education and ensuring that children show respect and courtesy in their daily interactions with other adults and students. There is nothing dramatically different or innovative here, except the fact that these parents are asked to pledge their allegiance to specified school policies. Although no fee is charged at Carlton, the contract purchases an enhanced level of commitment and expectations, something teachers say requires parents to "buy into this program." As one teacher observed:

> If the parents give me any problems I always say to them, "Well, you signed a contract." And it's like, "Yes, I did; yes, you're right." There's no, "It doesn't mean anything; it's just a piece of paper." I have yet to have a parent say to me, "Well, it's just a piece of paper," because they know if they say [that] they are not committed and I can say, "Gee, I guess you don't want to be here. This is not the right place for you." (teacher)

> Q. Can you be tougher with parents here because it's a choice school?
> A. I don't think so. I think where the difference comes is in the final response. That because they've bought into this program, in some way, shape or form, they're maybe a little more willing to hear it than maybe in another place where they haven't been told that there are any expectations for them. (teacher)

Despite the explicit level of commitment expected from Carlton parents, several teachers indicated that parents still resist the partnership role the school intends them to assume. The exigencies of time and the dual obligations of home and work lives make it difficult for some teachers to manage everything; they recognize that families face the same challenges. One teacher talked about the message she conveys to parents at Back-to-School Night each fall regarding the need to practice verbal communication, simple geography, and math facts with their youngsters:

> A lot of the time they don't want to hear it. They don't want to hear . . . "You mean you're not going to give them three hours of busywork for me to send them off with?" A lot of times I get a lot of groans at Back-to-School Night when I say that in the lower grades, it really has to be their responsibility.

> Q. Why do you think they are groaning?
> A. I don't think they have the time to do it. I know myself, as a working parent, it is absolutely exhausting. I do not turn on the TV in the evening. I do not sit down until my kids go to bed. When I sit down, I lie down. And

there's nothing in between. And I don't go out on the weeknights. It's between baseball and soccer, whatever, music lessons. And my kids know the same thing. School night is school night, and it means everybody is working. (teacher)

The expectations for teachers are also outlined in the contract in ways that help clarify their roles and relationships vis-à-vis parents. For both parents and teachers, the contract provides a language and a framework for interacting. It also provides a contractual basis—symbolically and substantively—to begin working on a partnership. Here are several different teachers' views:

**Q.** What kind of expectations do the parents have of you? What do you expect from parents?

**A.** They expect that I'm going to give these children the very best education that they can get—that we can give them within the framework. Their expectations of me are that I give them the very best. Then, what happens is, I expect them to back me up—if I make a decision. I expect that if they have a problem, that they'll come to me first and discuss the problem with me, and that they will not bad mouth me at home in front of the children. (teacher)

**Q.** How do you think about your role in your students' schooling?

**A.** It's my job to see to it that they become . . . that they get good study habits, that they learn self-discipline, and a sense of responsibility. Those are the three things. And I always say that if they have those three things they can do everything—even if they're not the most intelligent child in the whole world. (teacher)

**Q.** What do you think parents expect from you?

**A.** They do expect a lot. It's real challenging. They expect us to be prepared. They expect us to care about their children. They expect us to treat their children in a fair and humane manner. They expect us to be good role models. I think if I were to stop and really think about it, I'd really wonder whether I could carry this all. [laughs] But they have very high expectations and because they are very empowered in the school they don't have a big problem expressing those expectations. If they perceive that something doesn't seem to be the way they would want it to be, they're in here to visit the classroom. And we tell them that that's fine. That's their right and that's their choice. (teacher)

**Q.** In your mind, why does this school "work"?

**A.** I think from the staff point of view, there is a very high level of commitment to the program, a high commitment to kids and to teaching and education in general. I think from the parent point of view, because they have made a commitment in writing, somehow, like everything else . . . it's like Jenny Craig. It's paying that extra money and committing yourself to the program. It's not that it's magic weight loss. It's just that, you've given that extra level of yes, I will buy into that. I think that's what parents do here and so it gives them a vehicle to become more active. And I think some parents at other schools might even like to be as active as they are, but they don't know quite how to do it. Whereas here, we clearly lay out ways for them to be involved in their school. (teacher)

If the contract provides a blueprint for teachers and parents to construct a dialogue and set of relationships around a common set of ideas and expectations, it is the faculty that has built the bridges and executed the designs. The basic school program is a product of their joint efforts and shared goals. The next section examines the Carlton faculty and its collective influence on relations between parents and teachers.

## A Community of Teachers

Under the rubric of "faculty culture" researchers have described a heightened sense of collegiality among teachers in magnet schools (McNeil 1987; Metz 1986; Raywid 1988b). The research suggests that the specific curricular focus and organization of magnet schools contribute to a shared commitment to a way of teaching. The culture is founded and reinforced by these common perspectives and common practices (McNeil 1987).

The teachers at Carlton invoke similar language, refer to common symbols and strategies, and support a common ideology. If interaction and mutual dependence, the intention of longevity and permanence, communication, common and mutual sentiments, shared beliefs, and an ethic of individual concern constitute the elements of contemporary community (Raywid 1988b), the Carlton faculty can claim each and every marker.

Before Carlton became a magnet school with a specific curricular emphasis, much of the curriculum and discipline reflected the tenets of basic education but without the label. The program was created in a bottom-up fashion by a group of like-minded teachers with extensive tenures at Carlton, all of whom are still there. Incremental changes (the contract, required participation, strict homework policy) were made by the staff as they learned more about the intentions and design of a basic school. Nevertheless, the school's basic framework had been established long before the district's decision to call it by another name; now they had the means to enforce their ideas by attracting like-minded parents and their children. Consequently, the transition to the magnet program involved little disruption or discord. The teachers, in fact, had already "bought into" the program, or, as one teacher put it, they "were the ones who kind of invented it, actually."

What ideas about schooling have laid the foundation for the integration of basic school policies? Consider the responses from these three teachers:

**A.** I don't see anything that I'm doing right now as resulting in any kind of immediate [effect]. . . . I see myself as just kind of laying the groundwork for a long road. It's not going to be earth-shattering today, but I think long down the road, it's going to make a difference.

**A.** We only have them for a few hours a day compared to the length of time the parents have them. It really has to be a teamwork kind of an approach. And also children need to come to school with the idea that this is where learning in a particular way takes place. We can't cut their heads open and pour knowledge in. There has to be some kind of curiosity, some kind of desire to learn these things.

**A.** I try to get parents to realize they can only do so much and then after a while, the student must kick in. I think as students start getting into the third grade, they have to realize that they can do something on their own. And I try to get parents to see too that it doesn't always mean you must sit down and call the spelling test. Even if you're washing dishes, you can be doing spelling. Or if you're driving to school, you could be doing math facts. Education has to go on all the time.

The parallel and reinforcing ideas of a partnership with parents, student responsibility and self-discipline, and rigorous training in the basic subjects resonate with the perspectives and practices of Carlton teachers. Their individual biographies, visceral styles, and varied interpretations seem to coalesce around a shared vision of what schools ought to offer children and their families:

All of us have our different kind of interpretations, but as far as a whole, we're very committed to the goal of a basic school, so that gives us a lot of collegiality, so that all of us focus on what we want to be about. We may be a little different in our getting there, but we're all kind of focused about being there. And because we all kind of agree on that, we're all willing to help each other. So it's really a very high level of collegiality. In our lunch room, we talk about how we handle different things. We ask people's advice. There's not a stigma in me going to another teacher and asking her to help me out. So we just all work together. And I think that kind of teamwork is really different than at some of the other less successful schools.

I would say we probably have the best program in the city because these children here are going to get an education. And the other thing you're going to find here is with these children, they come first and we come second. Their needs come first and ours come second. . . . You don't see a lot of teachers going home early. They're here a long time and spend a lot of time.

We sell this to our parents because we're sold on it. Everybody is sold on it. Not just me. Not just the intermediate side, but the whole school is.

The heightened sense of commitment and demonstrated success has engendered a vocal and exuberant claim of ownership, as one veteran teacher answered the question:

**Q.** Does this school belong to someone, to some group?

**A.** The teachers and the children and the parents—it belongs to us. It's ours. You should ask the teachers around here. When you talk to the rest of us who have been here a long time, just don't . . . just be careful because we feel . . . we're the first to tell you when things are wrong but we're the first to tell you things are right. This is like family to us.

The consensus, common goals, and collective beliefs Carlton teachers share are translated to parents and students in a common language and set of consistent actions. The incentive is real and powerful: the intrinsic rewards associated with successful classroom experiences and supportive parents require a collective of like-minded parents and their children. The challenge of "selling the program" involves communicating this imperative. The next section examines the formal and informal channels of communication which provide a conduit for the promotion and maintenance of family-school interactions, and ultimately, the value community at Carlton School.

## Communication

Parents' knowledge of Carlton's requirements, activities, and the kind of homework their children are assigned, reflects a vast network of communication channels the principal and teachers monitor with attention and diligence. The channels include both written and telephone messages. They include the routine notices sent home with the student announcing special events, meetings, and testing dates. There are some additional lines which the school has developed to make sure news and information are communicated in a systematic, organized way.

Each grade level is assigned a chairperson who is responsible for organizing a telephone network system which alerts parents in that grade of any specific events, responsibilities, etc. The chairperson receives credit hours for his/her participation, as do any parents who participate in the telephone network. Each classroom has a room parent, whose duties include organizing class parties and arranging drivers for field trips. These duties count toward participation hours.

Additionally, a punitive system ensures that parents and students coordinate their efforts in receiving and returning notices. If students fail to return notices which require a parent's signature, they are penalized with minutes subtracted from their recess. The triad partnership and the responsibility that the basic program emphasizes extends to home-school communication.

Thus, the school's need and interest in keeping parents informed is well integrated with their need for volunteer support (an instrumental rationale for the participation requirement) and the basic school philosophy. If parents are well informed, perceive that their interests and concerns are being taken into account, and identify themselves as a member of the school community, their level of involvement can be expected to increase. The communication system draws from a ready pool of parent volunteers eager to satisfy the forty-hour requirement. A threat of punitive action acts as an enforcement mechanism. The policies parallel and reinforce one another.

The impact of an enhanced level of communication between home and school at Carlton is reflected in the rich, detailed knowledge of school policies and activities parents possess. In addition to this type of information, parents are kept abreast of their children's academic performance through what are called "weekly reports." Each Friday, teachers send home a comprehensive summary of the student's performance on homework, quizzes, class assignments, and tests. This way, say teachers and parents, there are few surprises.

Across social class backgrounds and regardless of their own schooling experiences or personal networks, the impression of uniformly well-informed parents is unavoidable. While a part of this is indisputably attributable to the natural by-products of exercising choice (i.e., parents being more likely to demonstrate a higher degree of commitment and sensitivity to these aspects of schooling), it is equally true that the accumulated effect of these processes and procedures provides the connections to ensure their sustained interest and loyalty. Several perspectives help illuminate this point:

Oh, they're real good at communication. They send home papers. So they're really good. And things that are really important, they have you sign and you have to take back. It's really a responsibility between you and your child to make sure that it comes back because if it doesn't, they get points, or minutes, where they have to stay in from recess. (mother; lower-middle class)

With Carlton, they let you know each week what's going on. If they've missed an assignment, then it comes on a sheet that you sign that goes back Monday. It has to be in. It's their responsibility to have it in, or they have to do time in study center. (mother; middle class)

It just seems like sometimes people throw their kids at school to baby-sit. Or parents don't find out what's going on until open house. Whereas at Carlton, we know what's going on all the time. We don't have to wait for an open house. (father; middle class)

I don't know if my parents were informed when I broke a girl's hand in fifth grade. I don't know if they knew until I told them later. I have no idea if the school contacted them or not. Now, if something like that had happened with one of these two [children], I'm sure we would get a phone call immediately. If not then, you can rest assured there would be a note on that cover sheet. (father; middle class)

They keep you involved, and they keep you aware of what's going on over there. The teacher-parent communication is really good. The teacher's always letting me know where they're at, what's going on, where they need help. (mother; middle class)

By encouraging parents to visit the school and their children's classroom "as often as possible," teachers strengthen the structural arrangements designed to sustain a fluid, consistent dialogue across family and school. Parent-teacher conferences are scheduled for thirty minutes, instead of the customary fifteen. At least one teacher offers parents a choice of holding the conference at the school or in their home. The conferences themselves seem to be structured around a variety of family and school topics, rather than narrowly focused on the student's report card. One teacher explained:

> We could very well send our report card home if that's all we're going to talk about. So we try to give you a little more. This is our purpose in structuring it for half an hour—to give you time so that if you know the conference is coming up, there's anything you want to discuss, now is the perfect time to give you that opportunity to bring up whatever you might want to bring up.

These established, customary rituals can become something more under these conditions; teachers may learn more about particular family problems which are making a child seem anxious or disinterested in her school work. As one teacher put it:

> With the conferences, as draining as they are, they are enlightening because I better understand why students do some of the things they do, and it makes me get to the point of readjusting my teaching, my approach to a particular student.

The various elements under the umbrella communication system solidify the organization of a value community by connecting individuals to a collective of parents with congruent values and shared belief systems. To be sure, the impact of these arrangements are enhanced by the synergetic effect of voluntary choice. That is, in a nonchoice public school, these same arrangements may not deliver the same potent meaning and value. The simple act of choosing delivers an immeasurable degree of sensitivity, incentive, and commitment to parents' social interactions with Carlton staff. The important point is to acknowledge that choice cannot alone promote or sustain a value community in schools. The portrait is incomplete without the addition of the organizational elements and processes discussed throughout this chapter.

## SUMMARY

The serendipitous nature of school choice is represented in the ways in which parents at Carlton School selected it for their children. Rather than pursuing a systematic review of school alternatives, the context of decision making reveals that a chance conversation or unsolicited advice prompted a look-and-see attitude for many parents discouraged by their unsafe or depressing neighborhood school. Their unfamiliarity with the basic school philosophy or the aims of the magnet program suggests that these parents do not resemble the characteristics of self-selected parents who opt for private schools.

Nevertheless, the exercise of choice and the corresponding organizational arrangements and policies combine to produce a pervasive sense of community at Carlton School. Although drawn from disparate neighborhoods throughout the city, the nature of social interactions among parents and staff reflect an intensive degree of solidarity, mutual support, and familiarity. The policy which requires parents to participate forty hours each year provides a symbolic as well as instrumental tool for promoting social cohesion. A sense of connection and interdependence is born through a series of interactions at school-based events. The incentive to earn participation hours provides the parameters for these occasions of face-to-face talk in which news and information about schooling is exchanged. For those parents whose social class positions do not provide the resources (education, social networks) through which to gain information about curriculum, testing, teachers' reputations, and middle/high school admissions, these social networks mediate the influence of cultural capital on parents' interactions with schools. Still, the organization of parents' work lives serves to disadvantage those parents whose full-time, inflexible work arrangements prohibit their involvement in school-based activities and the social networks which those activities promote.

A number of organizational conditions and arrangements seem to account for discernibly cooperative and respectful relations between parents and teachers. First, the contract teachers, parents, and students sign helps avoid frustrations and confusion by specifying expectations. Second, a palpable culture of community and ownership exists among teachers which provides a coherence and connection between the faculty and families. Finally, the established processes for communication between home and school promote understanding, awareness, and cooperation. Fueled by the attendant elements of choice (incentive, commitment, awareness), these organizational processes help promote and sustain the value community at Carlton School.

## NOTES

1. The racial breakouts for the school district population are as follows: 22 percent black; 20 percent Asian; 18 percent Hispanic; 40 percent white.

2. There are seven magnet and alternative elementary schools, two kindergarten through eighth grade magnet schools, three at the middle school level, and four high school magnets. The majority of these magnet/alternative schools were created between the years 1987–1989.

3. The median price of a home in this Northern California city is $135,000 (September 1992).

4. Two years ago, eight appeals were submitted by parents whose children were not accepted; of these, four were admitted upon review.

5. A total of eleven families was interviewed. Nine of the interviews took place in the family home (one parent was interviewed in her office and another parent in my home) and were audiotaped with the permission of the subjects. These cases reflect the range of backgrounds and family structures among the families at Carlton School.

6. According to the assessments of faculty and Carlton parents, and a review of parent information cards and free lunch eligibility data, the majority of families are middle to lower-middle class. Two of the eleven parents interviewed are upper-middle class.

7. These categories reflect composite definitions of social class and in some cases, respondents' self-identifications with a particular class category. Composite measures include income, occupation, education, and material resources. All names used here are pseudonyms.

8. In a 1988–89 district-wide survey of magnet schools, over 90 percent of the 171 Carlton School parents surveyed responded positively to questions regarding the school's discipline, academic, communication, and safety policies.

9. For some parents, their interest in safety extends beyond schoolyard fighting and is heightened by a concern about their own neighborhoods and neighborhood schools as places where children can be assaulted or abducted. These concerns were expressed by mothers who work full- or part-time, and are anxious about their inability to more closely monitor their children's time before and after school hours.

10. Although several of the families are active members of a church, including two sets of parents who are Mormon, none identified their religious beliefs or church teachings as a source of influence on their beliefs about education.

11. The principal reported that there has been a "significant" increase in parent participation since enforcement began last year. The impression among teachers suggests that although participation tended to be fairly widespread prior to enforcement, *more* parents are contributing *more* hours now.

12. That is, the ability of parents to fulfill the forty-hour participation requirement by performing certain tasks at home does not appear to be impacted by differential access to income or material resources. However, the ability of parents to assist their children with homework—a taken-for-granted element of parent involvement not accounted for by the policy—is necessarily influenced by the parents' own educational backgrounds and abilities.

13. Last year, in the first year that the participation requirement was formally enforced, twelve families (out of a total of 230) failed to complete their forty hours and were asked to register their child or children at another school for the following school year.

14. The proposal includes the creation of four new kindergarten classes: two of the classes to be filled by children from the sixteen feeder schools; one class to be filled with overflow from a neighborhood school. The board recommended that the basic school program not be eroded to accommodate neighborhood enrollees. Toward this goal, they suggested that Carlton take unspecified actions to ensure that new kindergarten students obtain the skills needed for the basic school first grade. Carlton would not be expected to enroll students who qualify for special education, bilingual education, or Chapter 1.

# 4

# *Western School*

Western public elementary school straddles a decidedly mixed neighborhood of middle-class homes and low-income apartments. The school is encircled by quiet, meandering streets dotted with modest three-bedroom homes valued at between $125,000 and $140,000. Some are neatly manicured with green, robust shrubbery accenting the front yards. Other houses resemble fortresses, with barred windows and waist-high chain-link fences around the perimeter of the yards; faded, peeling house paint and lawns littered with disemboweled cars make some homes look particularly aged and vulnerable for their twenty-odd years. American-model sedans, pickup trucks, and compact Japanese autos are scattered down these streets; a small fishing boat and trailer occasionally front a driveway.

Apartments, duplexes, and townhouse developments flank Western School on the south side. The newer apartment complexes have grassy knolls separating the Cape Cod-style units and list for $625 for a two-bedroom. The townhouse developments offer swimming pools and tennis courts for the owners of the two- and three-bedroom units. Moving out beyond these offerings, however, the apartments and duplexes which line the noisy, busy boulevards demarcating the school's attendance area feature accommodations far less attractive and desirable. Most of the residents here are unemployed and receive government assistance. The reputedly high volume of drug activity in these apartment complexes is evidenced by the frequent visits by police patrol cars.

The Western School campus features neatly trimmed lawns and green hedges, shady trees, and healthy-looking ivy and juniper bushes. The main office sits in the center of campus, providing an obvious starting point for school visitors. Classrooms are clustered on either side and toward the back in chunky blocks of four, in typical 1970s-style school architecture. The dark windows designed to dim the glaring effects of the sunshine make attempts to spy classroom activities difficult, if not futile. Beyond the classrooms, the generously sized, grassy athletic field and asphalt basketball courts form the "backyard" of the campus property.

As visitors enter the school office, a low counter topped with in/out mail trays, plants, and a sign-out sheet interrupts their forward momentum; on the other side sit two large desks fit together to form a seamless working space for the school secretaries. Rolodex wheels, files, telephones, typewriters, and computer terminals spill out over the desktops. A picture window reveals the principal's quiet, self-contained office to the left; a closed door on the right leads to the nurse's room. Just outside her office, a large bulletin board announces "PTA News" and "Volunteer of the Month." Across the room another bulletin board displays the colorful artwork and essays of Western's fourth graders. A photograph of the student council's "Teacher of the Month" is posted on the far wall, just above the copy machine. Two window-framed doors, exactly like the entrance doors, lead out the other side of the office to the central campus area, creating a busy footpath for teachers, aides, and students. Outside, in the corner of the entrance door, a handwritten sign affixed to the glass proclaims: "Welcome to Western. We are glad you are here."

## SIZE AND MAKEUP

Western School has two classrooms of 30–33 students in each grade from kindergarten through sixth. Typically, school enrollment is between 450–460. According to the most recent district figures (1993–94), the school population is 74 percent white, 7 percent black, 8 percent Hispanic, and 11 percent Asian, drawn from the school's surrounding neighborhoods.[1]

About 300 families send their children to Western School. As many as half of these families are headed by a single parent; of the other families, most are two-income families in which mothers are employed outside of the home at least part-time. Approximately two-thirds of the families at Western are middle class; one-third are low income and receive some kind of government assistance. Some of the middle-class parents attended college, but few hold a bachelor's degree; most terminated their formal education after high school or community college, or technical/trade school. These parents typically hold skilled jobs in construction, computers, or insurance. Many of the Western parents who hold college degrees work in semiprofessional occupations for the state government.

The full-time faculty at Western numbers sixteen (including two teachers responsible for the "special day class" for physically handicapped students), of whom fourteen are female. In addition, the staff includes a resource specialist, resource teacher, psychologist, music instructor, and speech therapist. The support staff is comprised of the nurse, secretary, clerk, parent coordinator, and librarian. A group of ten part-time aides assists teachers in remedial math and reading, bilingual classes, and computer instruction, as well as in the special day classes. The principal, who is female, has been at Western for four years and was a speech pathologist in the district before entering administration. Up until two years ago, most of the faculty members had taught at Western for a minimum of eight years and could be considered veteran teachers. Recently, however, transfers and retirements have resulted in five new teacher assignments.

## RULES AND POLICIES

The philosophy of Western School is embodied in an acronym: CARES. According to the school parent handbook, CARES stands for Cooperation, Academics, Respect, Effort, and Safety. "Pride Assemblies" are held the last Friday of every month so that students, staff, parents, and volunteers can be recognized for their achievement in these five areas.

In addition to rules governing student behavior on the playground, in the cafeteria, and during assemblies, Western has a schoolwide policy of "Responsible Discipline." The policy is designed to ensure consistency and clarity across classrooms and between teachers and students. Teachers select five basic rules which they deem appropriate for their classroom. Clearly defined consequences are attached to any violations of these rules. The "Pride Assemblies" are used to positively reinforce appropriate behavior for students who obey classroom, playground, and lunchroom rules. For students who misbehave, a series of increasingly severe punitive actions are imposed, including conferences with the principal, written paragraphs on the inappropriateness of their behavior, and restricted recesses. The five-step process culminates at the "serious concern level" with suspension.

Western participates in the Early Intervention Program, a district-wide program designed to help students in grades kindergarten through sixth who are experiencing stress and difficulty in their home and school lives. Aides work with students one-on-one (in the primary grades) and in groups (in the upper grades) to improve students' self-esteem and self-control and to guide them through problem-solving techniques.

The homework policy at Western states that the purpose of homework is to "strengthen academic skills, reinforce concepts taught by teachers, develop student responsibility and accountability, and promote parent awareness." Accordingly, homework is "generally" assigned on a Monday through Thursday basis. The amount of homework assigned "shall be related to the maturational and ability level of the students in a given class." By the sixth grade, the amount of time expected to complete these assignments should not exceed four hours per week. Finally, the policy suggests that students should understand, complete, and return homework assignments on the required day. Parents' responsibilities include setting a specific time and place for doing homework, monitoring their children's work, and providing assistance if needed. The homework policy does not specify any consequences of incomplete or missed homework assignments.

## GOVERNANCE

As part of the city's twenty-school unified school district, Western is governed by decisions of a five-member board of education and the district superintendent.

Western's school advisory council consists of twenty-one parents, three teachers, and one interpreter. The group meets three times a year to discuss the federal compensatory education program (Chapter 1) and the distribution of these funds. Most of these funds are used to pay the costs of four instructional aides who assist classroom teachers in providing special instructional services for students who score below the forty-eighth percentile in reading and math.

A total of eleven members serve on the school site council, including six parents, three teachers, the principal, and the parent coordinator. As part of the School Improvement Program (SIP), the council governs the disbursement of funds used for "school enrichment" items, including classroom aides, field trips, and assemblies. The council meets three times a year. These funds account for less than 5 percent of the school's total budget.

## PARENT-TEACHER ASSOCIATION (PTA)

Typical of many schools, the PTA serves a critical fund-raising function at Western. About 200 parents joined the Western School PTA last year for $2.50 per person. Events such as the annual jog-a-thon, candy sale, spaghetti dinner, ice cream social, and the ongoing sportswear sales generate over $8,000 in revenues annually. The PTA sponsors entertainment and educational assemblies for the school and provides many educational materials used in the classroom. Last year, for example, PTA funds paid for a new carpet in the school library, new curtains in the multipurpose room, and a handheld microphone system.

## ORGANIZATION OF FAMILY LIFE:
## THE CONSEQUENCES FOR SCHOOL INVOLVEMENT

### Family Profiles[2]

The Western parents interviewed for this study range from middle-class to low-income parents on public assistance. Their residences vary in size and value from a comfortable three-bedroom, one-story home in the quiet neighborhood near the school, to a cramped, roach-infested two-bedroom apartment off a heavily trafficked boulevard. The parents in six of the twelve families I interviewed have some college experience in either a community college or a four-year institution. Three families have at least one parent who dropped out of high school.

Half of the families interviewed are two-parent, dual-income (working) families; most include mothers who work full-time outside of the home. Five

Table III  Western School

| FAMILY | EDUCATION* | OCCUPATION | MARITAL STATUS | NUMBER OF CHILDREN |
|---|---|---|---|---|
| 1 | Father: B.S.<br>Mother: B.S. | High school teacher<br>Sales representative | Married | 3 |
| 2 | Father: H.S.<br>Mother: H.S. | Construction worker<br>Bookkeeper | Married | 2 |
| 3 | Father: H.S.<br>Mother: --- | Construction worker<br>Student (part-time) | Married | 2 |
| 4 | Father: H.S., A.A.<br>Mother: H.S. | Operations analyst<br>Retail sales clerk | Married | 2 |
| 5 | Father: H.S.<br>Mother: H.S., A.A. | Construction foreman<br>Insurance claims analyst | Married | 1 |
| 6 | Father: B.S.<br>Mother: H.S. | Computer analyst<br>Word processing supervisor | Married | 1 |
| 7 | Father: H.S.<br>Mother: H.S. | Mail carrier<br>Owner, crafts business | Married | 4 |
| 8 | Father: H.S., A.A. | Mortgage broker | Divorced | 2 |
| 9 | Father: H.S. | Construction worker | Divorced | 1 |
| 10 | Mother: H.S. | Insurance claims analyst (on medical leave) | Separated | 3 |
| 11 | Mother: --- | Unemployed | Separated | 3 |
| 12 | Mother: --- | Unemployed | Divorced | 5 |

\* B.S.—Bachelor of Science degree  H.S.—High School diploma
A.A.—Associate of Arts degree  --- —Left high school at age 16

of the families I spoke with are headed by a single (separated or divorced) parent. Only three of the families interviewed are members of a church and regularly attend church services. All of the parents interviewed have at least one child enrolled in the third or fourth grade at Western School.

The following composites portray families from each of the two social class groups predominant at Western: middle class and low income.[3]

## The Thompsons

The Thompsons live in a comfortable, three-bedroom, one-story home on a quiet street just a couple of blocks from school. They bought the house for $73,000 when they moved here from Michigan five years ago. They are just completing some modest renovations—new kitchen wallpaper and fresh paint in the bedrooms—and could sell the house for $135,000 in today's real estate market.

High school sweethearts, the Thompsons married shortly after graduation. Mr. Thompson started an apprenticeship in paving and heavy equipment operations. His wife found a job in the customer service department of the local telephone company. Since moving to California, Mr. Thompson has been promoted to a foreman position with a paving company, and Mrs. Thompson is a data processing supervisor for a state government agency.

The Thompsons say their busy work schedules rarely provide enough time to enjoy a family meal together with their two children, ages nine and seven. Saturdays are spent cleaning up around the house, doing yard work and occasionally, browsing at a garage sale or the local shopping mall. Last summer they took a camping trip up the Oregon coast for a week. They enjoy reading and playing Nintendo games when they are home together. With both of their boys involved in soccer and scouting, the Thompsons spend many weekends and weekday evenings at games, practices, and meetings. They are not members of any church.

## Mrs. Joiner

Mrs. Joiner lives in a small, two-bedroom apartment with her boyfriend and her three children, ages ten, seven, and three months. The rent is $450 a month. The window looking out to the parking lot is cracked, and there are several areas where the paint is chipped and peeling in the center room. One late night last month, Mrs. Joiner and her boyfriend spent 3 ½ hours spraying roaches after finding them in the kitchen, the bedrooms, and in the baby's crib. She says that drug use in the complex is common; her kids regularly pick up syringes from the parking lot.

Mrs. Joiner grew up in a nearby community and attended the local high school before dropping out in the middle of her sophomore year. She married when she was eighteen and had her first child shortly thereafter. Three years ago she divorced her husband, whom she says physically abused her; he also abused drugs and alcohol. She was living with her mother in an adjacent apartment until 1¹/₂ years ago, when she met her boyfriend. They recently had a child together.

Mrs. Joiner says she "likes to party" but no longer uses drugs. She has been unemployed for almost two years and receives AFDC. She enjoys watching rental movies with her children and taking drives in her boyfriend's car.

## Parents' Expectations and the Value of Education

Research suggests that "residential mobility" for those parents who can afford it—mainly middle- and upper-middle-class parents—provides a quasi-choice mechanism by allowing parents to select a home in a neighborhood with a reputedly high quality public school (e.g., see Peterson 1981; Tiebout 1956). In other words, parents' interest in and knowledge of schools often drive the selection of a neighborhood and a home.

The parents interviewed from Western School made decisions regarding their children's schooling in the opposite direction; they selected a neighborhood which offered reasonable homes for an affordable price with general expectations, not knowledge, of the local school. They made blanket assumptions that Western would offer a good education for their kids. Some parents based these ideas on a cursory review of the campus and the neighborhood. Other parents who moved to California from out of state (more than five years ago) were comforted by a general impression that California schools enjoy a strong reputation for quality:

**Q.** What did you know about Western when you moved here?

**A.** I knew it was right around the corner and I was glad of that. Other than that, not too much, except that it was a California school and I've been in different states, and I knew California had more money than other states. So because of that, I knew there was nothing wrong, immediately. Nothing to bicker about. (father; middle class)

**A.** I didn't know anything about the school, in fact, none of the California schools. I knew nothing about them. It looked nice from the outside and it was very close. I felt it was a good neighborhood. That's why we chose it. (mother; middle class)

Another parent who is a member of the local Catholic parish said he has not considered sending his sons to the parish school because:

Right now it's a situation where all their friends are here. It's close. It's convenient for me. They can walk to school and come home. There's no problem. (middle class)

Other parents were equally enthusiastic about the fact that Western is close and convenient to their homes, allowing their children to either walk or ride their bicycle to school. When asked what they thought about Western after a few years' experience with the school, their responses suggested a general satisfaction. As one parent observed, "We haven't had any problems, so we're happy." Since sending her son to Western, she has heard from other parents that Western is considered a top school in the district, along with the nearby elementary school that offers a gifted and talented program. Another parent noted that the teachers were "real supportive" in addressing their daughter's learning disability. A few others noted that the staff's attitude is emblematic of the school motto: CARES. One parent said she likes Western because "they always have a lot of things going on—special jog-a-thon, special pizza parties." A mother who attended Western School over fifteen years ago also said she "likes" the school:

> **Q.** What do you like about it?
> **A.** I don't know. It's just that I went there. I don't have that much experience with other schools. So, it's kind of hard to say. (low income)

These middle- and low-income parents did not systematically investigate the neighborhood school before making their decision to move into the community. Although they are pleased with the program and staff at Western, their satisfaction seems rooted in the *absence* of any problems or concerns, rather than in the *existence* of any particular attributes or features that the school offers.

To explore further the education values of these parents, they were asked to discuss the important outcomes of schooling, their goals for their children's education, and the ways in which they participate in their kids' education.

When I asked parents what they wanted their children to gain from their education or to name the most important outcomes of schooling, many parents identified particular skills and subjects which they consider vital for their children to grasp in order to be successful adults. For many of the parents who are low income, learning the "basics" has particular meaning and significance:

> **Q.** What would you like your kids to get out of their schooling?
> **A.** They should be able to read and write and to be able to have learned enough to decide what they want to do with their lives, basically, is what it boils down to. (mother; low income)
> **A.** To read. I think reading is the most important thing because a lot of people our age can't read. Reading and spelling is the most important thing. (mother; low income)
> **A.** The most important I think is basics because later in life you can always add if you have really solid basics in education. (mother; middle class)

Another parent suggested that "a real, basic, strong foundation of education" would help her daughters decide "what they want to do with their lives." She dropped out of high school during her junior year and after trying cosmetology and restaurant work, has not found what she wants to do. She hopes her daughters stay in school:

> Hopefully, they'll have a strong enough foundation and a little taste of things that they might get an idea of what they want, what they're the best at, or what they enjoy the most. Just some general math—you need math in life. You don't need algebra maybe, unless you use that in a career. (mother; lower-middle class)

Other parents coupled the need to acquire a basic education with the skills that will enable their children to take care of themselves. They suggested that the organization of schooling and the processes which establish certain expectations and obligations help reinforce the personal characteristics required for work lives. Thus, beyond the subject matter skills of reading, writing and mathematics, these parents envision the acquisition of responsibility and self-discipline during their children's schooling:

> **Q.** What is the most important outcome of your kids' schooling:
> **A.** Discipline. Discipline leads to everything. Discipline leads to doing well in school. If you've got the discipline to work, he'll do as well as he can. If he doesn't, then he'll never reach his potential. Making sure you go to school every day means you'll probably go to work every day and that you'll stick to it and do as well as you can. (father; middle class)
> **A.** All I care about is that my child learns to read, learns to write, has good attendance, gets into the habit of getting up every morning and being there, and gets his education. (father; middle class)
> **A.** To learn responsibility. I try to tell my children that when you go to school, if you don't learn to work hard at school and be responsible, that's exactly how you'll be when you get into the work field. You have assignments; you have to turn them in. You are going to have a boss who's going to ask you to do something by such and such a time. So they need to be responsible. They need to do their best. Whether it's an A or a C, you just do your absolute best. (mother; middle class)

Other middle-class parents, some of whom have college experiences in a four-year institution (including one who is a graduate of the state university), suggested some broader aims of schooling which transcend specific, marketable skills. These parents emphasized elements which focus on self-fulfillment and happiness, and the ability to reason:

> I'd like to say . . . I don't know, that with education, you can have independence, the ability to realize. You learn; the more you know, the more you can learn. It's an ongoing thing, and you can see that with us. (father; middle class)

I think that you should . . . well, there should be some basic knowledge there. You should be able to read and things like that, but that goes unsaid. I think it should help you build your self-esteem so that you feel good about yourself. And I can say that about Western. That's one thing they really promote is building a child's confidence in himself and making him feel good about himself. And that's important and a lot of times that doesn't come from family situations. It does come from school. (mother; middle class)

I would say pretty much the tools to live your life by, the ability to analyze a problem and come up with solutions. It's a training ground for thinking things through. What they're learning now isn't going to make diddley when they're out in the real world but it sets the pace. It sets a tone for them. That's all I can ask for. (father; middle class)

I want her to be happy in life and to be able to earn a good living for herself. I don't want her to be stuck in a ditch unless she wants to be. There's a difference between having to do it because that's the only thing you can do, and doing it because that's what you want to do. I want her to be happy . . . you've got to like your job because you spend a lot of time on them. (father; middle class)

While most of these Western School parents expressed an interest and desire to see their children graduate from college, several stated emphatically that the decision would not be forced upon their kids. Other parents made hopeful predictions that their kids would earn a college degree and, in doing so, enjoy material and career success in their adulthoods. A few parents suggested that meeting the cost of college would be difficult, but that "come hell or high water" sacrifices and scholarships would ensure that their children enjoyed the opportunities that the college credential could purchase:

**Q.** How far in school do you think your kids will go?

**A.** We want to give her more than what we had. We would like to see her go to college. We want her to be happy, and I think if you go to college and get a good education, her chance of happiness and achievement are better than if you don't. (father; middle class)

**A.** I'm hoping all the way to college. I'm hoping. I think my oldest daughter will go on to college. I hope she does. I'm encouraging her. She's been in beauty pageants and she's won a lot of them and I told her the main goal was for her to get a scholarship to a good college. (mother; low income)

**A.** Depends on money. I'm a firm believer he'll go to college. That's my attitude. It's the same as my parents. That he will go to college, come hell or high water. While we're still young, we worry about funds and all that. They are available. We don't have a college fund for him, or whatever, but we'd like to think that in ten years when it's time for him to go that they'll be available. He might go to a junior college, but we expect him to go to college. (father; middle class)

Some parents observed that learning a trade or joining other family members in the real estate/remodeling business diminished the need for college. These parents noted that hard work and diligence could provide their children with a number of choices, with college representing only a single path to success and fulfillment.

While some parents noted with sadness and regret their decisions to leave school early, others expressed pointed resentment at their parents' expectations that they attend college, regardless of their own interests and desires. To be sure, these experiences provide a powerful framework for considering their educational goals for their children:

> I just want them to finish high school with the chance to get a scholarship, with the chance to do something else. I don't want them to do like I did and so many other people do: give up because you think, your life, you know everything now and you can just work somewhere and waste time. (mother; low income)

Later, she recalled her efforts to falsify school records and to hide from her parents the fact that she had quit school:

> What a wasted . . . see, that's what I don't want to happen to my kids: totally wasted smarts. I spent so much smarts on being sneaky. If I had just applied it in the right way then maybe I would have gone straight to college and who knows what I could be right now.

This parent recalled a far different experience:

> In my family, you had to be a doctor, a lawyer, at least a nurse or a teacher. And I won't push in that way. If they go to school, and continue on, I want them to want that. If they want to go to trade school or be a mommy, or whatever they want, we want to support it. Their self-esteem is much more important to me than what they become. (mother; middle class)

It is hardly surprising that nearly all the parents identified their own upbringing as the primary influence on their ideas about schooling. Perhaps predictably, some parents expressed gratitude for the care and interest their parents had demonstrated during their schooling years. One parent said her mother could not afford to go to college but that she had demonstrated a lifelong interest in learning that was inspirational. Another father noted that "education was number one," when he was growing up and that there were always two things for sure, "I was going to be bald and I was going to go to college." Others, however, spoke with determined bitterness that they would do more for their children and would avoid the mistakes their own parents had committed:

**Q.** What has influenced the way you think about your kids' education?
**A.** The way we were raised. Neither one of us had good childhoods. My parents were alcoholics. I was nine years old and they used to leave for two weeks at a time. It was okay for them to do that. We won't do that to her. They've never been to a PTA meeting. They've never been to my school. They never met my teachers. And if they met my teacher it was because they met them in a bar. I won't subject my daughter to the same things that we did. We have the choice to change, so we made the choice. (father; middle class)
**A.** Maybe because I always went by myself. My oldest brother and I always felt alone, that it wasn't fair. I always . . . never had anybody to go with me. And when my mother ever did she was always drunk and it was embarrassing. And I swore my kids would have it different. And I kind of like it; it's fun going to school. It's kind of neat. (mother; low income)
**A.** My parents. The fact that they never knew anything that was going on. When I needed them the most, they were having problems and I was so mature for my age and very independent and they never had to pay any special attention toward me and so they thought . . . they were wrapped up in their very own problems so therefore, I quit school a year before they even knew it. (mother; low income)

Another parent, while noting her parents' positive influence on her values regarding education, contrasted these with some of her own experiences as a young student:

> Sometimes I think it's beneficial when you look back on your own education. You know, you thought you had really great teachers. I had a fifth grade teacher who said, "Here, take out your spelling books. Sit on it. Okay, now we've covered that." I can remember thinking it was great because I wasn't a great speller when I was in the fifth grade. But now, now you look back, and I go, I want my kids to have . . . to get a good education. (mother; middle class)

Finally, one parent cast his particular values and beliefs regarding schooling in more sweeping, inclusive terms of parenting, and offered a perspective for understanding parents who echo the theme of improving upon their own upbringing:

> I don't think it's about schooling. I think it's about the total package of the kid. There are certain things when you were growing up that you wanted different in your life, maybe. I don't know, but most people, there's something that you want to change. So you try and adjust for that or overadjust for it with your children. It's just that, you need more involvement, to show them that you care what happens and not just when the report card comes home. (father; middle class)

## Patterns of Participation

The organization of schooling reflects common understandings about what is appropriate and meaningful behavior. Social scripts provide a language and framework for parent and teachers alike. Over time, parents learn the circumscribed roles they are expected to assume. They learn to think of themselves as "monitors," "helpers," and "supporters."

The discussion with Western parents regarding their role in their children's schooling produced predictable and routine responses reflective of these social scripts. Parents identified their roles by context; that is, they expressed an overwhelming willingness to assume the role of teacher or monitor in their home; very few parents identified school-based activities within the realm of parent involvement. The nature of parents' activities, however, suggests that the process is driven almost exclusively by activities authored and sanctioned by teachers, namely, homework:

**Q.** How do you see your role in your children's schooling?

**A.** I don't understand half the stuff they do anymore. My role, I feel, is to try to help her when she comes . . . okay, she comes and she has a problem. She doesn't understand it, so we sit down, try to take it apart, step by step, try to see maybe there's something that by talking about it we can figure it out. (mother; low income)

**A.** Well, I think my role is to be supportive of what she's doing, to encourage her, to make sure she does the things that she's supposed to do. That's basically my role—to make sure that her homework gets done. (mother; middle class)

**A.** I'm not even sure how I'd answer that. I mean, we just. I don't really have the time to teach every individual [child]. Usually when one of them needs help with the homework, one of us will do it, usually [my boyfriend], because I'm doing dishes or dinner or taking care of the baby or something. (mother; low income)

This "relational" perspective—definition of the parent's role in relation to the role of the teacher or the arrangement of school activities—was echoed by most parents and underscored by this one:

If they are lucky enough to have a real good teacher, then my role in their education is reduced. I help them with their homework every night. I'll ask them what their homework is. . . . I don't have to teach them when they have a good teacher. I just have to help them remember what they already learned. When they have a bad teacher I have to teach them. (mother; lower-middle class)

Several parents recited an inventory of activities they assume in a coproduction model of schooling which dictates particular prescribed roles and expectations:

She [the teacher] teaches. She does the best to her ability, and we do the best to our ability. We make sure she gets the clean clothes, good breakfast, good amount of sleep, goes to school healthy. It's my feeling that it's her job to present the material so that my daughter will understand it. I will reinforce it; go over it; whatever it needs to, at home, to back that teacher up; to get her to understand and learn. (father; middle class)

While these parents take for granted a role in their children's education, there is little sense of discretion, creativity, or individuality. Their responses reflect almost robotic motions which seem to dampen initiative and foster a persistent sense of dread and frustration. The issue of homework highlights the point. For many parents whose own educational experiences were unhappy, unsuccessful, or short lived, helping their children with homework can be a painfully revealing exercise, as this parent relates:

The only participation I found in kindergarten is reading with them and helping them with their homework. With my older daughter, it's helping with her school work that . . . some of it I can't do, which is kind of embarrassing but I figure it out with her and then I can do it—just some of it. Some of it will come to me and other things, I'm like, guy, I never had this. Something she had about the globe, and I got the oceans wrong, and I felt like such an idiot. But she got them right. (mother; low income)

Homework presents particular challenges for parents who have fewer years of schooling, are low income, and do not have access to resources such as tutoring or a set of encyclopedias. However, for parents of both middle- and low-income social status, the organization of homework impacts family rhythms and routines in ways which are uniformly disruptive and divisive. Arranging time and space for homework activities in the hectic hours between 3:00 P.M. and bedtime often creates stress and discord. Consider the perspectives of these parents:

[My husband] seems to think that's a real easy thing but then again, he's not here and doesn't have to deal with that. It's not real easy to get someone . . . it's not that she can't do it, it's that her mind wants to be somewhere else. She wants to be doing other things. I mean, she's been at school all day. Who would want to come home and do homework? (mother; middle class)

Other parents, notably fathers, observed that homework often takes place in the evenings, after parents have worked all day and are anxious for some rest and relaxation. The fact that teachers are typically not available during the evening hours to help answer questions or clarify assignments, can create further anxiety. For single parents, the challenge of orchestrating the array of family, school, and work activities is even greater. This divorced father relates:

They were sending my son home for a while with three pages of homework, in the first grade, in the second grade. And gosh, I called them up and said, "What does he do in school? He's doing every bit of his work at home. What is this? I work for a living. I don't want to come home and spend two hours on homework." And some of this was pretty hard homework. (father; middle class)

A few parents painted their roles in far broader strokes, suggesting a relationship which transcends the institution of schooling and rests with good parenting. As one parent who is low income, put it: "I don't consider it taking a role in their schooling; it's just a role in their life, and that's part of their life." These parents emphasized the importance of communication—listening and talking to their children—as well as discussing at dinner what they and their children have done that day. In this more integrated view, reading at night with their children is considered a shared activity, not an arduous assignment.

## The Organization of Work and School

While homework provides an institutionalized niche for parents to engage in their children's schooling and to identify their roles vis-à-vis teachers, their ability to fulfill certain expectations is necessarily influenced by the parents' own educational backgrounds and abilities. To the degree that essential elements associated with social class (e.g., education and income) differentially exclude or weaken the abilities of certain parents to assist in their children's schooling (Lareau 1989), homework represents a pernicious and disabling school policy.

The organization of schooling, however, includes other institutionalized events and activities which involve parent participation, and Western School features all of them. Parent-teacher conferences, back-to-school night, open house, and PTA meetings reflect such ritualized events for parent-teacher-school interactions. Western also offers "reading nights" for parents and kids; "parent education day" to familiarize parents with classroom planning and curriculum; parenting classes; an annual spaghetti dinner and ice cream social to raise funds; and a "bring a parent to lunch" day. Although there is no school-wide policy,[4] some teachers invite parents to volunteer regularly in their classrooms. Western also features monthly assemblies to recognize the achievement of students.

How does social class influence parents' level of participation in these school-based events? The experiences and explanations of Western parents suggest that the organization of work critically influences patterns of participation among middle-class parents; for low-income parents who are unemployed, an interplay of home environment factors impacts their level of involvement in these events and activities.

Among the two-parent middle-class families interviewed for this study (there were six), four include a mother and father who work full-time outside of the home, and two include a mother who is employed part-time. The range of occupations include a high school teacher, computer troubleshooter, insurance analyst, paving foreman, and retail sales clerk. Regardless of status or type of work, the degree to which these occupations/jobs provide flexible work arrangements highly influences the nature and frequency of participation at school-based events. Part-time employment, flexible scheduling, and work hours which mirror school hours allow, respectively some mothers, a father who is a mail carrier, and a father who is a high school teacher to attend events which other parents cannot, due to constraints imposed by the organization of their work. Self-employed status (real estate/residential remodeling, and mortgage broker, respectively) permits two fathers who are single (divorced) parents to visit the school during school hours without rearranging work time or requesting time off from their employers.

When asked if anything prevented parents from participating the way they would like, the responses were immediate and remarkably similar:

> I'm always getting this coffee klatch notice that they're asking you to do, but it's during the day, at 9:30 in the morning. Now, I work. He works. We can't be over there at 9:30 in the morning. (mother; insurance analyst)

She also received a notice about the monthly Pride Assembly:

> I made it, but it was like I went to work at 6:00 A.M. to make up the time so I could drive like a crazy woman home, hop out of the car, go there, sit down, get her award, and leave before the assembly was over because it was running overtime and I had to get . . . be back at the office by 9:30. So I'm running back, get in, drop off my purse, go back out and listen to this guy speak for two hours.

Another mother enthusiastically described the opportunities the principal provides for parents to attend informational meetings and enrichment activities, and then added:

> I don't really go to school a lot. I don't volunteer for classroom stuff because I just can't. My job doesn't let me. (data systems supervisor)

Even for those parents with semi-flexible hours, school-based activities are often arranged with school hours in mind:

> They invited me to this meeting but it was at 2:15 in the afternoon, and it's real hard for me. I mean who can get off work at 2:15 in the afternoon? So I worked through my lunch and everything and I got there at, I think 3:15, and it was all over with. I felt bad about that. But I said, "You've got to think about people." It doesn't make sense when they do things like that. (father; mail carrier)

Other parents noted that a dual-income, two-parent, working family arrangement forced them to establish priorities, with limited involvement in school-based activities the price of an established middle-class lifestyle:

> If we had the money, then we could donate a lot more of the time. We can't be at the school and work too. So it's like one or the other. Well, we tend to like to eat and do things so we both work. We're involved in her life in other ways. (father; paving/construction foreman)

While parents considered the constraints imposed by the organization of their work lives, an implicit assumption undergirded their responses: These families have established a set of priorities, and across a continuum of discretionary and required activities, have created particular family rhythms and routines. The point here is to underscore the importance of work as an element of family life which influences participation in school-based activities. At the same time, it is worth noting the degree to which families' social, religious, and cultural activities are disconnected from school-related activities. As this mother relates, a full schedule of church, labor union, scouting, and sports activities—none of which intersect with school events—prevent her (or her husband's) attendance at an evening activity at Western School:

> Q. Is this "parents as partners" event something you would go to?
> A. Probably not, for one particular reason. We hardly have any time to do anything. With four kids, one working on Wednesday night. I go to Bible study Tuesday night. What do we do Friday night? He's got union meetings and these other meetings half the time. We do a lot of counseling. We have different things going on all the time. (mother; self-employed/crafts)

For low-income parents who are not employed, the environmental factors associated with poverty—poor health, emotional distress, violent or abusive family members, lack of child care and transportation—suggest patterns of coping and survival which sometimes leave little energy or opportunity to attend school-based activities. A mother of five children described the health problems afflicting various members of her family, including chronic asthma and acute anxiety attacks. In the last two years, she had suffered burns in a kitchen accident and had been hospitalized for two weeks following the recent birth of her baby. She seemed to spend most of her time caring for her infant son and her other four children, and driving to medical appointments.

Another mother described the difficulties she faces in attending meetings or other school-based events. She lives in an apartment complex known for its drug activity, domestic violence, and police busts. Since her daughter pricked her foot on a syringe last fall, she does not allow her to run around outside of the apartment. As a single parent, she identifies particular constraints:

> Just put yourself in the parents' shoes. Like sometimes they'll say, "Can you come to the school right now?" I said, "No, we'll have to make an appointment. I have twins. They're not in school. And I can't talk to you without them hanging on me." And she'll get really fresh and I'd get really frustrated but I say, "You're going to have to do it on my time. I can't do it on the regular time. I'm a single parent. You're going to have to deal with me the best you can." I think they should have a little more sympathy for single parents. It's really hard for single parents. And in the neighborhood I live in, I really don't trust anybody around here to watch my kids. (mother; low income)

The next week she had to cancel an appointment because the lights went out in the apartment laundry room, and she was afraid her clothes would be stolen if she left the complex without collecting them—which she could not do until the lights went back on. A rescheduled meeting was cancelled a few days later when her five-year-old twins came down with the flu.

In sum, middle-class parents' efforts to balance frenetic work and family lives require them to ration their limited time and energy. School-based activities like PTA meetings, spaghetti dinners, and reading nights are considered by many parents extras which they cannot afford. Unless their children are involved in an event or activity, there is little interest in making the effort. Even then, for such events as the Pride Assemblies, many parents find it difficult to adjust their work schedules to fit school hours. For these parents, evenings are just a blurry and brief respite before another work day; any expendable energy is spent preparing meals, organizing bath times, and helping with homework.

While the stressors associated with maintaining family life are shared by low-income families, other punishing and disabling factors associated with their socioeconomic status combine to limit their involvement in school-based activities, including parent-teacher conferences, back-to-school night, and open house. There is no hint of intimidation among these parents. Instead, the accumulation of multiple distractions and interdependencies deflect their energies and attention away from attendance at such events.

The next section examines the implications of these collective patterns of participation for the nature and quality of school community at Western. The impact of a neighborhood school fractured geographically and socially and the corresponding efforts by Western School to embrace the school population are explored. The discussion concludes with a focus on Western's efforts to construct elements of community amidst parent apathy and the faculty's own creeping cynicism.

## SCHOOL COMMUNITY:
## IMPLICATIONS FOR FAMILY-SCHOOL INTERACTIONS

### Parent Participation and Volunteer Opportunities

Western School invites participation from parents through a wide array of volunteer opportunities, special events and programs, and traditional school organizations. There are special workshops on parenting skills, helping children with their homework, and promoting children's self-esteem. Some workshops target specific subgroups, such as single parents and grandparents, who may be facing particular challenges and concerns in raising their children or grandchildren. Some of these events are onetime only affairs, while others are arranged on a weekly, yearlong basis. Western also features "Parent Education Day," in which parents are invited to sit in on classroom lessons, review a lesson plan, and examine curricular materials with the principal. There is a "Grandparents Day," a "Bring a Parent/Grandparent to Lunch Day," as well as the monthly Pride Assembly. These assemblies include a fifteen-minute "Principal's Chat" in which parents are invited to sit with the principal and enjoy coffee and cookies while engaging in a discussion on a particular topic selected by the principal. Finally, the PTA and the School Advisory Committee/School Site Council offer parents the opportunity to make decisions regarding school fund-raising and discretionary spending.

In addition, the weekly Western School bulletin regularly announces "special awards" for the Volunteer of the Month. Typically, the honorees are parents (or former parents) who volunteer part-time in the library or classroom, help during the lunch hour or on field trips, or organize a particular fund-raiser. A parent questionnaire is sent home each fall requesting parent volunteers for room parents, PTA officers, SAC/SSC members, the school library, computer center, classrooms, and field trips and clerical duties.

Western's interest and commitment to promoting a spirit of school volunteerism in evidenced by repeated announcements and notes of appreciation in the Weekly Bulletin. The parent handbook/school calendar includes a special page devoted to a description of the volunteer opportunities. Also, a small framed card, which hangs prominently in the front office bulletin board, reminds parents and visitors that "Volunteers are a real asset on the Western campus. . . . Your help can make the difference!!" The efforts seem to have paid off; Western has won the district award for volunteerism three years in a row.

The principal is the enthusiastic promoter behind the volunteer and parent participation programs at Western. In her message to parents on page one of the Western Parent Handbook, she focuses on parent involvement and the Pride Assembly—the forum designed to celebrate students' and parents' contributions to the school. She reminds parents that "parental involvement in a child's education is one of the major factors of how well a child does in school." Throughout the months of the school calendar, the box for Saturday lists such parenting tips as the following: "Take your child to the public library;" "Listen to your child;" and "Remember-Parents are their child's first teacher!!" When asked whether or not there were enough opportunities for parents and school staff to interact, she outlined her thoughts:

There aren't enough. You know, parents are tired after they work all day. They don't want to come in the evening. It's difficult to get off work. If they're not working, if they're on welfare, they're a little bit intimidated by coming to school to meet with the principal. You know, that's real scary to them. It's like pulling teeth to get parents into schools. And all those things are factors, the main one being if they're working, it's tough in a day and when you get home, you have to fix dinner, gotta get your kids ready for bed and then you've gotta go down to the school at 7:00. It's sort of like, I'm going to go and when the time comes you don't go.

In order to "get" the parents, her strategy involves attaching a student performance to as many parent events as possible. The principal observes:

They'll come to see their children—which again goes back to how much they care about their kids. So, if you can get them while they're here, you know, that's the thing to do and so if you have any kind of parent night, you always want kids performing or something to do with the kids.

How have parents responded to these opportunities? According to observations, teacher and principal reports, and parents' own accounts, despite the efforts of the school staff, only a small fraction of Western parents attend workshops, PTA or SAC/SSC meetings, or open house. The principal estimated that about fifteen parents attended the school's "Reading Night;" a handful participated in the weekly parenting class. The teachers interviewed reported that fewer than 50 percent of their parents typically attend the annual back-to-school night, although the numbers are often higher in the kindergarten and first grade classes. Several of the most active "parents," including the Parent Coordinator and PTA president, are parents of *former* Western students, long since graduated.

In line with the principal's strategy, the Pride Assemblies are well attended by parents whose children are receiving awards. (The "principal chats," which are held midmorning between the primary and intermediate grade Pride Assembly ceremonies typically attract 4–6 parents.) Although the principal noted her pleasure with even the smallest number of parents in attendance, she observed the tendencies of Western parents:

The PTA from the upper levels is trying to get PTAs focusing more on getting parents involved in the schools. I don't know if that will ever happen here. We don't get [support]. We have the jog-a-thon, and we get some parents to help, but we used to be able to have speakers and you'd get sixty parents. That doesn't happen here. Unless you tie in the kids, it doesn't happen.

## Multiple Categories, Tenuous Connections

Although the principal outlines an accurate account of the elements of family and work lives which impede parents' school-based participation, other fundamental characteristics associated with the nature and quality of community at

Western undergird the tenuous connections linking parents to one another and to the school. To be sure, the school shares few of the constitutive elements of community: interaction and mutual dependence; the intention of longevity and permanence; expressive ties; and shared beliefs (Raywid 1988b). If a portrait of school community is composed of a sense of commitment, solidarity, and mutual support, Western reflects only a sketchy outline. Instead, a sense of diversity and division—geographical and social—are expressed in the reverberating language of parents and teachers.

When parents were asked if they thought other Western parents were people like themselves, several used phrases like "a real mix" to describe the various socioeconomic backgrounds and values of the school families. Several middle-class parents referred to the apartment residents as the "drug abusers" and "bikers." They implied that the neighborhood of homeowners, while far more stable than the apartments, also includes families with histories of drug abuse and violence, and, as one parent put it, people who have "terrible kids that do terrible things." Here are some parents' impressions of other Western families:

**Q.** Are other Western families people like yourselves?
**A.** It's a mix of people. There are some children that I see that are on this block, they come home and they don't have any parents. That doesn't mean that they're not interested, but you can tell. I've had children in the second grade when I've worked at the school, and they've told me, "I don't care what you say. I don't have to listen to you." I was so shocked because I didn't even think like that in high school. (mother; middle class)
**A.** No, I don't think so. But there are a few. I've met some lately. (father; middle class)

Half and half. Most of the people that are there—the working class—I don't think you have a problem with their values because you get what you put into it. They're trying to raise their kids to get out what they have to put into it. It's the ones . . . it's your drug dealers. To me, it's the people on welfare. I think we have a little bit of everything here. (father; middle class)

I'd like to think so. Well, there's probably a big mix of people. I wouldn't say everybody is the same. I'm sure value wise, they have the same values for their kids and want them to do good and get a good education. Outside of that, I can't really say. I don't really know them. I would say the ones that I know in the immediate neighborhood, yes. (mother; middle class)

Within the neighborhood of middle-class homes, there is a sense that people know their neighbors as well as they want to know them. Although individual efforts may be reciprocated among neighbors, there is a corresponding sense of insularity driven by the exigencies of work and family life. If school parents know one another, their familiarity arises out of their children's friendships with other school children, or through the community soccer league, or perhaps from Camp Fire Girls. These occasions for face-to-face talk are typically brief, unpredictable, and unrelated. Thus, the broad brush generalizations about a "mixed" population of school parents prompts a parent's admission that she, "really doesn't know them." Parents' social networks are tied to their family, their church, or perhaps, their work associates. Consider these perspectives:

**Q.** Do you know many Western parents?
**A.** Not really, outside of the parents of the girls my daughter plays with. I really don't know any others. (mother; middle class)
**A.** Just the parents of the kids that my boys are friends with . . . the people I talk to. I talk to the mothers and some of the fathers of my son's friends but that's about it. (father; middle class)
**A.** You know, I have to say no because of the fact I am [a member of a particular church] so I do a lot with families there. (mother; middle class)

This parent, who lives in an apartment near the school, suggests the parent-parent familiarity is tightly bracketed around limited conversation across the complex:

I know some of the mothers because when my daughter was in the first grade, I led a Blue Bird group. So I met a few mothers. And there are several I know that live in this complex that the girls spend the night over their house. So I've gotten to know like that, which is nice.

**Q.** Do you think most of the families are people like yourselves?
**A.** Yea, maybe. I guess . . . I don't really know them personally enough. I know them enough to talk to them and have a small conversation, but we don't go places with them. I don't know what they do with their time. (mother; lower-middle class)

Another parent, who is middle class and one of the few Western parents in a professional occupation, observed that there is a core of Western parents who attend the fund-raisers, back-to-school night, and meetings regularly and, consequently, know one another quite well:

You're seeing the same parents all the time. So there are those who are highly involved and those who are rarely involved. And there doesn't seem to be a middle ground. (father; middle class)

## THE CONSEQUENCES OF SOCIAL NETWORK PATTERNS: NATURE OF SCHOOL KNOWLEDGE

To an immeasurable degree, parents' source of knowledge regarding schooling reflects their patterns of social networks. For low-income parents who live in the crowded, problem-plagued apartments, a sense of mutual dependence and shared misfortune binds parents in a network of rumor, speculation, and advice. These neighbors tend to know much more about one another because their living space is far more compressed and communal; families share walls, balconies, and telephones. The substance and tenor of a heated argument penetrate family dwellings easily under such conditions. As one parent responded when asked if she knows her neighbors: "It's kind of hard not to know them. They make themselves known." Many of these parents said they try to mind their own business, stay in their own apartment, and keep out of trouble. However, the constancy and frequency of assorted crises—trips to the hospital emergency room, the use of a neighbor's telephone when their service is disconnected, the unforeseen need for a baby-sitter at midnight—account for regular, accumulated incidences of extended face-to-face exchanges. Their social networks are limited to other low-income parents because few are employed, attend a church, or are members of the PTA; their children are not members of a soccer team or scouting troop. Few of these parents are familiar with particular teachers' reputations or the language and implications of learning disability classifications. To the degree that they recognize the implications of a deficiency notice, it is likely that this understanding is derived from their own, often limited, educational experiences.

The nature of parents' knowledge regarding schooling suggests that in the absence of organizational structures and processes which draw deeply and regularly from among the diverse population of Western parents, parents' familiarity with school programs and processes are lifted from the written communications sent from school. Parents are well informed regarding the time and date of school assemblies, PTA meetings, ice cream social fund-raisers, and parenting classes for single parents. The regular Wednesday newsletters contain pertinent information for parents regarding Early Bird/Late Bird reading group schedules and California Achievement Program (CAP) testing.

More fine-grained information, however, regarding such things as teachers' reputations and parents' rights under the special education program, are the stuff of "insider information," or parents' networks. The patterns of social networks at Western indicate that these interactions are bracketed around social class and geographical boundaries. That is, while some middle-class parents report occasional exchanges with other middle-class Western parents, most suggest rather insular patterns of interactions between families. Low-income apartment residents, in contrast, reflect an interwoven network of interdependence and information. In the absence of mechanisms which promote sustained social interactions across the population of families at Western, these patterns are fixed and self-sustaining.

Parents' knowledge of teachers' reputations provides an illuminating example of these information flows. Most of the parents interviewed knew the names of their children's teachers, were informed regarding the Pride Assemblies, and understood the concept of the "early birds" and "late birds" ability grouping for reading instruction. When asked whether or not they had ever requested a particular teacher for their children, only three parents said they had. Among these parents, one said they based their request on their children's suggestions; another parent said she knew who the better teachers were from her classroom volunteer experiences at Western. Only one parent observed that his family's information came from neighborhood parents with older children. A parent who is low income and was well informed regarding Wednesday newsletters, reading groups, and assemblies, said she did not realize she could request a teacher. The rest of the parents indicated that any knowledge of teachers' reputations was limited to their firsthand experience with their children's teachers.

Knowledge regarding academic programs not offered at Western also reflects a lack of social networking within Western School's geographical community. For example, one parent said she learned about the gifted and talented program from her in-laws and from some parents at another school who attend her church. Another parent noted he had heard about the gifted and talented program through parents at his children's former school.

## In the Absence of . . .

The nature and quality of community at Western School suggests a critical absence of social cohesion and communication. While there is some evidence of interaction and mutual dependence within a geographically isolated and socially differentiated subgroup of school parents, it is undergirded by corresponding elements of instability and uncertainty. Despite the vast array of programs and policies designed to enhance a sense of connection to the school, these parents reflect alternating patterns of insularity and distraction. In the absence of a robust community, these are tenuous connections among parents, and between parents and the school.

The next section examines the ways in which these qualities of community influence relations between parents and teachers and shape the nature of expectations each has for the other.

### RELATIONSHIPS BETWEEN PARENTS AND TEACHERS

## Teachers' Expectations

Echoing the rhetoric and research which suggests that a committed and equal partnership between parents and teachers in the enterprise of schooling is rewarding and beneficial for all parties, the teachers at Western School talked about the need for parents' "support" and "reinforcement." The notion of a joint production between themselves and parents—regardless of parents' particular educational or social class backgrounds—was strong and apparent:

**Q.** How do you see the parent's role in your student's education?

**A.** A lot of times it's very frightening to me as so often parents don't seem to realize how much of a partnership we have and that for their child to really be successful, they have to be as much a teacher as I am. They really are their child's first teacher. (teacher)

**A.** Those students who are successful students really have parents that are behind them and make sure that they provide time for the student to study on a regular basis. They're willing to help and get in and make sure they get things done. They help their child develop the skills necessary to be successful in terms of being organized, in terms of being responsible. And it just shows because the work comes in when it's supposed to. (teacher)

For teachers, the boundaries between their responsibilities and parents' are clear and specific:

> I think I'm responsible for what goes on in the classroom, and they're responsible for what I send home. And so they should have a workplace for their children, find out about their homework, and encourage them. And if I send a note home about a problem, they should respond. If I call, I want help. I don't expect them to come and find out about it from me first; I expect if I need it, I should go to them.

Another teacher offered a more foundational concept of parent involvement:

> I expect them to be involved in their child's education, and I talk about that a lot. And I don't mean volunteering in the classroom. I really try to change that emphasis because that's what it means to everybody. And that's what it means to teachers. And so I've said: that's not what I mean. I mean getting their child here everyday, clean and fed, on time. That's the very first thing I expect from them.

After the "basic stuff" is carried out:

> Then we talk about providing your child with a place to study, quiet time, turn the TV off. I expect you to do that. If you're able to help your child with their homework, fine. If you're not, the teacher will deal with that, but I expect you to make sure they're doing that. I expect if there's a problem to let us know. And I hope they will work with us. But basically, supporting us in the sense that saying to your child: school is the most important thing, and you must be doing it.

The faculty's consensus on what ought to be the relationship between themselves and parents was matched by an equally unanimous assessment of the discouragement and disappointment they experience with parents. They tended to lump parents in categories with identifying characteristics: single parent; divorced; drug addict; and alcoholic. The teachers also referred to more general and ultimately more troubling trends among parents at Western. Parents just are not interested; they're caught up in their busy work lives; they are inclined to leave more and more teaching for the teacher and assume smaller and smaller educative roles for themselves. Then there are the parents who do not have the skills to help their kids with homework.

There was a pervasive sense of this self-described cohesive, compatible, and supportive faculty fighting what they perceive to be unbridled apathy among parents and their own creeping cynicism. These two teachers observed:

> The parent that doesn't send their child to school on time is not one that I can depend on weekly. And the mother that supposedly is my room mother hasn't paid her telephone bill so she couldn't contact the other mothers for the party. So we had to gerryrig a situation just a few minutes ago. She hasn't known the time all year long.

> I gave up a long time ago thinking that anything that I said was going to change what parents do. But I keep trying. And if I can say I had the same experience and this is what I did, they might say, well maybe I could try it.

Another teacher, commenting on the fact that attendance at back-to-school night is often disappointingly low, observed:

> You're the person that their children spends six and eight hours a day with. What we teach, they'll pick up on that. I would like to know what kind of values my child was getting from that teacher. And yet they send them off to school and they say, "Oh, whatever happens, happens." And then if it doesn't happen the way they want it, we hear about it.

One teacher, who said that an alarming number of first graders use obscene language and lack social skills, added:

> As teachers, it's very hard sometimes for us to understand that some parents think that's okay, to be drunk in front of your children, to do drugs in front of your children, or to talk that way or to have a constant stream of male visitors in and out of your home. It's just not healthy for the kids. It's not healthy for the adults.

The explanations teachers offered for parents' actions or inactions revealed a heightened and primary focus on a particular subgroup of parents—those who are low income and live in the reputedly roach- and drug-infested apartments.[5] Regarding parents who don't help their children with homework:

> They just don't care about it. It's not a priority. It's not a priority. They're not thinking through that if their children miss this right now, they're going to miss other things later on and then they're not going to have good jobs and

then maybe they won't work at all and they'll still be supporting them when they're not wanting to support a child anymore or end up having trouble with that child later because they haven't instilled good patterns.

**Q.** Are you saying that those parents don't value education or that they don't think it's as important?

**A.** I think they haven't made the connection that the better education you have, the better life you have.

Other teachers' impressions:

**Q.** What are some things that prevent parents from participating the way they would like to or the way you want them to?

**A.** Lack of education. The self-esteem that goes with that. They don't want to put themselves on the line. They don't want to commit themselves to a certain amount of time every day or once a week. Time commitment. You know, one of the things about staying home is you're not committed to time. And they may not choose to tie up their time that way.

**A.** I think some parents are more organized than other parents. I think most all parents care about their children, but a lot of parents haven't developed the skills themselves. A lot of them really could use some parenting skills classes—really learn how to be parents.

A strikingly similar response was registered by parents when they were asked to consider the expectations that teachers hold for parents. A pervasive sense of entrenched pessimism and cynicism colored their remarks. Parents referred to other parents' childrearing practices, their own experiences at school-based events, and particular interactions with school staff to conclude that teachers' expectations of parents have been justifiably diminished by experience:

**Q.** What do you think teachers expect from you? How would teachers like parents to be involved?

**A.** I don't think teachers expect anything from parents anymore because parents don't usually give them much. I think they feel that the parents are sending their kids there to be baby-sat and taken care of. That's what I think they expect. In fact, I know that's what they expect because they have been real shocked that we've been as interested in our kids as we are. (mother; middle class)

**A.** Probably from experience, they don't expect a lot. But realistically, people just don't have the time. A lot of people just don't care. I found that out with a lot of parents I know—parents of his friends. Mothers who work full time during the day, their time is even more limited than mine. (father; middle class)

Other parents offered similar assessments of parents' actions and inactions when asked:

**Q.** How do you think schools define parent involvement?

**A.** I don't know if they wish parents would be more involved or if they think parents are a pain in the ass and they just wish they'd make sure their kids were clean and fed and rested and at school every day. I don't know. It depends. . . . I don't know if there's more pains than gains. (mother; lower-middle class)

**A.** They probably think it stinks. Parents aren't involved in school. Even the time I was involved in kindergarten and first grade, you didn't see parent involvement. You don't see parents in the classroom. (mother; middle class)

Her husband continued:

**A.** They don't care what happens to their kids. They're working. Some parents don't give a shit. My parents didn't go. My parents never made anything. So if that's the way they were raised, well my parents didn't go, why should I go to yours . . . (father; middle class)

## Communication

The widespread impression of parents' apathy is reinforced by the ubiquitous time and space formats undergirding relations between parents and teachers. These structured interactions delimit communication between families and schools to formal, abrupt, and incomplete exchanges. The scripts governing parent and teacher action promote predictability and internal control. Unannounced visits to the classroom are discouraged; parents are expected to check in at the front office counter or to make prearrangements with a school official. Evening meetings convene on school grounds, rather than in community centers or parents' homes. Meeting agendas are set internally and reflect school officials' registered concerns and priorities. Letters go home to inform, rarely to solicit input or to generate sustained dialogue. Telephone calls from school officials usually signal a serious problem, not a friendly inquiry.

Parents and teachers at Western School suggested that their interactions are often focused on students' misbehavior or learning problems. Perhaps predictably, there seems to be a degree of discomfort and miscommunication which colors these occasions. Nevertheless, parents and teachers did not characterize their relations as angry or hostile, just deeply frustrating.

The few occasions for face-to-face exchange assume heightened importance in the absence of more fluid, constant, and consistent interactions. The parent-teacher conferences, which are attended by an average 75–90 percent of Western parents (usually the mother), are recognized by both parents and teachers as a key opportunity to overcome the chasm fostered by structured relations. The reliance on such arrangements has obvious and direct implications for family-school relations. The quiet, comfortable distance between parents and teachers helps minimize expectations and carve out a degree of anonymity which buffers and protects parents and teachers from further instruments of intrusion and upset. Nevertheless, when a child's particular interests require coordinated and cooperative attention, the foundation for parent-teacher support and understanding can be a bit unstable, stiff, and brittle.

While parents' comments and observations reflect a generally high degree of satisfaction with the streams of information captured each week in the Wednesday bulletin, several identified the weaknesses and hazards of home-school relationships which must rely on such narrow bands for information exchange and social networking. Many parents said they were unaware of problems such as incomplete homework or in one case, a learning disability, until late in the school year or just before conferences. In some instances, parents were "surprised" with the information regarding their children's poor academic performance at the first conference. Telephone calls exchanged between parents and teachers were greeted with alarm and apprehension, and often, troubling suspicion. Some parents said they called teachers only as a last resort when they could not reach them after school. Indeed, it seems that problems and questions are typically collected in a repository of suspended inactivity until they become intolerable or until regularly scheduled conferences are held. The conferences tend to mirror in microcosm all the abrupt, incomplete exchanges between parents and teachers. They are scheduled for fifteen minutes; dialogue focuses on the report card. Most parents attend only the fall conference because the spring meetings are reserved for students whose academic performance or behavior necessitate a "risk conference." As one parent said:

> The parent-teacher conferences that we have every quarter seem more like this huge flow. We see them; we talk to them for a few minutes and promises are made, but nothing ever happens. So I'd like to see the teachers be a little more responsible for communicating back to the parents as to this information that we've talked about. (father; middle class)

Many teachers do make special efforts outside of the regular schoolwide events and announcements to enjoin parents in their children's classroom experiences. Some write a short note to each parent in the first few weeks of school introducing herself or himself. Others share their home phone numbers with parents and encourage them to call if there is a concern or problem. A recent policy promoted by the principal requires every teacher to make "good news phone calls" to every student's home in the beginning of the school year. A parent noted that this unexpected exchange with the teacher should encourage parent involvement by "making you feel more at ease so that if you need to talk to them about something, you can." Another teacher invites parents to talk to the class about his/her occupation.

Still, teachers noted with concern and consternation the parents who make appointments and fail to attend or even to cancel. Several teachers pointed out that it's often difficult to contact parents at work, and many parents who are unemployed do not have phones. The tightly scripted school day leaves little room for spontaneous exchanges, as this teacher explains:

> If they drop in, it's not a good time. Hardly ever is it a good time if they drop in because we have meetings, or I have class. There's always one thing or another. If they call and make an appointment, then it's a good time.

## Anonymous Lives, Parallel Institutions

In the absence of incentives or sanctions to promote sustained and meaningful interactions, parents and teachers at Western suggest a striking lack of familiarity with the social context of one anothers' lives. These parents and teachers come together through random assignment, not choice. Outside of Western's school motto, there are few organizational arrangements which promote a sense of ownership or help define collective goals and interests. Instead, lacking a sense of entitlement (for example, that Catholic school parents might feel) or the threat of punitive action (for example, that parents in a magnet/required participation school might experience), or a notion of self-interest (for example, that parents and teachers might possess in a choice school), family-school interactions at Western suggest ad hoc responses to the myriad of responsibilities associated with work and family lives.

The images of anonymous and parallel (rather than intersecting) social institutions—school and family—were underscored when parents were asked to consider what teachers know about them. The buffer zone which protects parents and teachers from further instruments of intrusion into their hectic, busy lives also militates against enduring and understanding relationships. In the absence of processes which promote social cohesion, relations between teachers and parents are necessarily confined to forced incidences of interaction, which prompt repeated cycles of disappointment and discomfort. Consider these observations:

> Q. What do you think teachers know about you?
> A. It seems like parents can be as anonymous as they want to be. If they don't want to deal with a teacher, the teacher figures that's just one less they've got to deal with. Something tells me the teacher is not going to go out of their way, unless this kid is going to fail their class, to contact the parent. These middle-of-the-road kids simply aren't going to get the attention unless the parents decide they want to have it. The parents aren't going to be known unless they want to be known. (father; middle class)

Several parents said they did not know what teachers knew or thought about them. Most suggested that any information would have to come from their children in casual conversations with their teachers, unless there had been specific incidences of academic or behavioral difficulties which had prompted the teacher to contact the parent. As one parent observed:

> If they're relying on a child's opinion, they're listening to an eight or nine year-old child who's generally not going to be very reliable. They're going to speak their emotions and that type of thing. It would be exaggerated. The teacher wouldn't know me. (father; middle class)

Not surprisingly, due to special arrangements, including home visits and smaller class sizes, several parents suggested that they know special education teachers better than their children's classroom teachers:

> Well, the special education teacher said she can tell I care about my kids. I explain that they have problems when most parents would hide it. And I don't hide it because they have to be recognized or else it's going to get worse. And then they know that I have problems too. (mother; low income)

Some low-income parents suggested that they shared more of their personal lives with the school secretary, with whom they were in contact on a much more frequent basis regarding tardiness, absenteeism, or other matters.[6] One mother said she had told the secretary about her former drug addiction and the fact that her children were placed in foster homes for a period of time. She had not shared this information with any teachers.

## SUMMARY

Western School invites participation from parents through a wide array of volunteer opportunities, special events, programs, and traditional school organizations.

The experiences and explanations of middle-class Western parents suggest that the organization of their work-lives critically influences patterns of participation at school-based events; for low-income parents who are unemployed, an interplay of home environmental factors impacts their level of involvement in these events and activities. Despite the vast array of programs and policies designed to enhance a sense of connection to the school, the parents at Western reflect a community fractured by geographical divisions and social diversity.

The nature and quality of community at Western School indicate a critical absence of social cohesion and communication. While some middle-class parents report occasional exchanges with other middle-class Western parents, most suggest rather insular patterns of interactions within families. Low-income apartment residents, in contrast, reflect an interwoven network of interdependence and shared information. In the absence of organizational processes which promote sustained social interactions and cohesion among the families at Western, these patterns are fixed and self-sustaining.

The nature of parents' knowledge regarding schooling indicates that in the absence of organizational structures and processes which draw deeply and regularly from among the diverse population of Western parents, parents' familiarity with school programs and processes are lifted from the written communications sent from school. More fine-grained information regarding such things as teachers' reputations are the stuff of "insider information," or parents' networks. In some schools (e.g., Carlton Magnet School), school-based social networks help parents whose social class position does not provide the particular resources (education, social network ties) which critically influence the ways parents interact with schools (Lareau 1989). Unfortunately, the patterns of social networks at Western indicate that interactions among parents are bracketed around social class and geographical boundaries.

The few occasions for face-to-face exchange between parents and teachers assume heightened importance in the absence of more fluid, constant, and consistent interactions. The reliance on such events as parent-teacher conferences to overcome the lack of a value community has obvious and direct implications for family-school relations. The quiet, comfortable distance between parents and teachers helps minimize expectations, and carve out a degree of anonymity which buffers parents and teachers from further instruments of intrusion and upset. However, when a child's particular interests require coordinated and cooperative attention, the foundation for parent-teacher support and understanding can be unstable and unreliable.

## NOTES

1. The district enrollment by ethnic groups: 75 percent white; 10 percent black; 6 percent Hispanic; 7 percent Asian; 1 percent Asian; 1 percent Filipino; 1 percent other.

2. A total of twelve families were interviewed. Eleven of the interviews took place in the family home; one parent was interviewed at his place of employment. These cases reflect the range of backgrounds and family structures represented among the population of families at Western School.

3. These categories reflect composite definitions of social class. Composite measures include income/material resources, occupation, and education. All names used here are pseudonyms.

4. Each classroom has a volunteer "room parent" who is responsible for coordinating holiday parties and carpool rides for field trips.

5. The principal observed that parents who are receiving government assistance (AFDC) and/or are habitual drug or alcohol abusers account for a "small" percentage of the total population of school families. She suggested that she needs to underscore this fact for teachers in order to redirect their attention and reinforce their spirit of optimism.

6. The visibility and accessibility of the school secretaries make them natural points of contact between parents and teachers. According to the Western School sec-

retaries, they "see the parents who have problems, all the time." These tend to be parents who live in the low-income apartments who, the secretaries said, "try to make every problem they have something that we can handle here so that they won't have to." Often, the secretaries tell the parents to call the police if they're calling regarding an incident in the apartment complex. Otherwise, they suggest that the parent contact either the principal or a teacher.

# 5

# Family Life, School Organization, and Community

## INTRODUCTION

These case studies provide illuminating evidence regarding the relationship between organizational processes and patterns of parents' participation in schools. Drawing on the experiences and explanations of parents and school staff, a vivid portrait of the nature and quality of a school community emerges from their collective and resonating voices. The case study analyses describe each school community, examine their organizational influences and antecedents, and explore the implications for connections across families and schools. The aim throughout these studies lies with underscoring the importance of family processes and routines on patterns of school participation and with exploring the ways in which choice, community, and programmatic commitment interact to mediate these family effects.

The next section reviews the conceptual basis underlying this study's focus on class culture and family-school interactions. Following that, I examine the nature of community in each of the three schools and the organizational arrangements and processes which help define them. The implications of these processes are underscored by revisiting the patterns of parent participation in each of these school settings. Observations are made regarding the parallel and divergent patterns of organization, community, and parent participation between the three school sites.

## SOCIAL CLASS AND PARENT PARTICIPATION

This study examines the concept of cultural capital and its application to family-school interactions by posing a set of questions regarding the influence of social class and school organization on patterns of parental participation. Recent research suggests that higher social class provides parents with more resources (derived from their education, income, occupational status, style of work, social networks) to intervene in schooling and to bind families into

141

tighter connections with social institutions than are available for lower-income families (Lareau 1989).

The findings from this multiple-case study indicate that income and material resources allow some parents (upper-middle and middle class) to do more than others (lower-middle and low income). At the Catholic and magnet school sites, the differences were evident in comparisons of upper-middle- and lower-middle-class parents, and in the neighborhood school, between middle- and low-income families. The differences in material resources affect parental involvement in both home- and school-based activities. Lower-income parents suggested that the need to work full-time prevents them from volunteering in the classroom or driving on field trips. Typically, they do not take day trips to San Francisco or summer vacations to diverse and faraway places. Children from lower-income backgrounds do not attend summer camp nor own a lot of magazines or books. Educational resources such as a set of encyclopedias and tutoring are extras which stretch beyond their parents' financial means.

Additionally, parents whose educational backgrounds and abilities are limited due to shortened and/or unsuccessful schooling experiences are hampered in their ability to assist their children with homework. These parents are also less likely to be familiar with the technical language used by teachers to describe curriculum, instructional strategies, and educational goals.

The findings from this study regarding the influence of social/occupational status and style of work, suggest the limited importance of those elements on family-school relations. The effects of parents' social/occupational status appear to be salient only at the extreme positions. Professional status provides an added degree of confidence for parents and a recognized status differential between them and the teacher. Unskilled/semi-skilled status creates a degree of intimidation and discomfort for other parents. The fact that parents in these case studies universally consider homework an inseparable, important, and necessary element of schooling seems to discount the importance of the influence of differential styles of work on family-school connections.

These case studies underscore the value and importance of exploring other elements of family and work life to better understand the nature and quality of interactions between families and schools. Specifically, I posit that the intersection of work and family lives produces patterns of stress, and corresponding rhythms of accommodation and adaptation which direct families in their relationships with schools. The analyses indicate that the primary influence of parents' level of participation at school-based events is the organization of their work lives, not the amount of their paycheck. That is, the observed differences in income and material resources among families who are upper-middle class to lower-middle class are dwarfed by overarching and pervasive similarities which transcend social class. This symmetry is grounded in the nature of family organization in response to both parents working outside the home. Lower-income parents may not be able to volunteer in the classroom or drive on field trips, but neither are their middle or upper-middle counterparts; just about everybody works. Regardless of status (e.g., professional, skilled, technical) or type of work, the degree to which these occupations/jobs provide flexible work arrangements highly influences the nature and frequency of participation at school-based events. Part-time employment, flexible scheduling, and work hours which mirror school hours allow some parents to attend events which other parents cannot, due to constraints imposed by the organization of their work. For example, self-employed status permits some parents to visit the school during school hours without rearranging work time or requesting time off from their employers. Likewise, an upper-middle-class, college-educated mother who works full-time as an administrator with a law firm experiences the same constraints as a high school educated, lower-middle-class mother who works as a data processor in a medical office.

Another critical influence on the nature of parent involvement in schooling is an overlooked and underestimated by-product of the demands of family and work lives. Across social class and school setting, parents referred to an accompanying state of general weariness and a lack of discretionary time as elements which structure their involvement in schooling. For many parents, the exigencies of work and family lives demand deliberate rationing of their limited time and energy. School-based activities like PTA meetings, spaghetti dinner fundraisers, and parenting workshops are considered extras which they cannot afford. Unless their children are involved in an event or activity, there is little interest in making the effort. Even then, many parents find it difficult to adjust their work schedules to fit school hours. While some parents expressed regret and made apologies, most seemed comfortable in depositing their energies around the family at home. For these parents, evenings are just a blurry and brief respite before another work day; any expendable energy is spent preparing meals, organizing bath times, and helping with homework.[1]

The next section traces these critical similarities in family life across social class and school setting and reexamines the influence of school organization on promoting various elements of school community and in shaping the observed differences in parent participation across the three school settings.

## FAMILIES AND COMMUNITIES

### Portrait of Family Life

Across schools and social class, the parents interviewed for this study revealed a high degree of stress and exhaustion. As they considered the demands of balancing work and family lives, these parents described a frenetically paced lifestyle which allows little time for discretionary or spontaneous activities.

For dual-income, middle-class families, the layered responsibilities of parenting and employment turn typical evenings and weekends into tightly ordered time grids, with children's soccer practices, work meetings, and meals somehow squeezed into particular temporal slots. Cleaning up the kitchen after dinner, organizing bath times, returning phone calls, even reading the newspaper, seem to require immense amounts of effort and energy.

Although the degree of stress is shared by low-income parents who are not employed, the sources are strikingly different. The environmental factors associated with poverty—poor health, emotional distress, violent or abusive family members, lack of child care—create patterns of coping and survival which often leave little energy or optimism.

Family structure parallels and often compounds the stressors associated with socioeconomic status. Single parents identified particular constraints and challenges embedded in this social structure which impose the overwhelming responsibilities of parenting on a single individual. Regardless of whether or not they are employed and have access to additional resources, these parents' voices reverberated with images of loneliness, fear, and despair.

The ways in which families spend their time together reflects the fragmentation which arises from multiple obligations, conflicting schedules, and endless chores. For many families in the study (excluding low-income families), organized family interactions center around sports or religious activities. Church-related obligations and functions tend to tightly organize the social activities of families who are members of a Christian fundamentalist church. Likewise, parents whose children are actively involved in school or league sports programs such as soccer or Little League find their leisure time neatly bracketed around practices and games.

## Social Networks

The ways in which family lives are organized has implications for the kinds of social networks—social contact and the exchange of information—parents establish. As a consequence of some parents' patterns of social interactions, for example, they may tend to connect themselves socially and physically to other church members, or perhaps, families who are similarly active in organized sports.[2] Some families in this study, typically those who are upper-middle class, identified their neighborhoods as physical parameters for social networks with other adults and their families. A more common linkage expressed repeatedly was that of a kinship network. In the absence of social ties rooted in organizations, immediate and extended family interactions predominated the descriptions of social networks and adult socializing for parents across social class and school setting. To a large degree, this pervasive sense of insularity is driven by the exigencies of work and family lives. Nevertheless, this book highlights the potential power and influence of schools to unify disparate sets of parents in a community of shared interests and sustained interactions.

## Organization of School Communities

The degree to which parents' social networks include accessible channels to the community of parents whose children attend the same school is impacted in critical and fundamental ways by certain school organizational processes and structures. Collectively, the studies of a Catholic elementary school, a magnet elementary school, and a neighborhood elementary school suggest mechanisms which tend to either promote or constrain social contacts and information exchanges across geographically and socioeconomically differentiated families. In doing so, these studies highlight the issue of social networks and their effects on parental involvement in schooling as outlined by Lareau (1989). While affirming the significance of social networks as a mechanism for the exchange of information, advice, opinion, and rumor regarding schooling, these portraits of school community capture the ways in which school-based social networks mediate the effects of class-based social ties. Thus, in building upon the conceptual models which undergird this study, a central and fundamental question is addressed: How does community (and its attendant elements—social networks) alter the effects of social class on the nature and quality of family-school relations?

In each of the three schools, parents consistently characterized other school parents as "a real mix." There were repeated remarks and observations regarding differences in socioeconomic status, philosophical/religious beliefs, family structures, and ethnicity to greater and lesser degrees within each school setting. Amidst these cleavages, however, parents from the Catholic school and the magnet school invoked a far different language to suggest overarching commonalities which transcend individual differences. In sharp and striking contrast to the parents whose children attend the public, neighborhood school, these parents identified processes which create a widespread sense of social cohesion and community among a collection of differentiated members. What are these organizational processes? The following represents a continuum of school communities, from the most cohesive and robust (magnet school) to the most insular and elusive (public, neighborhood school).

### Carlton Elementary (Magnet)

Carlton School parents perceive themselves as members of a separate, elite public school community. Although drawn from widely scattered neighborhoods, the sense of community at Carlton is palpable and pervasive. In the absence of natural familiarity and occasions for face-to-face talk which may be evidenced in geographical communities, Carlton School reflects a constructed community undergirded by a sense of shared values, solidarity, and commitment.

Three integrated elements of the school's organization account for the processes which construct the social network and value community at Carlton:

required parent participation; the three-way contract between students, parents, and teachers; and established communication policies.

Both substantively and symbolically, the forty-hour participation requirement binds parents in a sense of solidarity and "family." Parents have a clear incentive to attend school-based events such as fund-raisers, meetings, and social get-togethers, or to work part-time in the classroom, computer lab, or library—they earn hours. These occasions for face-to-face talk with other school parents accumulate over time, contributing to a sense of familiarity and connection. The process creates perfect redundancy: parents have an incentive to attend school events (forty-hour requirement); the more events they attend the more relationships they form with other parents; and consequently subsequent occasions for face-to-face talk provide the opportunity to exchange information, thus providing additional incentives to attend school events.

While the participation requirement is instrumental in providing a mechanism to establish social networks among parents and between parents and school staff, it also marks parents as members of a particular group or *Gemeinschaft* community (Tonnies 1963). That is, rather than being tied together solely by legal or formal means such as by law or contract (*Gesellschaft* communities), Carlton parents are bound by a perception of shared interests and mutual goals embodied in the act of public choice. Just as a willingness to pay for education seems to purchase a sense of mutual commitment and membership for Catholic school parents, the promise to fulfill the participation requirement specified in a written contract is the badge that provides Carlton parents with a manifest sense of belonging to this value community. The fulfillment of the contract acts as a kind of standard which ensures a collection of homogeneous and compatible members who have "bought into the program."

Carlton School has established a vast network of communication channels which solidifies the organization of a value community by connecting individuals to a collective of parents who perceive themselves to be like-minded. The communication system, for example, draws on a ready pool of parent volunteers eager to satisfy their forty-hour requirement through their participation in a phone network system which alerts parents in each grade regarding specific classroom events and responsibilities. Additionally, a punitive system ensures that parents and students coordinate their efforts in receiving and returning notices. Parents are kept abreast of their children's academic performance through what are called "weekly reports." Each Friday, teachers send home a comprehensive summary of the student's performance on homework, quizzes, class assignments and tests. Thus, the school's programs and policies reinforce and parallel one another: parents are kept well informed, perceive that their interests and concerns are being taken into account, identify themselves as a member of the school community, and maintain an active level of involvement in school activities.

The basic school program at Carlton and the corresponding culture of community reflect the faculty's unity of purpose and social cohesion. The common practices and collective beliefs Carlton teachers share are translated to parents and students in a common language and set of consistent actions. They are the agents and the enforcers of the organizational processes which create community and social networks at Carlton.

Choice is a fundamental component in the construction of the value community at Carlton. The fact that these parents have chosen a school voluntarily rather than through coercion or mandate, solidifies a sense of commonality around a particular set of values and expectations. The simple act of choosing sensitizes parents to particular benefits that might otherwise go unnoticed and inspires a level of commitment to ensure that the choice is rewarded (Erickson 1982).

Nevertheless, it is vital to underscore the evidence which suggests that socialization, rather than self-selection, accounts for the influence of school organization on parent-school interactions. The serendipitous nature of school choice is represented in the ways in which parents at Carlton School selected it for their children. Rather than pursuing a systematic review of school alternatives, the context of decision making reveals that a chance conversation or unsolicited advice prompted a look-and-see attitude for many parents discouraged by their unsafe or depressing neighborhood school. Their unfamiliarity with the basic school philosophy or the aims of the magnet program suggest that these parents do not resemble the typical characteristics of self-selected parents who opt for alternatives to their neighborhood public schools. It is clear that rather than *matching* parents' particular expectations for a school, Carlton helps *define* and *develop* them.

## Consequences for Patterns of Parent Participation

The sense of familiarity and social cohesion have direct and immediate implications for patterns of parent participation at Carlton School. Knowing "lots of parents" provides particular benefits to all parents who are members of this community. These relationships are neither tenuous nor temporary; rather, they are stable and predictable sources of information and referral. Reputations of particular teachers, the types of homework he/she assigns, deadlines for applications to the basic middle school, reputations of high schools—access to this kind of "insider" information provides an invaluable tool for parents who are engaged in their children's academic experiences. The social network established easily and naturally through Carlton's array of school activities provides the channels for shared information, advice, and referral.

Social networks with Carlton parents who possess particular knowledge about schooling may help parents whose social class position does not provide similar resources and who, for example, may be unfamiliar with the language of competency testing and curriculum or with school policies regarding alternative academic programs and special education assignments. Thus, these school-based, reconstituted social networks may mediate the influence of at least some of the elements of social class (e.g., education and social networks) which critically influence the ways parents interact with schools.

The impact of an enhanced level of communication between home and school at Carlton is reflected in the rich, detailed knowledge of school policies and activities parents possess. As a result of the fluid, consistent dialogue between parents and teachers, there are few surprises regarding students' performance. Established, customary events like parent-teacher conferences barely resemble the uncomfortable and forced occasions of face-to-face interactions that most school teachers and parents dread. The widened zone of comfort and familiarity between parents and teachers allows these events to become something like a friendly conversation about mutual interests and concerns.

## St. Martin's School (Catholic)

There is little sense of traditional Catholic community at St. Martin's School. Generational divisions, philosophical/religious differences, and partisan demands have ruptured the heart of this former functional community. The punishing demands of work and family and the corresponding constraints bounding time and space have widened these chasms.

Interviews with parents from St. Martin's School create the striking impression that they reject notions of cohesion and consensus that most observers would expect in a Catholic school community (e.g., see Coleman and Hoffer 1987). There is a sense of their separateness and individuality, rather than their collectivity and mutual dependence; a sense of distinctive beliefs, rather than shared values. To be sure, the functional community described by Coleman and Hoffer (1987) in their study of Catholic schools is absent here.

One institutionalized, schoolwide activity provides the seeds for sustained social interactions among this disparate set of parents: school sports. Nearly all the parents interviewed indicated that their children—and by necessity, they themselves—were actively involved in the tightly organized and highly competitive worlds of volleyball, basketball, football, and softball. With an average of three practices a week and a game on Saturdays, these events provide the time and place for casual, if perhaps abbreviated, social exchanges between families from different backgrounds and school experiences. Parents exchange information about teachers' reputations, ability-grouping, and high school admissions strategies. They provide an opportunity to discuss issues ranging from Parent's Club fund-raisers to the condition of the lunch room.

Despite the integral role of school sports, the St. Martin's school community reflects only some shadowy dimensions of the constitutive elements of community. There is a sense of community there, but it is neither absolute nor aggregative; it is neither rooted nor ephemeral. Rather, the nature of community embraced and fostered at St. Martin's is grounded in an alliance of accommodation and differentiation. That is, there is an implicit understanding among families and school staff that internally, the St. Martin's community may be differentiated, but externally, against the backdrop of a larger community of school parents, set apart. Individual differences between classes, occupations, neighborhoods, and religious faiths, are leveled at the intersection of private choice. These parents' collective actions—to enroll their children in a Catholic school—assume public dimensions by providing the link to bind these disparate families to a "school community."

The "common ground" shared by parents at St. Martin's is cultivated by the act of choosing and the attendant features of monetary investment. Parents at St. Martin's pay directly for the educational services their children receive. Individually, tuition expenses may be viewed as a necessary sacrifice to obtain highly valued services. But collectively, a willingness to pay for education seems to purchase a sense of commitment and a membership in a group which is decidedly separate from any other group of school parents. Tuition is the badge, the currency of commitment, that provides parents with a manifest sense of belonging to this community. There is an unfounded belief that if they care enough to pay, they must value education more than parents who simply send their kids to the neighborhood school. Thus, rather than being internally derived from a homogeneous collection of necessarily like-minded school families, a sense of community is externally driven.

The "common ground" which parents describe is tended and cultivated by the school principal using the tools of humor and laughter, an uncanny ability to remember names, and a deep sense of caring. The principal's popularity seems to neutralize the discordant voices which rumble just below the surface of this community. Her tireless promotion of an ethic of caring and compassion unifies St. Martin's, generating feelings of inclusion and comfort. The principal's leadership works to promote a cohesive social network across a self-described differentiated school community.

## Consequences for Patterns of Parent Participation

The school sports program serves as an important channel for parents to establish regular, predictable social network ties and to exchange information regarding school activities. These opportunities for face-to-face interactions with other school parents are critical repositories for parents engaged in managing their children's school experiences. The knowledge and understanding of school processes and programs gained from these parent-to-parent interactions are realized by their enhanced ability to negotiate their children's academic careers. For parents whose social class position does not provide the resources (social network ties, education) from which other parents may draw, the organized school sports program diminishes or mediates the influence of cultural capital on these parents' interactions with schools.

Parents at St. Martin's have voluntarily elected to send their children to a private school and to commit certain resources to gain admission. This badge of membership includes a package of expectations, which undergirds relations between parents and teachers in this school of choice, and serves to flatten differences associated with parents' and teachers' educational and occupational status. Although several of the parents interviewed did not graduate from college and hold jobs which are not equivalent in occupational status to teaching, there were no indications of deference, discomfort, or an unwillingness to challenge teachers. Rather, the fact that these parents have "literally bought into the system" seems to purchase status and a sense of entitlement. Both parents and staff are cognizant of the ways in which parents' heightened expectations engender an increased level of responsiveness and concern.

## Western School (Neighborhood)

The nature and quality of community at Western School suggests a critical absence of social cohesion and communication. While there is evidence of interaction and mutual dependence within a geographically isolated and socially differentiated group of school parents (low-income apartment residents), it is undergirded by corresponding elements of instability and uncertainty. Despite the school's programmatic commitment to parental participation—the vast array of volunteer opportunities, special events and programs, and traditional school organizations designed to enhance a sense of connection to the school—Western School parents reflect alternating patterns of insularity and distraction. In the absence of a robust community, there are tenuous connections among parents, and between parents and the school.[3]

## Consequences for Patterns of Parent Participation

The nature of parents' knowledge regarding schooling suggests that in the absence of organizational structures and processes which draw deeply and regularly from among the diverse population of Western parents, their familiarity with school programs and policies are lifted from the written communications sent from school. Parents are well informed regarding the time and date of school assemblies, PTA meetings, ice-cream social fund-raisers, and parenting classes for single parents. The regular Wednesday newsletters contain pertinent information for parents regarding "early bird/late bird" reading group schedules and California Achievement Program (CAP) testing.

More fine-grained information, however, regarding such things as teachers' reputations and parents' rights under the special education programs are the stuff of "insider information," or parents' (limited) social networks. Parents' knowledge of teachers' reputations suggests rather insular patterns of social interactions and information exchange among Western families. Of the twelve parents interviewed, only three said they had requested a particular teacher for their children. Only one parent said that the information came from another Western parent. A parent who is low income and well informed regarding Wednesday newsletters, said she did not realize she could request a teacher. Scant knowledge regarding alternative academic programs not offered at Western suggests a lack of information exchange among Western's socially and economically differentiated families.

PARENTS AND TEACHERS

Relations between parents and teachers are nested within a larger social context of families and schools. The organizational elements and processes which promote the formation of value communities and social networks within schools necessarily impact these relations as well. Nevertheless, the case studies reveal a set of institutionalized roles and responses which parents and teachers assume. This section reviews the roles and expectations of parents and teachers which are evidenced across school settings. The ways in which these patterns vary are related to particular organizational arrangements.

### Parents' Roles

The organization of schooling is institutionalized to produce common understandings about what is appropriate and, fundamentally, accountable behavior. Social scripts provide a language and a framework for parents and teachers alike. Over time, parents learn the circumscribed roles they are expected to assume. They learn to think of themselves as "monitors," "helpers," and "supporters."

The discussion with parents in this book regarding their role in their children's schooling produced predictable and routine responses reflective of these scripts. Most parents described their patterns of involvement as managing, supervising, and assisting their children with school activities. Typically, parents identified their roles by a familiar context; that is, they expressed an overwhelming willingness to assume the role of teacher or monitor in their home. Few parents identified school-based activities as within the realm of parent involvement.

Despite the almost seamless pattern of responses, these conversations produced different perspectives, or lenses, through which parents view and catalog their behavior. Many parents consider their role *in relation* to the role of the teacher or the arrangement of school activities. These parents tend to invoke the language of manufacturing or co-production—using terms such as "partnership," "joint effort," and "technical stuff."

In contrast to the "relational" perspective, some parents consider involvement in schooling within a broad definition of parenting roles and frame their participation in terms of the integral social institutions which comprise their children's social worlds. Given the focus of this book on the effects of social class on parent involvement, it is important to note that these perspectives are not associated with parents from a particular social class or school. Although parents from the middle and upper-middle class dominated the integrated viewpoint, there were lower-class parents in each of the three schools who echoed their perspectives. While they expressed an interest in participating in their children's education and acknowledged the value of school involvement, these parents tended to define this involvement in terms of a general awareness of their children's lives and a deep interest in their well-being.

## Homework

Within the predominant "relational" role which parents assume, their experiences and explanations suggest that the process is driven almost exclusively by activities developed and sanctioned by teachers, namely, homework. Through this home-based activity, the partnership between parents and teachers moves beyond a rather imprecise joint effort to one with explicit and easily identifiable goals and roles for parents and teachers alike. Helping with multiplication tables, checking the spelling list, and listening to their children read—these tasks help parents identify their appropriate roles vis-à-vis teachers. Across social class and regardless of occupation, there is an unquestioned acceptance that homework is inseparable from the experience of schooling.

At the same time, parents from all three schools suggested that homework can have divisive and destabilizing effects on family life. In the context of family rhythms and routines, homework establishes the pace and priority of after school and evening activities. It tends to impose certain restrictions on already dense and rigid time grids slotted with basketball practices, soccer games, meetings, and meals. Thus, while the idea of homework seems to resonate with parents' interest in education and their commitment to supporting their children's academic achievement, parents indicated that actually allocating their (scarce) discretionary time to working out math problems or helping to write a book report was burdensome. For some parents, homework introduces other particularly difficult and painful challenges. When parents perceive that, due to their own unsuccessful or short-lived educational experiences, their own abilities are insufficient to help their children with homework, they tend to feel frustrated, defeated, and angry. Sometimes these feelings lead to a gradual disengagement from their children's school work (particularly after the primary grades); other times it leads to parents reconfiguring their roles. Given the frames in which they and teachers portray their roles, these consequences are not surprising, nor are they trivial.

## Teachers' Expectations

Echoing the rhetoric and research which suggests that a committed and equal partnership between parents and teachers in the enterprise of schooling is rewarding and beneficial for all parties, the teachers at each of the three schools reiterated the need for parents' "support" and "reinforcement." Their expectations, they said, were simple and traditional—reading to their children, helping with homework, attending conferences and back-to-school nights. At the neighborhood school, which among the three schools has the largest low-income population, teachers also underscored the need for parents "to be parents"—to make sure their children are rested, fed, and dressed for school on time.

These teachers' consensus on what ought to be the relationship between themselves and parents was matched by an equally unanimous assessment of the discouraging and troubling trends they are witnessing among school families. Many of the teachers suggested that parents' increasingly fractured lives are leading more and more parents to bracket their roles into smaller, manageable units, leaving teachers with larger chunks of responsibility for the education of their students. There was an implicit message that the increase in the number of mothers who work outside their home is producing a deleterious effect on children; hectic work lives mean additional distractions and constraints and add little value to the educational or social lives of students. Teachers also worried that with more children starting preschool at age three or four, parents are completely dismissing their primary educative role by reducing learning situations to their most organized, school-like forms. Many suggested that it is a constant battle to remind parents that learning exceeds the boundaries of a classroom or the bindings of a book.

## SHARED DIFFERENCES

Despite the almost seamless accord struck by these faculty members regarding parent-teacher relations, some critical differences emerged which are grounded in the issues of choice, communication, and accommodation. These issues produce contrasting characterizations of parents from the teachers' perspectives. Magnet school teachers perceive parents as *committed partners*; Catholic school teachers see parents as *meddlesome intruders*; and the neighborhood school teachers view parents as *distracted absentees*.

### Carlton School (Magnet)

The contract which parents and teachers sign at the magnet Carlton School clearly articulates the expectations of each group. From the teachers' perspective, the contract encodes what good parenting is all about—maintaining an active, supportive, and encouraging role in children's education and ensuring that children show respect and courtesy in their daily interactions with other adults and students. There's nothing dramatically different or innovative here, except the fact that these parents are asked to pledge their allegiance to specified school policies. Nevertheless, the contract helps clarify roles and relationships. For both parents and teachers, the contract provides a language and framework for interacting. Most importantly, it provides a contractual basis—symbolically and substantively—to begin working on a partnership.

The contract's life and force, however, stems from the fact that parents have chosen Carlton, or, as several teachers put it, "have bought into the program." For school officials, the contract provides the leverage and clarity to justify expulsion procedures against parents and students. It sets the tone for this school of choice: if you don't follow the rules, you are out. Consequently, the document is more than a piece of paper filed away somewhere; it carries the threat and authority of a forced exit from Carlton. Quite simply, it gives teachers an edge in their expectations of parents.

Additionally, the communication system at Carlton draws on a set of incentives and punitive actions to ensure that parents and teachers maintain constant and fluid interactions; there are few surprises here. The established processes promote understanding, awareness, and cooperation between families and the school.

## St. Martin's School (Catholic)

Relations between parents and teachers at St. Martin's School are driven by parents' expectations and defined with apparent regularity and clarity. These expectations are incredibly high, teachers claim, due in large part to the fact that parents pay directly for the educational services their children receive. There is a corresponding dependency on these tuition dollars. While school policies provide for the forced exit of students and their families, there is an organizational imperative (survival) which exacts a level of accommodation from the school and its faculty. These arrangements prompt a subtle but simmering sense of resentment among teachers who note that they are sometimes asked to make special efforts to keep parish family members in the school, although these members may be better served in another school setting. The heterogeneous school population (Catholics, non-Catholics, nonparticipating Catholics) also triggers a flashpoint of opposition from teachers who are deeply committed to the tenets of a Catholic education. For the staff, the gulf between home and school is widened by parents who fail to reinforce Catholic values and traditions at home. Parents' emphasis on different educational and social goals and the corresponding undercurrent of entitlement provide the parameters for teachers' impressions of parents and their attendant strategy designed to buffer their relations with parents.

## Western School (Neighborhood)

In the absence of incentives, contractual understandings, and systematic communication between home and school that shape and define parent-teacher relations and without the sense of entitlement that a private school promotes through tuition and the explicit acknowledgement of self-selection, a quiet, comfortable distance has been carved out between parents and teachers at the neighborhood school. Western teachers lack the leverage that the faculty in a magnet school enjoy with the threat of forced exit and the corresponding self-interest which motivates parents to respond enthusiastically to school programs lest they be remanded to a less desirable or second choice school. Consequently, Western teachers rely on an array of both traditional and innovative programs designed to attract and motivate parents' interest in their children's school. The distracting and disabling elements of family and work lives which necessarily shape parent-teacher relations across the three schools, assume unaltered proportions here. Without the organizational processes to sharply define relations, and the attendant force of choice, these efforts fall far short of their goal of enhancing connections between families and the school. Parents' patterns of insularity and distraction create a degree of anonymity which buffers and protects them and teachers from instruments of perceived intrusion and upset. The few occasions for face-to-face exchange between parents and teachers assume an uncomfortable degree of importance in the absence of more fluid, constant, and consistent interactions. The result is an incomplete and distorted view of one anothers' experiences and expectations.

## RECONSIDERING COMMUNITY

The images of functional school communities drawn by Coleman and Hoffer (1987) are contradicted by the case study of the Catholic school. Their research on public and private schools suggests that a Catholic school acts as a repository for bonding among geographically, socially, economically, and ideologically homogeneous families. The portrait of St. Martin's School reveals a far different picture—one of a diverse, differentiated Catholic school community—and argues strongly for the need to explore broadly the varied nature of these schools and the families which they serve. Moreover, the case study of the magnet school suggests that a richly endowed, robust school community can be promoted and sustained in the absence of the structurally reinforcing elements which serve as the basis for Coleman's and Hoffer's concept of functional communities. Although their notion of a value community is helpful in describing the magnet school community, the researchers' descriptive model offers only a partial glimpse of the elements which comprise communities in public, public-choice, and nonpublic schools.

Collectively, the case studies suggest the need to underscore the value and importance of school communities and, in effect, "bring community back in" to the discussion and research surrounding families and schools. The concept of community invoked by Newmann and Oliver (1968) is perhaps most helpful here; that is, it is important to consider each element of community—social cohesion, commitment, communication, shared values, familiarity, sense of membership and ownership (among others)—along a continuum and to explore the ways in which school organizational processes and structures promote or constrain their development.

## THE PARADOX OF CHOICE

These case studies suggest that choice is a powerful engine for creating the constituent elements of community. These elements seem to coalesce when choice mechanisms organize like-minded individuals who view themselves as separate from other nonchoice individuals or, in the words of one, as "a better class of parents." Badges of community typically reflect standards which must be overcome to prove oneself worthy of inclusion into the community. Community members have an obvious and vested interest in working to maintain a community of conformity to ensure a collection of like-minded families. Nevertheless, these issues raise serious and troubling questions which are typically not addressed in the research and rhetoric on school choice. Is this "spirit of elitism and separatism" pernicious? Do the organizational arrangements which promote social cohesion and social networks militate against certain elements of diversity? Can schools promote value communities and social networks in the absence of choice? The final chapter considers these issues and others associated with the influence of school organization on family-school relations, in an examination of the policy implications and future research directions prompted by this study.

## NOTES

1. While the stressors associated with maintaining family life are shared by low-income families, other punishing and disabling factors associated with their socioeconomic status combine to limit their involvement in school-based activities.

2. Some families active in scouting identified this group as a source of adult friendship and socializing. Only two parents identified work associates as a source of social networking; both are high school teachers.

3. Western School may be considered more heterogeneous in terms of the school's student population because it offers programs designed for students with special needs (e.g., bilingual, special, and compensatory education programs). St. Martin's and Carlton School do not offer these programs and, as a consequence, may enroll a more homogeneous student population. The relative homogeneity in these two schools may account, in part, for the greater potential and realization of social cohesion among parents at St. Martin's and Carlton.

# 6

# The Call for Community

## INTRODUCTION

The case studies in this book demonstrate that the context of family life and school organization must be linked in ways which examine the interaction between community-building strategies and parents' social networks. If the problem rests with the promise of parent involvement, the fault is found in the generic qualities of participation strategies which ignore context. Absent a consideration of the stressors and the supports associated with social status, family structure, and neighborhood, the promise of parent involvement falls far short of stated goals. These cases demonstrate the value of situated strategies nested within the everyday rhythms and routines of families and educators.

## SOCIAL NETWORKS AND COMMUNITY BUILDING

Thomas Sergiovanni (1994) observes that "there is no recipe for community building—no workshop agenda, no training package. Community cannot be borrowed or bought" (p. 5). Nevertheless, repeated calls for greater community across recent social theory literature (e.g., Bellah et al. 1991; Barber 1992) and educational research (e.g., Bryk, Lee, & Holland 1993; McLaughlin, Irby, & Langman 1994) coalesce around core elements of commitment, shared beliefs, interdependence, and communication. These values initiate the process of community building and lead to the stable and predictable relationships which provide sources of information and referral.

The value of this case study research rests with the prominent attention and importance paid to social networks as a central aspect of community building. The reconstituted organizational form of interest extends beyond the visceral elements embraced in a *gemeinschaft* model of community and the sterile, commercialized concept of singular parent involvement strategies. Social networks provide a way of enhancing our understanding of the salient properties of social class culture. The focus on the personal networks of parents moves the unit of analysis from a "social address" (Bronfenbrenner 1966) to a more dynamic view of the social processes associated with class distinctions.

The conceptual and empirical work in the area of social networks establishes the significance of personal associations to the development of particular social and cognitive competencies, including caregiving and parenting (Cochran 1990). Social networks provide access to the resources which are central for parents in managing and enhancing the educational experiences of children. The relative resource accounts of social networks, however, are directly related to members' social structural position (Cochran 1990; Cochran & Brassard 1979; Lareau 1989). For poor and undereducated parents, issues of neighborhood stability and isolation, limited access to transportation and civic organizations, and occupations which disallow workplace associations, reduce dramatically the pool of potential members of primary social networks[1] (Cochran 1990; Lareau 1989).

The primacy assigned to the role of parents' primary social networks in this study is a function of the importance of information gathering and exchange to the ways in which parents participate in their children's educational experiences. Reputations of particular teachers, requirements for special enrichment programs, deadlines for applications to magnet middle schools, and reputations of high schools—access to this kind of information provides an invaluable tool for parents to maximize their children's educational and academic success. Social networks with parents who possess particular knowledge about schooling may help parents whose social class position does not provide similar resources from which to draw this kind of information. Thus, school-based social networks may mediate the influence of at least some of the elements of social class which critically influence the ways in which parents interact with schools.

The policy proposals[2] which flow from this position require a shift from a focus on individual families to the social context which supports family life—the naturally occurring social system. While personal choice shapes the pattern of all parents' social networks, these choices tend to be far more constrained for low-income families. The effort here rests with affirming the mediating role of schools in reconstituting parents' primary social networks in ways which provide broad access to a deep pool of social network members.

## BUILDING COMMUNITY AMONG PARENTS

The next section highlights the organizational features which account for and help promote the reconstituted social networks evidenced in the magnet and Catholic school case studies. Following this discussion, this study explores the troubling and negative aspects of school characteristics and an alternative proposal for creating the constitutive elements of community.

### Community in Schools of Choice

At Carlton Elementary School, the promise to abide by items specified in a written contract exclusive to a particular school purchases a sense of mutual commitment and membership in a value community. The fulfillment of the contract acts as a kind of standard which creates a shared perception that, rather than a disparate set of parents, the school population reflects a collection of compatible and like-minded individuals who have "bought into the program."

The key element of the contract is the forty-hour parent participation requirement. Substantively and symbolically, the requirement binds parents in a sense of solidarity and commitment. The occasions for face-to-face talk with other parents accumulate over time (given the incentive to attend fund-raisers, meetings, social get-togethers, etc.), contributing to a sense of familiarity and connection. The participation requirement provides a mechanism to establish social networks among parents of various socioeconomic backgrounds, thus mediating the influence of social class on the nature of family-school interactions.

Each of these organizational arrangements raises powerful and potentially troubling issues. On the one hand, the Carlton School contract embodies what many parents consider the elements of good parenting and "commonsense stuff"—the promise to maintain an active, supportive, and encouraging role in their children's education. For some observers, however, the imposition of a contract implies an asymmetry of power, knowledge, and control—elements appropriated by school officials. They may find a contract anathema to the sense of mutual respect, shared commitment, and sustained cooperation which it is intended to foster. The imposition of a single set of sociocultural norms and the failure to recognize the rich diversity within and between families of varied social and cultural backgrounds may also be a concern.

## Vision Statement

An alternative approach might involve parents more substantively in developing ideas for their participation in schooling. For example, parents might be asked to develop a "vision statement" of their educational goals for their children. The statement would establish a set of guidelines for achieving these goals—ideas which would involve meaningful and sustained interactions between the family and the school. This document would reflect parents' expectations, desires, and self-imposed obligations. The process involved in asking parents what they want for their children and in what ways they can contribute to these goals may work to nurture and sustain meaningful relations between them and school officials.

In the absence of choice arrangements, this modified agreement process seems more appropriate and meaningful, particularly since regular public, neighborhood schools lack enforcement capacity (i.e., forced exit). Under a choice arrangement similar to Carlton's magnet program, however, the contract reflects the parallel convictions and intentions of parents and school officials to impose a certain boundary of expectations around participants. Since parents have voluntarily selected this school, there is little sense of institutional control or power play.

## Diverse School Activities

Despite the organizational, philosophical, and geographical divisions among parents at St. Martin's Elementary School, the established school sports program engages a broad spectrum of students and parents in weekly athletic and social activities. This schoolwide activity provides the seeds for sustained social interactions between disparate sets of parents. These events establish the time and place for casual social exchanges between families from different backgrounds and school experiences.

As organizational elements which promote community in schools and social networks among parents, required parent participation and established school sports programs require relatively less scrutiny. These case studies suggest that the organization of work lives, to a larger degree than salary or occupational status, influences parents' level of participation at school-based events. Observed differences in income and material resources (within a certain band of social class—upper-middle class to lower-middle class) are dwarfed by the overarching and pervasive similarities found in the nature of family organization in response to both parents working outside the home. Nevertheless, parents whose work lives make it difficult to attend school events or to simply volunteer occasionally in their children's classrooms (i.e., those who do not have flexible work arrangements or who work full-time) are objectively disadvantaged under a required participation scheme; they may not have access to particular knowledge or to the school-based social networks that these activities promote.

The Carlton case study indicates that the wide variety of activities parents can fulfill at home (e.g., correcting homework, making signs and buttons, baking cookies) seems to level the effects of social class derived from differences in income or material resources. Thus, the value and benefits of required participation evidenced at Carlton Elementary School seem to outweigh the potential for disadvantage experienced by certain working families, since the nature of "inventoried items" are generously varied. Still, in the absence of some system of incentives and sanctions (such as a forced exit and forfeiture of some benefit), the enforcement of such a requirement is problematic.

In addition to a school sports program, which may exclude some students whose interests and abilities fall outside of athletic competition, other events, such as season-long academic olympiads or musical/dramatic programs, could be adopted in an effort to provide opportunities for face-to-face interactions among disparate sets of parents. The case study of St. Martin's Elementary School provides persuasive evidence of the importance of these events for establishing regular, predictable social ties which can be utilized to exchange information regarding school activities.

## School Choice

At Carlton School, voluntary choice contributes to a sense of commitment and cohesion by connecting individuals to a collective of parents with perceived congruent values and shared belief systems. The simple act of choosing promotes a heightened sense of awareness to the value and importance of social interactions with other parents and school staff.

Nevertheless, the choice mechanism itself may contribute to large-scale inequities which are ultimately more troubling than any contract arrangement. By establishing admissions policies which exclude certain students who require educational services such as bilingual education or special education (for emotionally, physically, or educationally handicapped students), particular school choice arrangements may create a de facto, multi-tiered school system which sets aside certain schools for certain classes of students. While the advocates of a magnet/thematic curriculum school such as Carlton Elementary School may argue that most students can benefit from a back-to-basics program, depending upon the level of parental commitment to the program, it is evident that "special needs" students are excluded from this alternative in the selective admissions policy. It is certainly the case that some students, in order to negotiate the process of schooling, require educational services which Carlton does not offer. In this sense, the spirit of elitism and separatism which binds Carlton parents in a mutually reinforcing sense of social cohesion and unity of purpose is undercut by rather pernicious tones of selectivity and exclusion. By selecting out certain elements of diversity and disadvantage, these conditions seem predictable, and perhaps, inexcusable. The educational opportunities of these excluded students and their families demand thoughtful and vigorous attention in any discussion of choice and its stratifying effects.

## CONNECTIONS BETWEEN PARENTS AND SCHOOL STAFF

These case studies suggest that trusting, cooperative, and mutually supportive relations between parents and teachers act as a linchpin to promote rewarding and successful academic experiences for students. Conversely, ambiguity, conflict, and distance may undercut the level and nature of social interactions between these groups, producing a pattern of inconsistent and incomplete information exchanges. When parents' patterns of insularity and distraction create a degree of anonymity, the few occasions for face-to-face exchange assume an uncomfortable degree of importance. The result is often a distorted view of one anothers' experiences and expectations and their individual contributions to students' schooling experiences.

The case studies indicate both striking similarities and profound differences in relations between parents and teachers at the three school sites. Institutionalized teacher practices and variable organizational conditions account for these patterns.

The communication policies at Carlton Elementary School ensure fluid, consistent dialogue (verbal and written) between parents and teachers. The process links incentives and punitive actions with responses to requests to promote a set of expectations which would otherwise be undercut by parents' distractions and disinterest. Maintaining regular and predictable contact reduces feelings of distrust and distance, which often color parent-teacher interactions. A widened zone of comfort and familiarity between parents and teachers might minimize the likelihood of unexpected and unplanned for reports of academic or behavioral problems, which parents uniformly dread and resent.

The contract at Carlton, which parents and teachers sign, clarifies expectations, roles, and relationships. For both parents and teachers, the contract provides a language and framework for interacting. It also establishes a contractual basis—symbolically and substantively—to begin working on a partnership. The contract is a blueprint for teachers and parents to construct a dialogue around a common set of ideas and expectations.

The Carlton School contract requires parents to participate forty hours each year in school-related activities. By providing a formal incentive for parents to attend meetings, fund-raisers, social get-togethers, and conferences, the contract provides a means of enhancing parents' knowledge and understanding of the school. The requirement also promotes parental involvement in more elemental activities, such as supporting teachers, enforcing rules, and assisting with home-based assignments. Involvement in school and home-based activities becomes an unavoidable, integrated part of family routines.

While the contract and required participation stand as powerful organizing structures which enhance relations between parents and teachers, their potential weaknesses (described earlier) suggest limited applications in nonchoice schools.

In the absence of choice mechanisms which provide force and authority to these elements, alternative arrangements should focus on the organizational structures and processes which delimit parent-teacher interactions to formal, abrupt, and incomplete exchanges. These integrated proposals cut deeply into the established professional practices of teachers. Although some of these elements are embedded within particular educational programs in schools in the United States, Japan, and Germany, embracing the assumptions undergirding these arrangements requires a fundamental reconceptualization of the roles of teachers within the broader social context of student, family, and community life.

## Home Visits

The issue of home visits prompted a range of vocal and vigorous responses from teachers at each school site. Teachers at St. Martin's School angrily objected to the idea and said such arrangements placed teachers in a "menial" position. They suggested that such a policy constituted yet another assault on the teaching profession.

Teachers at the two public schools, Carlton and Western, issued somewhat different objections and concerns. They said that they would not be welcome in a lot of family homes, many homes would not be safe, and the densely packed school day imposed unalterable time constraints. Several of these public school teachers, however, recalled making visits to the homes of their special education students. These experiences left them with an enduring sense of insight and understanding. One teacher said that knowledge of a student's home life helped her "attack the situation differently" and "give a certain child more . . . because he may not have what it takes at home to get him over this hump." Another teacher observed that in some ethnic cultures, schools are frightening and unfamiliar places. For families whose children are in bilingual education programs, for example, a home visit may pay an immediate dividend for a teacher by demonstrating a "willingness to go into their world a little bit so they'll be a little more willing to come into yours."

When teachers measure parents' interest in education by the number of visits parents make to the school, the number and type of "extras" (backpack, glue, pencils) students bring to school, and whether or not parents return teachers' telephone calls, the absence of their knowledge regarding the social and economic context of those families' lives can have serious and negative implications for students' academic success. That is, the teachers' expectations for a student may decline as a result of teachers' perceptions that the family does not value schooling. Interestingly, only teachers who work with learning and physically handicapped children typically make home visits. These programs include special organizational arrangements (small classes, aides, flexible scheduling) which help accommodate time away from the school site. It is obvious that all teachers, parents, and students could benefit immeasurably by expanding this practice so that teachers' understanding of family life is not limited to speculation and rumor.[3] As a parent who is low income observed:

> In many ways, I think [home visits] would be good. Sometimes I think it would help the teachers see their children—the students—as people with a life. Sometimes I wonder if they understand that people have a life outside of school. They might understand the challenges that they face—why they're strong and why they're weak in different areas. We might see each other all more as people and understand each other better. I can see how that would happen.

## Teacher-Student Cohorts

The interviews with teachers in each school revealed that they typically possess only shadowy knowledge of their students' family backgrounds. Many teachers noted that parent-teacher conferences were helpful in providing a glimpse of their students' home lives but that it took most of the school year to extend their knowledge and understanding of students' family lives beyond the information listed on the parents' data card. Each fall, teachers begin with a cleared, or empty, base of knowledge regarding the context of their students' lives.[4]

Schools could create teams of two or three teachers which would follow the same cohort of students for three-year periods (first through third grade; fourth through sixth grade). Similar to the imperative of maintaining a "continuity of care" in medical treatment and training, this arrangement would provide sustained, dependable, and continuous interactions between the same group of teachers, students, and their families. This continuity may promote enduring relationships based upon trust, familiarity, and mutual understanding.

## Communication Networks

Carlton's extensive network of communication channels helps bridge the insularity and distractions that often color family school relations. Under the "open door policy" which encourages parents to visit the school and their children's classroom as often as possible, Carlton teachers promote an image of the school that reflects support, trust, and understanding. The physical presence at school of parents who would not otherwise feel welcome is an obvious aim of broader efforts designed to promote frequent interactions among socioeconomically diverse parents. Altering the established routines and rituals that typically delimit parent-teacher interactions may also have a profoundly liberating effect on the way that parents and teachers view one another. For example, rather than schedule fifteen-minute parent-teacher conferences to focus on student academic progress, these could be expanded to thirty minutes (a Carlton School practice) to help promote a richer *conversation* about a variety of family and school topics.

## Rethinking Homework

Beyond the need to fracture some of the brittle structures which organize relations between families and schools, the case studies clearly demonstrate the value of rethinking other institutionalized instructional practices, particularly the nature and purpose of homework. To be sure, this routinized activity makes the roles for parents more easily identifiable and explicit. Nevertheless, the value and design of homework should be reassessed by addressing the disruptive and disabling effects of home-based activities on family routines and rhythms. Activities which involve the reinforcement of concepts and skills could be performed during school hours, if necessary, with the advice and supervision of aides and volunteers. Activities could be explicitly designed to promote family learning opportunities and to underscore the importance of parental educative roles. These could be assigned with longer-term or more flexible completion dates. These activities might include family histories, community and cultural portraits, and science projects.

## Organization of Work

Finally, these case studies suggest the need to reexamine those aspects of the workplace which limit the ability of employees to participate in school-based activities. Schools tend to structure school-based activities for traditional, stay-at-home mothers. At the same time, a large number of households include parents who are employed in full-time occupations that provide little flexibility and opportunity for parents to leave work during school hours. As schools begin to rethink the purpose and organization of their parent involvement activities, employers should reevaluate workplace policies which hinder the kind of parental commitment to educational excellence that organized business groups are demanding in the current debate on the quality of our nation's schools.

## NOTES

1. Primary social networks are distinguished from peripheral networks by the central importance, high value, and multiple functions/roles network members represent to parents (Cochran 1990).

2. The policy proposals presented here are aimed at establishing organizational features which will promote school community among families, students, and staff in an elementary school. It is vital to underscore the target population of schools and families to which this discussion is directed. First, the scope of findings, conclusions, and policy proposals is limited to elementary schools. The age and maturity of older students, the roles of parents vis-à-vis their older children, and the organization of high schools require a different set of assumptions and analyses. Second, with the interest of mediating the effects of cultural capital which influence the ways in which parents interact with schools, this discussion focuses on school populations which are diverse in socioeconomic status. While socioeconomically homogeneous school populations could benefit from most of the issues raised here, the intention rests with building communities and social networks between socially and economically differentiated families.

3. To integrate home visits into the organization of school, a longer school day may be necessary to accommodate a midafternoon breakout period for teachers. During this time, paid or voluntary aides (parents, retired adults, etc.) would supervise students while they perform review and skill reinforcement exercises (which would normally be assigned as homework). In addition to home visits, this breakout period could be used by staff for a myriad of planning and organizational activities.

4. Knowledge and familiarity can accumulate over time when teachers instruct the siblings of former students. Schools with low transiency rates, such as Carlton Magnet School, provide the continuity for enhanced teacher knowledge of family backgrounds.

# Appendix A:
# Research Methods

## DATA COLLECTION

The questions generated by the conceptual model in chapter 1 are grounded in the research literature on cultural capital and school organization. These questions shape the methodological strategy adopted for this study.

The conceptual framework requires a methodological design which can be used to explore parallel and divergent patterns across organizationally different school sites. A "comparative" (see George 1979) or multiple-case study design (see Yin 1989) serves the explicit interests of the research questions by establishing a framework to examine the degree to which school organizational processes mediate the influence of cultural capital on family-school interactions. Each individual case study is treated as a "whole" study, in which convergent evidence is sought regarding the facts and conclusions for the case (Yin 1989). The individual cases and multiple case results (cross-cutting themes) are the focus of chapter 5.

A Catholic school and a magnet school were selected to examine the influence of choice on public and nonpublic sectors. A public, neighborhood school (nonchoice school) served as the comparative model against which to contrast the conditions of the choice schools. The three schools selected satisfy the conditions necessary to examine different school community compositions and the degree to which these elements mediate the influence of cultural capital on family-school interactions. As a parish school, a Catholic school is formally and organizationally connected to a Catholic (parish) community, a condition which Coleman and Hoffer (1987) associate with "functional communities" and favorable family-school connections. The families whose children attend the Catholic school in this study are more geographically dispersed than those whose children go to the neighborhood school; they are less dispersed than the magnet school families. The magnet school reflects the conditions associated with "value communities" (Coleman & Hoffer 1987)—geographically dispersed families who share few social or organizational ties outside of the school which their children

167

attend. Their commonality is anchored in their association with a school which espouses a particular educational philosophy or set of values. In contrast, the families whose children attend the public, neighborhood school comprise, by definition, a geographical community.

In order to examine the ways in which cultural capital influences family-school interactions, schools were selected which are comprised of families from different social class backgrounds or, in other words, who differ in the amount of cultural capital they possess. Each of the three schools selected for the study include students whose families vary across a continuum of social class backgrounds, from upper-middle class to low income. Since the research questions for the study focus solely on the interaction between social class and school organizational structures and processes, participation was limited to white parents from each of the three schools in order to control for the effects of race and ethnicity on family-school interactions.

The data collection strategy for this study involved a series of in-depth interviews with at least ten families from each of the three elementary schools. The parents selected for these case studies were drawn randomly from a sample of white families in socioeconomic categories which range from upper-middle class to low income (defined as qualifying for Aid to Families with Dependent Children—AFDC). School records and parent data cards provided the necessary information indicating parents' income, education, and occupation. Interviews were arranged at the convenience of the participants and audiotaped with their permission. The interviews with parents were conducted in their homes, with a few exceptions. One parent from each of the three schools scheduled the interview at their place of employment. An interview with a parent from the magnet school took place at my home.

Teachers (third and fourth grade), principals, school secretaries, parent-school liaisons, and PTA officers were interviewed at each school site. Interview sessions lasted two to three hours. In addition to interviews, I observed both formal and informal interactions between parents and school officials over the course of the fifteen-month study. These included: back-to-school night, parent-teacher conferences, PTA and School Advisory Committee (SAC)/ School Site Council (SSC) meetings, and holiday pageants. Letters, newsletters, handbooks, budget reports, meeting minutes, and other school documents were analyzed. (See Appendix B: Interview and Observation Schedule and Appendix C: Document List.)

The three elementary schools selected represent organizationally different school settings in terms of choice/non-choice, type of school community (value, geographical, religious/philosophical), and programmatic commitment. The three schools are located within the same northern California county and are similar in the socioeconomic status of their student/family populations. (See Appendix D: Description of Schools.)

## CULTURAL CAPITAL

In order to examine the dimensions of cultural capital expected to influence family-school interactions, questions were designed to elicit information regarding parents' education, social status, income and material resources, style of work, and social networks. Questions were also pegged to differentiate the possession of cultural capital with the active use of these resources in the context of schooling. Observations conducted during parent-teacher conferences supplemented data collected in interviews. (See Appendix E: Interview Guide for Parents.)

## ORGANIZATIONAL CHARACTERISTICS

To examine the influence of affirmative *choice* on family-school interactions, I asked parents questions related to the level of perceived responsiveness of the school to their needs and interests. The focus here rests with the degree to which affirmative choice and the option of "exit" alters the nature of requests and responses exchanged between parents and schools. I also asked about the degree to which parents and teachers perceive a collectivity of shared values within the school community. Observations made during parent-teacher conferences and organized meetings between parents and school officials supplemented interview data. (See Appendix E: Interview Guide for Parents and Appendix F: Interview Guide for Teachers.)

Probes designed to explore the nature of *community* were addressed to parents in each of the three schools. Questions focused on the degree of value consistency (value community), and the degree of uniformity and cohesion in social institutions (functional community) as well as the factors which both enhance or diminish the sense of community experienced in these schools. (See Appendix E.)

The array of policies and procedures developed in connection with each school's programmatic *commitment* to parent participation were examined through interviews with school staff, an examination of written documentation (newsletters, parent handbooks, PTA/SAC/SSC minutes, and letters) and observations of Back-to-School Night, parent-teacher conferences, and meetings. Interviews with parents supplemented the findings related to formal structures designed to organize parent involvement. (See Appendices E and F.)

## INTERACTIONS BETWEEN FAMILIES AND SCHOOLS

Relations between parents and school officials were explored using probes which reveal the nature of requests and the types and quality of responses exchanged between families and schools. Parent-teacher conferences, formal and informal meetings between families and school officials, written communications exchanged between home and school, as well as in-depth interviews provided valuable data from which to examine the nature of these interactions. (See Appendices E and F.)

## DATA ANALYSIS

Case study analyses followed the theoretical propositions undergirding the study design and data collection strategy (Yin 1989). Data analysis focused primarily on three major areas: (1) the nature of cultural capital operating within families of different social class; (2) the nature and quality of family-school interactions; and (3) the ways in which organizational arrangements in three different types of schools mediate the effects of cultural capital on the nature and quality of family-school interactions.

I transcribed the audiotapes over a period of six weeks. This process provided an invaluable opportunity to revisit and reconsider the issues raised in interviews. As I listened to parents' and teachers' voices, their inflections and intonations, the emphasis which was attached to certain comments, or the disappointment and pain which colored other responses, this analytical exercise contributed to a fine-grained exploration and rich understanding of emerging patterns and themes.

Interview transcripts and observation notes were coded and summarized according to general descriptive categories generated by the conceptual framework. The detailed summaries were used to further analyze and interpret the data. Pattern coding (Fetterman 1989; Miles & Huberman 1984; Yin 1989) was used to discover patterns among individuals and schools. In addition, pattern coding was used to identify relations among individual families, schools, and the influence of various organizational arrangements. Pieces of information from three sources—interviews, observations, and documents—were sifted and sorted for patterns of thought and behavior.

Patterns emerged through repeated transcript analysis. I developed working propositions based on these analyses which were compared within schools and between sites. For example, one proposition that emerged was that organizational processes and activated choice empower parents within different social classes to positively influence the process through which parents interact with schools. Before making any conclusions about a pattern, I looked for data that opposed or was inconsistent with my conclusions.

Converging pieces of information from interview transcripts were cut up into small strips and arranged across a large desktop according to broad themes and categories, such as parent-teacher relations, issues associated with community, family background information, and school data. Subcategories included topics such as parents' knowledge of schooling, patterns of participation, goals for children's education, homework, and perceptions of other school parents. The arrangement of the data resembled that of the popular game show, "Jeopardy."

In order to identify the possession and operation of the key elements of cultural capital that affect patterns of parent involvement, interview transcripts and observation summaries were coded according to the categories specified in the conceptual framework. Items related to parents' schooling were coded *education*; items related to the occupations of parents were coded *social status*; items related to the relevant income and material resources were coded *income and material resources*; items related to the characteristics of the parents' employment environment were coded as *style of parents' work*; and items related to kinship and friendship associations were coded as *social networks*.

Interactions between families and schools were coded according to the nature and quality of requests and responses exchanged between the two groups. Observed exchanges as well as interview transcripts were coded for the content and context of interactions. Codes for content included request— (along with a subcode for initiator—parent, teacher, principal) and response. Codes for context included indicators of circumstance and physical setting (e.g., parent-teacher conference, telephone call, chance meeting at church).

Several factors may account for the degree to which cultural capital or social class influence patterns of parent involvement. I asked parents to identify factors and describe how they influenced the nature of their interactions with schools. If they mentioned any elements associated with cultural capital, then that condition was viewed as influencing the process through which parents participate in schools. For example, statements by parents regarding conflicts with work, child-care, and transportation which make it difficult for them to attend parent-teacher conferences provided evidence of the impact of cultural capital (or lack of it) on parent involvement.

Pattern coding was used to identify these associations within families and between sites. The relative importance of that element was determined by a simple ranking of all influential factors as reported by parents and teachers. After parents and teachers identified these elements, I looked for patterns between schools in order to generate propositions about the mediating influence of organizational characteristics.

When parents and teachers did not mention any element of cultural capital as influencing their interactions, then that was evidence that cultural capital did not play a central role in the nature and quality of their relationships. In an effort to determine why cultural capital plays little or no role in these interactions, specific probes were used to assess factors which account for their absence. These factors were examined to discover the impact of organizational characteristics.

In order to identify the organizational characteristics, interview transcripts and observation summaries were coded to the categories specified in the conceptual framework.

## CONTRIBUTIONS AND LIMITATIONS OF THE STUDY

This study was designed to explore the relationship between social class and organizational processes in order to understand how schools can better organize themselves to meet the wide array of interests and abilities of parents. The intent rests with moving toward a better understanding of parents' motivations, expectations, and experiences as voiced through their own words during moments of reflection; it is a modest effort to supplement large survey studies with descriptive and meaningful explanations of the social context of parent involvement. With a relatively small sample, however, the study does not attempt to test hypotheses; rather, it attempts to enhance our understanding of these processes and direct our efforts toward valuable research initiatives. The findings will contribute to the ongoing discourse among school officials, policymakers, and researchers about the importance of school organization to the experiences and opportunities of students and their families.

# Appendix B:
# Interview and Observation Schedule

## ST. MARTIN'S ELEMENTARY SCHOOL (CATHOLIC)

*Interviews*

- principal
- teachers (2)
- teachers (2)
- former Parent's Club officer
- parents (10 families)

*Observations*

- back-to-school night
- parent-teacher conferences (8–10 conferences with each of two teachers)
- Parent's Club meeting
- open house; Mass celebration and school reception

## CARLTON ELEMENTARY SCHOOL (MAGNET)

*Interviews*

- principal
- teacher
- teacher
- teachers (2)
- school secretary
- parents (11 families)

*Observations*

- back-to-school night
- parent-teacher conferences (10–12 conferences with each of two teachers)

- winter holiday musical program
- PTA meeting
- school office daily activities

## WESTERN ELEMENTARY SCHOOL (NEIGHBORHOOD)

### *Interviews*

- principal
- teacher
- teacher
- teachers (2)
- PTA president
- outreach/intervention counselors
- school secretaries (2)
- parents (12 families)

### *Observations*

- back-to-school night
- parent-teacher conferences (8–10 conferences with each of two teachers)
- Pride Assembly (3)
- SAC/SSC meeting
- parenting class/discussion
- school office daily activities

# Appendix C:
# Document List

ST. MARTIN'S ELEMENTARY SCHOOL (CATHOLIC)

- student-parent handbook
- registration contract
- student demographics report
- weekly newsletters
- diocese teacher salary schedule
- parent roster
- parish bulletin
- Parent's Club financial report
- school budget report

CARLTON ELEMENTARY SCHOOL (MAGNET)

- parent handbook
- district magnet school brochure
- three-way school contract
- parent survey response results
- miscellaneous letters from the principal to parents
- principal's parenting group topic list
- 5th grade class schedule
- weekly report forms
- student list
- parent information cards
- parent participation record form
- CAP test results
- progress report card form
- school calendar
- PTA news bulletin
- residential real estate fact sheets (school neighborhood)

## WESTERN ELEMENTARY SCHOOL (NEIGHBORHOOD)

- parent handbook and calendar
- weekly newsletters
- miscellaneous letters/announcements from school
- elementary intervention program pamphlet
- student list
- parent information cards
- CAP test results
- PTA budget reports
- SAC/SSC meeting minutes
- residential real estate fact sheets (school neighborhood)

# Appendix D:
## Description of Schools

### ST. MARTIN'S ELEMENTARY SCHOOL (CATHOLIC)

- 315–320 students
- one classroom in each grade first through eighth
- 75 percent white, 13 percent Asian, 8 percent Hispanic, 4 percent black
- 240 families (111 parishioners); upper-middle to lower-middle class
- school philosophy: Catholic
- organizational elements: tuition, selective admissions/forced exit option
- parent organizations: Parent's Club

### CARLTON ELEMENTARY SCHOOL (MAGNET)

- 340–345 students
- two classrooms in each grade first through sixth
- 49 percent white, 23 percent black, 14 percent Hispanic, 10.5 percent Asian, 3.5 percent Native American
- 230 families; middle class to low income
- school philosophy: basic school program
- organizational elements: contract, lottery admissions policy/forced exit option
- parent organizations: PTA, SSC

### WESTERN ELEMENTARY SCHOOL (NEIGHBORHOOD)

- 440–450 students
- two classrooms in each grade kindergarten through sixth
- 74 percent white, 11 percent Asian, 8 percent Hispanic, 7 percent black

- 300 families; middle class to low income
- school philosophy: CARES (cooperation, academics, respect, effort, safety)
- organizational elements: volunteer program
- parent organizations: PTA, SSC, SAC

# Appendix E:
# *Interview Guide for Parents*

## BIOGRAPHICAL DATA

- How long have you lived in this neighborhood?
- How many children in school? What ages?
- Are you employed? If so, what do you do?
- Are you married?
- Do you own or rent this home?
- How many years did you attend school?
- How do you spend any free time you might have?
  What do you like to do?
- Do you belong to any clubs, organizations, sports teams, etc.?
- Are you a member of a church?
- Do you have any friends who work in schools? What do they do?

## KNOWLEDGE OF THE SCHOOL

- What is your child's teacher's name?
- Did you know anything about him/her before this year?
- Have you ever requested a teacher? If so, what did you know about the teacher? Where did you get the information?
- What is your child studying this year? What books do they read? What arithmetic do they have to know?
- What programs does the school offer for parents?
- Did you attend parent-teacher conferences this year? What did you think? What did you find out?
- Do you visit school at any other times?

## MEANING AND VALUE OF SCHOOLING

- What do you want your children to gain from schooling? What is the most important outcome?
- How much schooling do you think your children should have?
- How far do you expect them to go in their schooling?
- When you think about schooling, how does it line up in terms of other experiences?

## ROLE OF PARENTS IN SCHOOLING

- What is your role in your children's education? Is it different than the teacher's role? How?
- Do teachers expect things from you? What do they expect?
- Do you participate in your children's schooling? Why?
- How do you participate?
- What are some things that keep you from participating the way you would like to?

## RELATIONS BETWEEN FAMILIES AND SCHOOLS

- How would you describe your relationships with school staff?
- What do you think about the teachers?
- What do you know about your child's teacher?
- What does your child's teacher know about you?
- How do you hear about things going on at school?
- Have you ever contacted a teacher? Why?
- If you're concerned about something at school, what do you do?
- Do you think your opinion counts?
- What kinds of decisions should parents be involved in?
- Does this school belong to someone?

## CONCEPTIONS OF PARENT INVOLVEMENT

- What does "parent involvement" mean to you?
- How do schools tend to think about parent involvement?
- Does anyone from the school talk to you about parent involvement?

## SOCIAL NETWORKS

- What has influenced the way you think about schooling? What has influenced the way you think about your role in your children's education?

- How often do you see other family members? Do they live nearby? Do you ever talk about school with them? What do they say?
- Do you ever talk about school with your neighbors?
- What do you think other families in the neighborhood think about this school?
- Do you ever talk about the school or education with other adults?
- Who do you and your spouse tend to see for social occasions?
- Do you know other school parents? When do you see other school parents?
- Do you think other school families are people like yourself (in terms of values, economic background)?
- How would you describe the parents at your child's school?
- Is there a sense of community at the school?

## CHOICE AND COMMUNITY

### *Magnet and Catholic School*

- What are your expectations of this school? Are they any different than they would be at a public, or non-choice school?
- Why do you send your kids to this school?
- How did you find out about the school?
- What did you know about it when your child started school here?

### *Magnet School*

- What do you think about the 40-hour participation requirement? How do you fulfill it? Any problems?
- What do you think about the contract?
- What do you think about the proposed changes, e.g., expanded kindergarten program?

### *Catholic School*

- Are you Catholic?
- Are you a member of the parish?
- Do you attend religious services regularly? If so, where?

# Appendix F:
## Interview Guide for Teachers

### BIOGRAPHICAL DATA

- How long have you been a teacher?
- How long have you taught here?
- In general, how would you describe your teaching experiences in this school?
- Do you live in the neighborhood?
- Do you have any children?
- Are you a member of any school committees?
- Have you ever taken any classes or attended any workshops on parent involvement?

### THE ROLE OF PARENTS IN SCHOOLING

- What is your role in your students' education?
- What is the parents' role and how is it different? Where do parents' responsibilities end and yours begin? Are they blurred?
- What do parents expect from you?
- Do you think parents think it's important to participate in their children's schooling?
- How do you know when a parent thinks education is important? What are some indications?
- How do parents participate in their children's schooling?
- How would you like to see parents participate? What are some things they should be doing?
- Are there adequate opportunities for parents to participate in their children's schooling?
- Are parents "qualified" to participate in their children's schooling? Are they all "equally" qualified?

- What are some things that prevent parents from participating in their kids' schooling?
- What could you or the school do to encourage broader participation?

## ATTITUDE AND BEHAVIOR TOWARD PARENTS

- How do you behave with parents? Do you behave the same way with all parents? What kinds of things are you conscious of?
- Why do you think parents and teachers sometimes feel uncomfortable around one another?
- How well do you know these parents? What do you know about them? What do they know about you?
- Do you know the social class backgrounds of your students? If so, how do you know? Is that information helpful?
- If a parent asks you to help them help their children, what do you say?
- What people or events have influenced the way you think about parents or the way you behave around them?

## RELATIONS BETWEEN PARENTS AND SCHOOLS

- Do you see yourself and parents as competitors? collaborators?
- Should teachers listen to parents?
- Do parents ever contact you to tell you you're doing a good job, or that their child is happy? Why do you think they do/don't?
- What decisions should parents be involved in? When should parents be contacted or consulted?
- Are you satisfied with the way you (or the school) communicate with families/parents?
- Is it important to have "good" relationships between families and schools? Why? What should that relationship be?
- How would you change relations between families and schools?
- Does this school belong to someone? Who?

## COMMUNITY

### Magnet Only

- This is not a "neighborhood school" in the sense that this school serves children from neighborhoods far from this surrounding one. Does that make a difference in terms of the climate here? In terms of family-school relations?
- Is there a sense of community here? A sense of shared values?
- How do you respond to parents' interests and concerns?

### Catholic Only

- Do most of the families who send their children here know one another? Are most of them parishioners and regular church-goers?
- Is there a sense of community here?
- How do you respond to parents' interests and concerns?

## CHOICE

- Parents make an affirmative decision to send their kids to this school. How does that affect their attitude toward you? How does it affect your relationship with them? Does it give you (and parents) certain rights and obligations? Does it affect the way you respond to parents' interests, concerns, or requests? Does the issue of choice impact the way they respond to your interests, concerns, or requests?

## COMMITMENT

- What programs does this school offer to parents? PTA? Site Council? Advisory Council? Volunteer program?
- Do they "work"?
- Back-to-School Night. Is it important? What do you try to get across to parents?
- Parent-teacher conferences. What's going on during these? Do you consciously try to control the conversation?
- Are these events merely rituals? Do they have meaning apart from their tradition and symbolism?

### Magnet Only

- Mandated forty hours of parent participation. What do you think about that? What are some of the problems with it? What are some of the benefits?
- Is the contract meaningful to you? to parents?

## FUNDING

- Traditionally one of the most important roles for parents has been fund-raising. Is that important here? How do parents contribute?

# *Appendix G:*
# *Carlton School Contract*

## Student

### *Academic Achievement*

1. I will do the best work at all times.
2. I will take advantage of every opportunity to learn.
3. I will have in class the necessary tools for learning.
4. I will complete assigned work neatly, accurately and on time.

### *Attendance*

1. I will go to school every day unless I am ill.
2. I will go to bed by 9:00 P.M.

### *Citizenship*

1. I will know and follow district, school and classroom rules.
2. I will respect the rights of others at all times.
3. I will follow the dress code.

### *Homework*

1. I will set aside time after school each day to review what I have learned.
2. I will complete (neatly, accurately, and on time) the assigned homework.

## Parent

### *Academic Achievement*

1. I will encourage and support my child's efforts to learn.
2. I will maintain contact with the school and my child's teacher(s).

3. I will review my child's progress with his/her teacher throughout the year.
4. I will seek help from the school when needed.

### Attendance

1. I will assume responsibility for the regular and prompt attendance of my child.
2. I will get my child to bed by 9:00 P.M.

### Citizenship

1. I will know and support district and classroom rules for acceptable behavior.
2. I will teach my child to respect the rights and property of others.
3. I will send my child to school with instructions to pay attention in class, and to be respectful.
4. I will assume responsibility that my child follows the dress code.

### Homework

1. I will provide a quiet time and place for study without TV.
2. I will know the school's homework policy.

### Parent Involvement

1. OUR FAMILY WILL CONTRIBUTE FORTY HOURS OF VOLUNTEER TIME TO THE SCHOOL AND ITS PROGRAMS. WE UNDERSTAND THAT IF WE DO NOT, OUR CHILD/REN WILL BE DISENROLLED AT THE END OF THIS SCHOOL YEAR.

## Teacher

### Academic Achievement

1. I will encourage the student to do his/her best work.
2. I will serve as a good example through my enthusiasm for teaching and learning.
3. I will evaluate student progress and report to student and parent at regular intervals.
4. I will have a written grading policy that is available to student and parent at the beginning of the year.

### Attendance

1. I will motivate good attendance through high quality instruction, incentives, and positive communication with the students.

***Citizenship***

1. I will have written classroom rules and will discuss them with parents at Back to School night and with students on the first day of school.
2. I will endorse all rules fairly and firmly.
3. I will maintain an attractive and well-managed classroom, conducive to good student behavior and learning.

***Homework***

1. I will provide homework designed to reinforce what has been taught in class.
2. I will provide student and parent with written information about the homework policy in my class.

# References

Anyon, Jean. 1981. "Social Class and School Knowledge." *Curriculum Inquiry* 11(1): 1–42.

Archibald, Douglas A. 1988. "Magnet Schools, Voluntary Desegregation, and Public Choice Theory: Limits and Possibilities in a Big City School System." Unpublished doctoral dissertation, University of Wisconsin, Madison.

Baker, David P., Hans Oswald, and David L. Stevenson. 1988. "School Charter and Parental Management in West Germany. *Sociology of Education* 61(October): 255–265.

Baker, David P. and David L. Stevenson. 1986. "Mothers' Strategies for Children's School Achievement." *Sociology of Education* 59(July): 156–166.

Barber, Benjamin. 1992. *An Aristocracy of Everyone.* Oxford: Oxford University Press.

Becher, Rhoda McShane. 1986. "Parent Involvement: A Review of Research and Principles of Successful Practice." In *Current Topics in Early Childhood Education*, ed. L. G. Katz, vol. 6. Norwood, NJ: Ablex Publishing.

Becker, Howard J. and Joyce L. Epstein. 1982. "Parent Involvement: A Survey of Teacher Practices." *Elementary School Journal* 83(2): 85–102.

Bellah, Robert N., et al. 1991. *The Good Society.* New York: Knopf.

Bird, T. and J. W. Little. 1986. "How Schools Organize the Teaching Occupation." *Elementary School Journal* 86(March): 493–511.

Bourdieu, Pierre. 1977a. "Cultural Reproduction and Social Reproduction." In *Power and Ideology in Education*, ed. J. Karabel and A. H. Halsey. New York: Oxford University Press.

Bourdieu, Pierre. 1977b. *Outline of a Theory of Practice.* New York: Cambridge University Press.

Bourdieu, Pierre and J. C. Passeron. 1977. *Reproduction in Education, Society, and Culture.* Beverly Hills, CA: Sage.

———. 1979. *The Inheritors: French Students and their Relation to Culture.* Chicago, IL: University of Chicago Press.

Brandt, Ronald S. 1979. *Partners: Parents and Schools.* Alexandria, VA: Association for Supervision and Curriculum Development.

Bredo, Eric. 1987. "Choice, Constraint, and Community." *Journal of Education Policy* 2(5): 67–78.

Bronfenbrenner, Urie. 1966. "Socialization and Social Class Through Time and Space." In *Class, Status, and Power,* ed. R. Bendix and S. M. Lipset. New York: Free Press.

Bronfenbrenner, Urie, Phyllis Moen, and James Garbarino. 1984. "Child, Family, and Community." In *Review of Child Development Research,* ed. R. Parke, vol. 7. Chicago: University of Chicago Press.

Brown, Patricia R. and Kati Haycock. 1984. *Excellence for Whom?* Oakland, CA: The Achievement Council.

Bryk, Anthony and Mary Driscoll. 1988. *The High School as Community: Contextual Influences and Consequences for Students and Teachers.* Madison, WI: National Center on Effective Secondary Schools.

Bryk, Anthony and Peter Holland. 1984. *Effective Catholic Schools: An Exploration.* Washington, DC: National Center for Research in Total Catholic Education.

Bryk, Anthony S., Valerie Lee, and Peter Holland. 1993. *Catholic Schools and the Common Good.* Cambridge, MA: Harvard University Press.

Chubb, John E. and Terry M. Moe. 1987. "No School is an Island: Politics, Markets, and Education." *Journal of Education Policy* 2(5).

———. 1990. *Politics, Markets, and Schools.* Washington, D.C.: Brookings Institution.

Clark, Reginald M. 1983. *Family Life and School Achievement: Why Poor Black Children Succeed or Fail.* Chicago: University of Chicago Press.

Clarke-Stewart, K. Alison. 1983. "Exploring the Assumptions of Parent Education." In *Parent Education and Public Policy,* ed. R. Haskins and D. Adams. Norwood, NJ: Ablex Publishing.

Cochran, Moncrieff. 1990. *Extending Families: The Social Networks of Parents and Their Children.* New York: Cambridge University Press.

Cochran, Moncrieff and Jane Brassard. 1979. "Child Development and Personal Social Networks." *Child Development* 50: 601–616.

Cochran, Moncrieff and C. R. Henderson, Jr. 1986. *Family Matters: Evaluation of the Parental Empowerment Program,* A Summary of a Final Report to the National Institute of Education. Ithaca, NY: Cornell University.

Coleman, James. 1987. "Families and Schools." *Educational Researcher* (Aug.–Sept.): 32–38.

———. 1988. "Social Capital and the Creation of Human Capital." *American Journal of Sociology* 94. Supplement, S95–S120.

Coleman, James and Thomas Hoffer. 1987. *Public and Private High Schools: The Impact of Communities.* New York: Basic Books.

Comer, James. 1980. *School Power.* New York: University Press.

———. 1984. "Home-School Relationships as They Affect the Academic Success of Children." *Education and Urban Society* 16(3).

———. 1985. "The Yale-New Haven Primary Prevention Project: A Follow-Up Study." *Journal of the American Academy of Child Psychiatry* 24(2): 154–160.

———. 1986. "Parent Participation in the Schools." *Phi Delta Kappan* (February): 442–446.

———. 1988. "Educating Poor Minority Children." *Scientific American* 259(November): 42–48.

Connell, R. W. et al. 1982. *Making the Difference: Schools, Families, and Social Divisions.* Sydney, Australia: Geo. Allen and Unwin.

Cookson, Peter and C. Persell. 1985. *Preparing for Power: America's Elite Boarding Schools.* New York: Basic Books.

Crespo, Orestes I. and Patricia Louque. 1984. *Parent Involvement in the Education of Minority Language Children: A Resource Handbook.* Rosslyn, VA: National Clearinghouse for Bilingual Education.

Criscuolo, Nicholas P. 1986. "Parent Involvement in the Testing Program." *Clearing House* 59(7)March: 330–331.

Davies, Don. 1980. "Co-production as a Model for Home-School Cooperation." In *A Two-Way Street*, ed. R. Sinclair. Boston, MA: Institute for Responsive Education.

———. 1987. "Parent Involvement in the Public Schools." *Education and Urban Society* 19(2): 147–163.

Davies, Don, P. Burch and V. Johnson. 1992. *A Portrait of Schools Reaching Out: Report of a Survey on Practices and Policies of Family-Community-School Collaboration.* Baltimore, MD: Center on Families, Communities, Schools and Children's Learning, Report No. 1.

Delgado-Gaitan, Concha. 1992. "School Matters in the Mexican-American Home: Socializing Children to Education." *American Educational Research Journal* 29(3) March: 495–513.

Deutch, M. 1967. "The Disadvantaged Child and the Learning Process." In *The Disadvantaged Child*, ed. M. Deutch. New York: Basic Books.

DiMaggio, Paul. 1979. "Review Essay: On Pierre Bourdieu." *American Journal of Sociology* 84(6).

Education Commission of the States. 1989. *A State Policy Maker's Guide to Public School Choice.* Denver, CO: Education Commission of the States.

Elmore, Richard. 1987. "Choice in Public Education." *Journal of Education Policy* 2(5).

Epstein, Joyce L. 1983. *Effects on Parents of Teacher Practices of Parent Involvement.* Baltimore, MD: Center for Social Organization of Schools, Johns Hopkins University. Report No. 346, October.

————. 1985. "Parents' Reactions to Teacher Practices of Parent Involvement." *The Elementary School Journal* 86(3): 277–294.

————. 1987. "Toward a Theory of Family-School Connections: Teacher Practices and Parent Involvement." In *Social Intervention: Potential and Constraints,* eds. K. Hurrelmann, F. Kaufmann, and F. Losel. New York: De Gruyter, 121–136.

————. 1990. "Single Parents and the Schools: Effects of Marital Status on Parent and Teacher Interactions." *Change in Societal Institutions,* ed. M. Hallinan. New York: Plenum.

————. 1992. "School and Family Partnerships." In *Encyclopedia of Educational Research,* ed. M. Alkin. New York: Macmillan.

Epstein, Joyce L. and Howard J. Becker. 1982. "Teachers' Reported Practices of Parent Involvement: Problems and Possibilities." *The Elementary School Journal* 83(2): 103–114.

Epstein, Joyce L. and S. L. Dauber. 1988. *Teacher Attitudes and Practices of Parent Involvement in Inner-City Elementary and Middle Schools.* Paper presented at the annual meetings of the American Sociological Association, Atlanta, GA.

Erickson, Donald A. 1982. "Disturbing Evidence about the 'One Best System.'" In *The Public School Monopoly,* ed. R. Everhart. San Francisco: Pacific Institute for Public Policy Research; Cambridge: Ballinger.

Espinoza, R. 1988. "Working Parents, Employers, and Schools." *Educational Horizons* 66: 63–65.

Feinberg, Walter and Jonas F. Soltis. 1992. *School and Society.* New York: Teachers College Press.

Fetterman, David M. 1989. *Ethnography Step by Step.* Newbury Park, CA: Sage Publications.

George, Alexander L. 1979. "Case Studies and Theory Development." In *Diplomacy: New Approaches in History, Theory, and Policy,* ed. P. G. Lauren. New York: Free Press.

Goodson, Barbara D. and Robert P. Hess. 1975. *Parents as Teachers of Young Children.* Washington, D.C.: Bureau of Educational Personnel Development, DHEW, Office of Education.

Gordon, Ira. 1979. "The Effects of Parent Involvement in Schooling." In *Partners: Parents and Schools,* ed. R. Brandt. Alexandria, VA: Association for Supervision and Curriculum Development.

Grant, Gerald. 1985. "Schools That Make an Imprint: Creating a Strong Positive Ethos." In *Challenge to American Schools: The Case for Standards and Values*, ed. J. H. Bunzel. New York: Oxford University Press.

Hallinger, Philip and Joseph Murphy. 1986. "The Social Context of Effective Schools." *American Journal of Education* 94(May): 328–355.

Heath, Shirley Brice. 1982. "Questioning at Home and at School: A Comparative Study." In *Doing the Ethnography of Schooling*, ed. G. Spindler. New York: Holt, Rinehart, & Winston.

Henderson, Anne. 1981. *Parent Participation-Student Achievement: The Evidence Grows*. Columbia, MD: National Committee for Citizens in Education.

———. 1987. *The Evidence Continues to Grow: Parent Involvement Improves Student Achievement*. Columbia, MD: National Committee for Citizens in Education.

Herrick, S. C. and J. L. Epstein. 1991. *Implementing School and Family Partnerships in the Elementary Grades: Two Evaluations of Reading Activity Packets and School Newsletters*. Report 19. Baltimore: Johns Hopkins University Center on Research on the Effective Schooling of Disadvantaged Students.

Hirschman, Albert O. 1970. *Exit, Voice, and Loyalty*. Cambridge: Harvard University Press.

Hobbs, Nicholas. 1978. "Families, Schools, and Communities: An Ecosystem for Children." *Teachers College Record* 79(4).

Hoover-Dempsey, Kathleen V. et al. 1987. "Parent Involvement: Contributions of Teacher Efficacy, School SES, and Other School Characteristics." *American Education Research Association Journal* 24(3) fall: 417–435.

Keesling, J. Ward and Ralph J. Melaragno. 1983. "Parent Participation in Federal Education Programs: Findings from the Federal Programs Survey Phase of the Study of Parental Involvement." In *Parent Education and Public Policy*, ed. R. Haskins and D. Adams. Norwood, NJ: Ablex.

Kohn, Melvin L. 1969. *Class and Conformity*. Homewood, IL: Dorsey Press.

———. 1971. "Social Class and Parent-Child Relationships." In *Sociology of the Family*, ed. M. Anderson. Middlesex, England: Penguin Books.

Kreinberg, N. and V. Thompson. 1986. *Family Math: Report of Activities*. Berkeley: University of California Press.

Lareau, Annette. 1987. "Social Class Differences in Family-School Relationships." *Sociology of Education* 60(April): 73–85.

———. 1989. *Home Advantage*. New York: Falmer Press.

Leichter, Hope Jensen, ed. 1979. *Families and Communities as Educators*. New York: Teachers College Press.

Levin, Henry M. 1989. *The Theory of Choice Applied to Education.* Stanford, CA: Center for Educational Research at Stanford, Stanford University.

Lightfoot, Sara Lawrence. 1975. "Families and Schools: Creative Conflict or Negative Dissonance." *Journal of Research and Development in Education* 9(1).

———. 1978. *Worlds Apart.* New York: Basic Books.

———. 1980. "Exploring Family-School Relationships: A Prelude to Curricular Designs and Strategies." In *A Two-Way Street*, ed. R. Sinclair. Boston: Institute for Responsive Education.

Litwak, Eugene and Henry J. Meyer. 1974. *School, Family, and Neighborhood.* New York: Columbia University Press.

Litwak, Eugene and Ivan Szelenyi. 1971. "Kinship and Other Primary Groups." In *Sociology of the Family*, ed. M. Anderson. Middlesex, England: Penguin Books.

Marjoribanks, Kevin. 1979. *Families and Their Learning Environments.* London: Routledge and Kegan Paul.

McLaughlin, Milbrey, Merita Irby, and Juliet Langman. 1994. *Urban Sanctuaries: Neighborhood Organizations in the Lives and Futures of Inner-city Youth.* San Francisco: Jossey-Bass.

McLaughlin, Milbrey W. and Patrick M. Shields. 1986. *Involving Parents in the Schools: Lessons for Policy.* Paper presented at the Conference on the Effects of Alternative Designs in Compensatory Education, Washington, D.C.

McNeil, Linda M. 1987. "Exit, Voice, and Community: Magnet Teachers' Responses to Standardization." *Educational Policy* 1(1): 93–113.

McPherson, Gertrude. 1972. *Small Town Teacher.* Cambridge, MA: Harvard University Press.

Medrich, Elliott A. et al. 1982. *The Serious Business of Growing Up.* Berkeley, CA: University of California Press.

Metz, Mary Haywood. 1986. *Different By Design: The Context and Character of Three Magnet Schools.* London: Routledge and Kegan Paul.

———. 1988. "In Education, Magnets Attract Controversy." *NEA Today*, Special Issue (January): 54–60.

Miles, Matthew B. and A. Michael Huberman. 1984. *Qualitative Data Analysis.* Beverly Hills, CA: Sage.

Moore, Donald and Suzanne Davenport. 1989. *School Choice: The New Improved Sorting Machine.* Chicago: Designs for Change.

Murphy, Joseph. 1991. *Restructuring Schools: Capturing and Assessing the Phenomena.* New York: Teachers College Press.

Nault, Richard L. and Susan Uchitelle. 1982. "School Choice in the Public Sector: A Case Study of Parental Decision Making." In *Family Choice in Schooling*, ed. M. Manley-Casimir. Lexington, MA: Lexington Books.

Newmann, Fred and Donald Oliver. 1968. "Education and Community." *Harvard Educational Review* 37(winter): 61–106.

Ogbu, John. 1974. *The Next Generation*. New York: Academic Press.

Peshkin, A. 1986. *God's Choice*. Chicago: University of Chicago Press.

Peterson, Paul. 1981. *City Limits*. Chicago: University of Chicago Press.

Raywid, Mary Anne. 1982. "The Current Status of Schools of Choice in Public Secondary Education." Project on Alternatives in Education, Hofstra University, Hempstead, NY.

———. 1984. "Synthesis of Research on Schools of Choice." *Educational Leadership* 41(April): 71-78.

———. 1988a. "The Mounting Case for Schools of Choice." Unpublished manuscript.

———. 1988b. "Community and Schools: A Prolegomenon." *Teachers College Record* 90(2): 197–209.

Reissman, F. 1962. *The Culturally Deprived Child*. New York: Harper and Row.

Rich, Dorothy. 1985. "Helping Parents Help their Children Learn." *Educational Leadership* 42(7).

———. 1987. *Schools and Families: Issues and Actions*. Washington, D.C.: NEA Press.

Rich, Dorothy and C. Jones. 1977. *A Family Affair*. Washington, D.C.: Home and School Institute.

Romero, P. Cesar. 1982. *Strategies to Involve Parents in the Schools*. Los Gatos, CA: Paradox Press.

Rubin, Lillian B. 1976. *Worlds of Pain*. New York: Basic Books.

Rutter, Michael et al. 1979. *Fifteen Thousand Hours: Secondary Schools and Their Effects on Children*. Cambridge: Harvard University Press.

Scherer, Jacqueline. 1972. *Contemporary Community: Sociological Illusion or Reality*. London: Tavistock.

Schultz, Theodore W. 1963. *The Economic Value of Education*. New York: Columbia University Press.

Scott-Jones, Diane. 1987. "Mother-As-Teacher in the Families of High- and Low-Achieving Low-Income Black First-Graders." *Journal of Negro Education* 56: 21–34.

Seeley, David. 1982. "Education Through Partnership." *Educational Leadership* 40(2): 42–47.

Sergiovanni, Thomas. 1994. *Building Community in Schools.* San Francisco: Jossey-Bass.

Shields, Patrick M. and Milbrey W. McLaughlin. 1986. *Parent Involvement in Compensatory Education Programs.* Center for Educational Research at Stanford, Report No. 87–6, Stanford University, Stanford, CA.

Shirley, Dennis. 1986. "A Critical Review and Appropriation of Pierre Bourdieu's Analysis of Social and Cultural Reproduction." *Journal of Education* 168(2).

Smrekar, Claire. 1989. *The Voices of Parents: Rethinking the Intersection of Family and School.* Paper presented at the annual meeting of the American Educational Research Association, San Francisco, CA.

Stearns, Miriam S. and Susan Peterson. 1973. *Parent Involvement in Compensatory Education Programs.* Menlo Park, CA: Stanford Research Institute.

Steinberg, Laurence. 1989. "Communities of Families and Education." In *Education and the American Family,* ed. W. Weston. New York: New York University Press.

Stevenson, David L. and David P. Baker. 1987. "The Family-School Relation and the Child's School Performance." *Child Development* 58: 1348–57.

———. 1988. *Developing a Comparative Institutional Perspective of Family-School Relations.* Paper presented at the annual meeting of the International Education Society, Atlanta, GA.

Strodbeck, F. L. 1958. "Family Interactions, Values, and Achievement." In *Talent and Society,* ed. D. D. McClelland. New York: Van Nosrand.

———. 1965. "The Hidden Curriculum of the Middle Class Home." In *Learning and the Educational Process,* ed. J. D. Kromboltz. Chicago: Rand McNally, 91–112.

Sung, B. L. 1987. *Chinese Immigrant Children in New York City.* New York: Center for Migration Studies.

Swap, Susan. 1987. *Enhancing Parent Involvement in Schools: A Manual for Parents and Teachers.* New York: Teachers College Press.

Tiebout, Charles M. 1956. "A Pure Theory of Local Expenditures." *Journal of Political Economy* 64(October): 416–424.

Tonnies, F. 1963. *Community and Society.* Ed. and trans., C. P. Loomis. New York: Harper and Row.

Valentine, Charles A. 1968. *Culture and Poverty.* Chicago: University of Chicago Press.

Waller, Willard. 1932. *The Sociology of Teaching.* New York: Wiley.

Wilcox, Kathleen. 1978. "Schooling and Socialization for Work: A Structural Inquiry into Cultural Transmission in an Urban American Community." Unpublished doctoral dissertation, Harvard University, Department of Anthropology.

Wolfendale, Sheila. 1983. *Parental Participation in Children's Development and Education.* New York: Gordon and Breach Science Publishers.

Wright, James D. and Sonia R. Wright. 1976. "Social Class and Parental Values for Children: A Partial Replication and Extension of the Kohn Thesis." *American Sociological Review* 41(June): 527–537.

Yin, Robert K. 1989. *Case Study Research.* Newbury Park, CA: Sage Publications.

# Index